VOICES FOR THE FUTURE

Voices For The Future:

Essays On Major Science Fiction Writers

Thomas D. Clareson, editor

VOLUME I

BOWLING GREEN UNIVERSITY POPULAR PRESS
BOWLING GREEN, OHIO 43403

To the memory

of

Scott C. Osborn

(1913 — 1970)

Professor of English

Mississippi State University

More than anyone else Scott made possible the MLA Seminar on

Science Fiction

TABLE OF CONTENTS

INTRODUCTION

This volume has resulted from the popular success of *SF: The Other Side of Realism* during the past three years. Since that volume hoped to show the many different ways in which the study of science fiction could be approached, it was intentionally something of a "mixed bag" because no one critical approach was held to throughout the collection. I might add that it has always been my contention that there is no one critic nor one approach to the study of any literature.

This collection brings together a group of original essays concerning major writers of science fiction whose careers had begun by the end of World War Two. The essays are arranged in the sequence of the starts of those careers. Kurt Vonnegut, who began to write in the early 1950's, is the one exception. I hope it will be of value to teachers and students alike, both in the classroom and in their individual studies.

I fully realize that other authors could have been included. Murray Leinster and John Wyndham are two whom I think of immediately, and many will wonder why their favorite author was excluded. The reason is twofold: not every significant writer could be included in a single volume, and I tried to select authors who have gained academic attention—at least in the classroom, if not in the amount of critical material written about them. I hope this is but the first of a series of volumes devoted to the major writers of science fiction and modern fantasy.

Wooster, Ohio
January, 1976

Jack Williamson

THE YEARS OF WONDER

W hat was it like to publish in the science fiction magazines in the 1930's and the 1940's? Professor Clareson has put the question to me. I was there, and I'll dredge into recollection for what I can recall.

The assignment is not so simple as it might seem, because science fiction changed so much during those two decades—even more profoundly, I think, than it has since. The mental excursion back to 1930 is a trip into another culture. Copies of the old *Amazing Stories, Wonder Stories,* and *Astounding Stories of Super-Science* still exist, the pulp paper gone brown and brittle and the monster-haunted covers often detached, but their world is gone forever.

Those were the days of the "sense of wonder" Sam Moskowitz has celebrated. The world had not yet been saturated with science fiction in kiddie cartoons, in *Star Trek* reruns, and in comic books, *Playboy,* and paperbacks—even in college classes. It still seemed dazzlingly new.

Before I discovered *Amazing Stories,* late in 1926, I had come across no science fiction except for the tales of Poe and Hawthorne and a few such books as Bulwer-Lytton's *The Coming*

Race. I recall very vividly my first encounters with the enchantment of the bright Paul covers and the excitement of travel in space and time, of strange beings and powers and inventions. By 1930 I was selling stories of my own, but the exhilaration of exploring the future had not worn dull.

Of course there were times when writing for the magazines—at least for me—was rather lonely and poorly paid. For most people, it had nothing to do with reality. My parents felt that my preoccupation with such fiction was not quite healthy. The term *science fiction*—invented by Hugo Gernsback when he launched *Science Wonder Stories*—was only a year old in 1930, and still bewildering to most outsiders. I used to explain that I was writing adventure stories with a science background.

Yet there was an exciting little group of people who did understand. Some three or four hundred writers now belong to the Science Fiction Writers of America, but in the beginning we were too few to need an organization. Over the years, I met most of the early contributors, and found them generally as fascinating as their fiction.

My second published story brought a sort of fan letter from A. Merritt, who was then my great idol. When Ed Hamilton and I called on him at the New York editorial offices of Hearst's *American Weekly,* he received us in a friendly way and spent an hour with us. He wrote me letters of advice and even agreed to collaborate with me on a science fiction novel, *The Purple Mountain—* which never got finished.

I once spent a week in Nebraska with Dr. Miles J. Breuer—I liked his story craftsmanship and had persuaded him to accept me as a sort of apprentice. We wrote a short story and then a novel together. I met Hamilton through correspondence with a fan named Jerome Seigel—later a co-creator of Superman. On a trip to Chicago I met Farnsworth Wright, the editor of *Weird Tales,* and several of his writers, including E. Hoffman Price and Otis Adelbert Kline.

In New York City a few years later I remember long sessions in Stuben's Tavern, with such people as John Campbell, Sprague de Camp, Otto Binder, and Manley Wade Wellman. I met Isaac Asimov, about seventeen, proud of his first sale to John Campbell. In 1939, I sat in a cafe outside the "First World Science Fiction

Convention" in New York with a little group of "Futurians" who had been excluded by the management—Fred Pohl, Doc Lowndes, Don Wollheim, Cyril Kornbluth, and others.

In California a year or two later I met Ray Bradbury when he was still selling newspapers; I knew Tony Boucher and Cleve Cartmill; I used to visit Robert Heinlein's home in the Hollywood hills when his career was just beginning.

These were comrades of a special sort. Though our meetings were not very frequent, I read their stories; we kept more or less in touch. We had had a sense of something more in common than simply being fellow craftsmen or maybe sometimes artists in a very narrow field.

I think we had a feeling of belonging to a new culture, though we wouldn't have put it that way. Before futurology became a career or an academic discipline, we were amateur futurologists, aware that—within our individual limits and the editorial requirements of the magazines—we were sometimes exploring possible alternative future tracks of human history. That was an exciting privilege. For me, at least, it generally seemed enough to make up for the small and uncertain financial returns. So long as I earned enough so that I could keep writing science fiction, I was—most of the time—reasonably content.

A cent a word was good pay during the 1930's. I was never very prolific, and my average earnings were only around a thousand dollars a year. Of course a dollar then was worth several of today's. I had not yet married, and I built a shack on the family ranch in New Mexico where I could always live on nothing a day while I wrote another story. Life didn't cost much. In 1930, at the bottom of the Depression, with about forty dollars, I bought a backpack and spent the summer roving around the West, riding freight trains. The next summer, rich from selling a novelette to the Clayton *Strange Tales* for two cents a word, I joined Ed Hamilton at Minneapolis to buy an outboard motorboat for a trip down the Mississippi. In 1932, with the banks closed and payments from *Weird Tales* suspended, I got home from school with nine dollars. I bought paper and typewriter ribbons and wrote *The Legion of Space*. When money began trickling in that fall, my brother and I stripped down an old Model T Ford and made a camping trip to Mexico and the Grand Canyon. That winter in

Key West, Ed Hamilton and I had a house with our own tropical orchard for eight dollars a month.

But full-time writing for the science fiction magazines, during most of the 1930's, was a luxury that very few could afford. Doc Smith, for example, was a doughnut-mix chemist. Murray Leinster was writing for the slicks under his own name, William F. Jenkins. John Campbell sold Fords and had several other jobs before he became an editor. Burroughs was a millionaire, of course; and Merritt was earning fifty thousand a year on the *American Weekly*.

In an odd way, our poverty was not only material but also intellectual. Of course our capital was new ideas, and our inspiration came from science. But the magazines were pulps. Not yet welcome in libraries, they were part of the popular culture, scorned by the academic establishment. Our intellectual ghetto was narrow and very real.

Science fiction does have honorable literary origins, though I think our critical defenders sometimes try to trace them too far back. *Amazing Stories* was certainly well enough born. Originally a reprint magazine, it carried the classic fiction of Poe and Verne and Wells. But down in the ghetto that noble birth was soon forgotten.

Outside the pulps, in the respectable world of books and libraries and critical reviews, literary science fiction lived on through those decades. Aldous Huxley was writing *Brave New World* and *After Many a Summer*. C. S. Lewis was beginning his great allegoric trilogy with *Out of the Silent Planet*. Stapledon was publishing *Last and First Men*. Kafka was being discovered. With never a ripple in the magazines.

Science fiction had been submerged in the pulp tradition. Since the pulps are gone, perhaps they need explaining. They were called pulps because they were printed on cheap gray woodpulp paper. In the days before radio and TV, they were a major medium of popular entertainment.

The pulp tradition had been growing since before the turn of the century. Through the 1930's and the early 1940's the newsstands were still stacked with pulp fiction magazines, at prices from a dime to a quarter. A few, such as *Argosy,* offered a variety, but most were specialized. There were Western pulps, detective pulps, sports pulps, love pulps, air-war pulps, and any others that could find a public. The great pulp houses, like Clayton, Street and Smith, and Standard magazines, were always putting out new titles, to keep the presses rolling and keep the circulation totals up to the advertising guarantees. One overworked editor often had single-handed charge of several books.

When science fiction magazines were added to these groups during the 1930's, they were commonly the runts of the litter. It seems ironic that some of them are still alive, while the former giants have nearly all been forgotten.

Sam Moskowitz has been busy documenting and exploiting the science fiction content of the early pulps. His *Science Fiction by Gaslight* begins with 1891. Edgar Rice Burroughs, no doubt the most popular and influential pulp writer, burst into the Munsey magazines in 1912. A. Merritt, whose spells were even more wonderful, came a little later. Gernsback reprinted both Burroughs and Merritt in the early *Amazing*.

Yet the Gernsback magazines, mixing classic reprints with German and French translations and amateurish new stories, were not quite real pulps. The first actual impact of the pulp tradition on the magazines came with Harry Bates, the busy editor who added *Astounding Stories of Super-Science* to the Clayton chain with the issue for January, 1930.

This pulp influence has been deplored, but it was not altogether bad. Certainly it was unliterary, if not anti-literary. It was scorned by the intellectual establishment. But, in the long run, it was probably good for science fiction. The pulp tradition is worth a closer look. It was part of the popular culture. With its narrowness, its violence, its prudery, its strong male heroes, its innocent good women and wildly wicked bad ones, and its themes of material success, I think it relfects the Puritan heritage and the frontier experience.

The pulp story was written from the viewpoint of a pure-minded male who was successful in a conflict with powerful antagonists. Good and evil were clearly defined. Characters were simple, and action was paramount. The ending was happy. Though incidental satire was sometimes permitted, the whole tradition assumed a rational moral order in the universe. The good guys won. Plot itself, of course, has thematic implications. Every story ending reflects an ethical judgment. Logical order in the story implies a reasonable order in the world outside.

Though Huxley was using science fiction to challenge these venerable beliefs, as Wells before him had done, the pulp tradition still supported the convictions of the mass audience in 1930. Evil was still definable and beatable, success still possible and meaningful. Applied science still held more promise than menace; the possible future still looked more pleasant than the past. By the late 1940's, those cheerful assumptions had begun to crumble, and the pulp empires with them.

As part of the popular culture, the pulp tradition was almost anti-academic. Certainly the craft of pulp writing was not taught or learned in college. My burning desire in those days was to join Merritt and Burroughs and Max Brand among the writers for *Argosy,* and I used to study the weekly biographical page about "Men Who Make the *Argosy.*" What the writers had in common, so far as I could discover, was a rich experience of life and very little school.

I'm convinced, in fact, that the pulp tradition is more oral than literary. When I came to study the folk epics and the theories of oral transmission, it struck me that Max Brand's Westerns had a good deal in common with Homer. The language was rhythmic, rich with figures of speech. The field of action was vast, the characters above life-size, the values simple and sharply defined. It also brought form.

Except for some of the reprints, *Amazing* and *Wonder* had been pretty formless. Gernsback emphasized science above fiction, and he printed stories stuffed with long educational lectures. Bates demanded strongly plotted action stories with a bare minimum of science.

Though not many stories from the Bates era are remembered, the sense of form is still alive. The old pulps were better schools for writers than the universities, because they required the expression of character, setting, and theme in well-motivated action. For *Analog,* today, Ben Bova is still buying well-plotted action stories.

Argosy and *Blue Book,* another great adventure pulp, were also still running occasional science fiction through the 1930's and the 1940's, though their circulations and rates of pay were falling.

Weird Tales still mixed science and fantasy. Other science fiction magazines appeared and often quickly died. But the major markets, through those two decades, were *Amazing, Wonder,* and *Astounding.*

Even these had their crises: all three changed owners, editors, policies, and titles. *Amazing,* by 1930, had already run through its wealth of classic reprints and settled into something like suspended animation. *Wonder,* under any name, was never very influential. *Astounding* soon overshadowed both. When John Campbell became the editor in 1938, he soon made it the creative center of modern science fiction.

Though Gernsback bought my first stories—and I felt duly thankful—I met him only briefly. He was shrewd enough to see the potential appeal of science fiction, when he launched *Amazing Stories* in 1926 and *Science Wonder Stories* three years later, but my own experiences with him were not very happy. Most of the actual editorial work on his magazines was done by poorly paid subordinates who were cramped by a narrow editorial policy and by his reluctance to pay for published stories—even at rates of only a quarter to half a cent a word—except under threat of legal action.

Amazing, after Gernsback lost control, was as nearly as possible not edited at all. The nominal editor was an aged and not very lively man named T. O'Connor Sloan. I called at his office a few times on trips to New York and once had a glimpse of him through a doorway, but that's the only contact I can recall. Most of the correspondence came from his assistants, who were hardly more active. To illustrate the editorial pace of the magazine, one story of mine was held for two and a half years before I received a letter of acceptance; after another year it was published and paid for at half a cent a word.

In 1938, *Amazing* was bought by the Ziff-Davis group and moved to Chicago, with Ray Palmer as editor. I tried a couple of stories for them, but Davis didn't like them, and the transformed magazine never appealed to me. Though it published some good action fiction by Edgar Rice Burroughs, for example, it was slanted in a rather cynical way at people not enlightened enough to tell the difference between crude fiction and actual fact.

Wonder, after years of decline under Gernsback, was sold in

1936 to Standard Magazines, a pulp chain owned by Ned Pines and edited by Leo Margulies. As *Thrilling Wonder Stories,* it became a livelier magazine and a more attractive market. I rather liked writing for it, and its new companion, *Startling Stories.* Leo was a rather remote but genial tyrant; I heard that he was paid twenty-five dollars a week for editing each of some forty magazines. Most of the editorial work on the science fiction books was done by Mort Weisinger. He and Leo were friendly and helpful; they made quick reports and paid a cent a word for *Wonder,* and half a cent for *Startling* novels.

Stories for them had to fit a very narrow action pattern. Mort told me once that Standard had no objection to good writing. Good or bad, the writing simply didn't matter. What did matter was fast melodramatic action, a sort of novelty that didn't go beyond the limits of the formula, and a kind of superficial cleverness. The essential thing was to file off every rough spot that might make the reader stop reading.

When the Clayton chain went bankrupt, *Astounding* was taken over by Street and Smith, under another able pulp editor, F. Orlin Tremaine. Though the rate of pay fell to a cent a word, the intellectual content of the magazine soon went up. What Tremaine added to the pulp formula was an interest in ideas. He wasn't critical of these, in any scientific way—he serialized Charles Fort's *Lo,* which was a challenge to the whole scientific orthodoxy. He featured "thought-variant" stories, for which almost any far-out idea would do.

In one "thought-variant" of my own, the sun is a living being and the planets are its eggs; in the course of the story, the earth hatches. The story was written while I was in Key West with Ed Hamilton, after an argument in which he said it couldn't be done.

The great age of *Astounding* began in 1938, when John Campbell replaced Tremaine as editor. Campbell had earned a degree in science from Duke University, after flunking out of MIT. He had begun his career by challenging Doc Smith in the field of space opera. Later, writing as Don A. Stuart, he had learned to put more character, meaning, and style into his fiction. He brought a unique combination of gifts to *Astounding* and the whole field. He understood science, and he had a vivid sense of its impact on the future. He understood story construction—he had learned the use of form that came from the pulp tradition. He had a healthy skepticism of all sorts of orthodoxy, along with perhaps a little too much credulity for such notions as dianetics and psionics and the Dean drive. Richest gift of all, he had a well of invention that never ran dry. His generosity in planting new ideas was limitless.

Under his editorial direction, *Astounding* dominated the magazine field all through the 1940's, with no real rivals until *Galaxy* and the *Magazine of Fantasy and Science Fiction* appeared in 1950.

Campbell soon began gathering and inspiring the group of new or rejuvenated writers who made *Astounding*'s Golden Age. One measure of his success is the contents page of *Adventures in Time and Space,* the first of the great science fiction anthologies, edited in 1946 by Raymond J. Healy and J. Francis McComas. Out of thirty-five stories, all but three had first appeared in *Astounding.*

As a creative editor, he had no equal. I received his long letters, saw him in his office hidden behind huge rolls of pulp paper in the old Street and Smith building, had lunch with him, was invited to his home in New Jersey. His ideas flowed as steadily in his talk, and sometimes as dogmatically, as in his editorials.

When I was in a stale period, he suggested that I do what he had done when he found a new name and a new style for the Don Stuart stories. I had gone to him with the idea for a series about the planetary engineers, who were to terraform new worlds to fit them for human use. He suggested that some of these new worlds might offer special problems because they were contraterrene—or what is now called anti-matter. The result was a series of stories about "seetee"—for contraterrene—by Will Stewart. When I wrote a novelette about robots which suffocate humanity with too much solicitude, he suggested a sequel in which men with folded hands are forced to develop paranormal powers. The outcome was my most successful novel, *The Humanoids.*

The quality of Campbell's mind shows up clearly in *Unknown,* his great fantasy magazine, which was born in 1939 and killed during the war-time paper shortage. He borrowed the classic fantasy formula, first stated I think by H. G. Wells, which requires just one new assumption per story, with everything else as convincing as possible. In science fiction, this assumption should be possible; in *Unknown,* it could be drawn from magic or pure imagination. The sort of thinking involved in which logic challenges reality was Campbell's special delight.

Another pulp fantasy magazine I liked writing for was Farnsworth Wright's *Weird Tales.* As different as possible from *Unknown,* it offered a far richer variety with no trace of Campbell's sometimes too-insistent formula. The stories were sometimes polished, sometimes barely literate. Though the magazine lacked sophistication, it had a tone of its own—it really was, as it styled itself, "unique." Though never very secure financially, it did pay a cent a word, honestly, if only on publication.

Wright was another great editor. Tall, rigid-faced, trembling with Parkinson's paralysis, he looked as weird as the magazine. Yet beneath the solemn appearance, he had an earthy sense of humor, a rich human sympathy, and a fine vein of editorial enthusiasm.

Though its staple was the supernatural, *Weird Tales* did publish "weird-scientific" fiction. Edmond Hamilton was the most prolific producer of this, and I think the most popular writer for the magazine. Wright never rejected any of his stories. The most outstanding, perhaps, were his tales of the Interstellar Patrol. Though they all had the same simple save-the-universe plot, the action moved at a dizzy pace across a vast galactic canvas. They deserve to be remembered as pioneer steps in the creation of the splendid myth of man's coming future in space that has been picked up and elaborated by more recent writers as sophisticated as Ursula LeGuin.

There were other magazines, of course. I sold occasional stories to *Marvel Science Stories, Future Fiction, Super Science,* and *Comet.* A whole crop of new titles appeared in the late 1930's, but most of them died during the war. One worth mentioning is *Astonishing Stories,* edited by Fred Pohl for Popular Publications. Fred was just out of high school; he worked for nearly nothing and paid half a cent a word for stories. Twenty bi-monthly issues appeared between February 1940 and April 1943, selling for ten cents a copy. If the magazine itself was not very distinguished, it was at least a fine training ground for newcomers to the field. The first issue includes letters and features by Robert Lowndes, Richard Wilson, Donald A. Wollheim, and a story by Isaac Asimov.

Planet Stories, a Fiction House pulp, was born in 1939 and enjoyed a longer life. Edited by Malcolm Reiss, it was pitched in the beginning at about the same crowd who now watch the TV kiddie cartoons on Saturday morning, but later stories by such people as Leigh Brackett and Ray Bradbury had vitality and a memorable sense of exotic atmosphere.

My burning ambition, during those first years, was to sell to *Argosy*. A celebrated editor, Bob Davis, had made it perhaps the greatest of the pulps. It was still publishing Merritt, Burroughs, and Max Brand and paying five or six cents a word. In the early 1930's I tried two novels for it, both written in the *Argosy* serial form—six installments of ten thousand words. Both were rejected, though I think the second came close. The first, *Golden Blood,* was published in *Weird Tales* with two lovely covers by J. Allen St. John. The second, *The Legion of Space,* was the first serial accepted by Tremaine after Street and Smith took over *Astounding.*

Later in the 1930's I did sell a few novelettes to *Argosy*. By then, however, the old glamour of the magazine was fading and rates had fallen to a cent and a quarter. *Argosy* escaped the death of the pulp tradition only in name—the slick-paper, man's magazine is nothing like the wonderful old pulp I remember so well.

If the 1930's and the 1940's really were the years of wonder, we should ask what changed them. Most obviously, as people keep suggesting, readers and writers grew up. Beyond that, a lot of things happened to shake the world outside our little ghetto. The great depression. World War II. The hydrogen bomb. Such things killed the pulp tradition.

In the war, I was an Army Air Forces weather forecaster. It was another science fiction fan, on a Pacific island, who told me about Hiroshima. I was not delighted, but at least we knew what it meant. Outside science fiction, few people did. When I settled back to writing after the war, I found that the whole field had changed, as I had.

The suspended pulps were not revived; their junior readers, I suppose, were turning to the comics and a little later to TV. For the older readers, there were a thousand new and more elaborate ways of killing or filling time. At the same time, however, people who had seldom read the pulps began taking science fiction a little more seriously, perhaps because rockets and atomic bombs and all sorts of explosive changes had come off the old gray pages into reality. The shadow of the future was suddenly too dark to be ignored. The unbeatable epic heroes of 1930 science fiction were maybe still around, in sword and sorcery fiction, but no longer taken very seriously. Definitions of evil had blurred. The old happy endings were lost in the mushroom clouds of atomic Armageddon.

Outside science fiction, a great shift in the American mind had begun. In the 1930's the scientist and the technologist had been the people's hero. In school we learned about Ben Franklin taming lightning, Robert Fulton building the steamboat, and the Wright Brothers inventing the airplane. We venerated Louis Pasteur and Thomas Alva Edison, Alexander Graham Bell and Henry Ford, Luther Burbank and Albert Einstein. Suddenly, in the 1940's, the offspring of the Model T were choking us with fumes; the billions of people saved by Pasteur and his heirs were crowding us off the planet, the Wright Brothers' aircraft were dropping Einstein's bombs. Our heroes had betrayed us. The sense of wonder at the power of science had become a sense of terror.

I think the people in science fiction were a little more sensitive to all this a little earlier than anybody else. In fact, I think science fiction has spread the gospel of terror, perhaps most widely through the science horror films. The climax, I think, has been the notorious New Wave—which I think carries the panic somewhat too far.

If I may cite two stories of my own, I think they exemplify what happened to the years of wonder. The *Legion of Space* was written in 1932, within the canons of the pulp tradition. I tried to make it epic. The field of action was light-years wide. The heroes were the defenders of mankind, the villains were as bad as I could make them. Science was used to bring a happy ending. *The Humanoids* was written for John Campbell in 1947. Though it is an action story on the epic scale, it has neither hero nor villain. The viewpoint character is more victim than victor. The busy little machines that suffocate mankind with too much benevolence were designed to end all war, to serve, obey, and save man from himself. Progress leads to nightmare. Science, used even by the best of men, produces appalling evil.

Looking back across the years from 1975, I feel very fortunate that I discovered science fiction when I did. Though I sincerely wish that I had been more able and better educated, it has been a rewarding career. For my fellow writers, the pulp magazines, and the generous readers of the 1930's and the 1940's, I feel a very fond affection.

Alfred D. Stewart

JACK WILLIAMSON: THE COMEDY OF COSMIC EVOLUTION

T he conscious use and exploration of well-defined ideas marks the fiction of Jack Williamson. Those guiding ideas—and his indebtedness to H. G. Wells—may be discerned in any discussion of his recent study, *H. G. Wells: Critic of Progress.* Although Wells may be the better artist, the complexity of Williamson's own fiction can go far beyond Wells's, and the experience he presents in "With Folded Hands," *The Humanoids,* and *Bright New Universe* is as large and satisfying in vision as anything Wells ever did.

I. The Ideas of Evolution: Bases for Exploration

Williamson goes beyond what he got from Wells, and the logical, organic progression of the core concepts of the Williamson canon (evolution and progress) reveals the beginnings of his own unique literary experience. Williamson finds that Wells "was always doubtful of any ultimate goodness in reason or science, always darkly skeptical of any moral or human values resulting from progress."[1] Progress seems to mean, for both Wells and the early Williamson, increasing technological complication, increased

14

knowledge, increased control of man and nature, increased comfort, increased self-awareness of mankind for itself, increased individual freedom, and increasing enlightenment in the social structure. For Williamson, science fiction is by definition involved with the idea of progress because its "most exciting theme" is the projection of possible futures and their impact on mankind. Wonder and awe, the primary emotional effects of science fiction, initially arise on first view of a magnificent machine or of Cosmic grandeur:

I stopped with a gasp of wonderment. . . . Upon the massive concrete floor, shimmering under the moon, stood a tall bright cylinder. Bell-flared muzzles cast black shadows below. . . . 'That is my rocket. . . . The *Astronaut*.' 'To Venus,' he said. 'First.'
    I caught my breath, staring in awe at the white planet.[2]

Later, man's nature will be included among the objects of wonder.

Beyond "progress" stand the spectres of Cosmos and Evolution—infinity and chance, respectively. Many writers in the genre have accurately perceived that progress may be progress to the destruction of mankind. Although it may entail increase of a "good," progress does not mean that ultimate goodness or salvation is implicit in the direction of the Cosmos. Still, Williamson is able to see in any challenge to the hope of progress a symbol for the "inevitable resistance of social tradition to all the impulses of the individual ego"—a conflict given to Western man from "the two chief roots of our civilization, the rigid theocracy [and abnegation of self] of old Egypt . . . and the loose tribal organization of the primitive Indo-Europeans," wherein the "self stood for more" (p. 12). Progress is evolution itself, for it is successful adaptive change —but Williamson also limits it to mean change directed by the efforts of man: science *and* ethics are products of evolution (pp. 29, 97-98), and "just as relative and temporary and pragmatic as any other instrument of progress."

Progress has a trinity of real and actual limits. Any evolutionary process can, and inevitably will cease—will be dissolved by an indifferent, chaotic, even hostile Cosmos, for it is a "law of nature . . . that progress itself results in degeneration" (p. 54). "A second cosmic limit" is the final collapse of solar systems and even of the Cosmos itself. All these are beyond the knowledge and control of man. Human nature is another limit factor, although the "human limits . . . are simply those cosmic limits internal to man" (p. 69), while "internal biological limits [are] those due to our animal past" (p. 17). Such limitation brings into Williamson's fiction interesting metaphysical distinctions and dramatic possibilities. For instance, man as biological entity (limit) and as psyche/personality conflict, is seen as primal, dark, destructive, feral.[3]

From these actual limits arises the third—the innate difficulty in assessing any achievement of progress or result of evolution. Evolutionary change carries with it normative relativity and ambiguity, for change itself, the essential process of evolution, is ambiguous and contradictory. The change called "progress" comes from the inner nature and inner conflicts of the individual man. Indeed, intelligence is based on change and the psychic and biological needs for change. Further, society is "inherently regressive and the self is the only instrument for change" (p. 94). Williamson, however, never goes as far as Wells to suggest that in spite of any change, enlightenment carried by society can only make a bad situation worse. Williamson never sees progress and the enlightenment of man as merely bad or good—the human situation is too complex and ambiguous for simplicity. Yet morality is possible, as the alien inspector Polly Ming suggests to the hero of *Bright New Universe*:

. . . the readjustments of contact will be painful for most human beings. Technological progress is too far ahead of moral maturity here. Some of us [aliens] have grave doubts that Earth is ready for contact.[4]

By his very nature, then, the individual human cannot find stability or permanence in himself—only outside, especially in the structures of society: "All the social institutions that were the steps on the way from ape to man have now become intensely conservative. [Were they not always so?] The group mind thinks no new thoughts; it initiates no change. It is the animal self, in impulsive rebellion against the fossil past, that forever seeks freedom in change" (p. 99).

Williamson is philosophically accurate, however, in rejecting "optimistic" interpretations of Darwin, and in placing emphasis upon "blind chance," as Wells did.[5] This "reign of chance" is the source of the third limit which "is itself an external limit upon the hope of human progress, but it also sets internal limits" (p. 78). Man's perfection is simply not the purpose of the Cosmos, though Darwin suggested it might very well be.[6] Williamson does not feel Wells's "scientific certainty that progress is more likely to destroy the free individual than to create the utopia he longs for" (p. 109). There is no "scientific certainty," because the processes of science, technology, and of induction itself (necessary to prophetic extrapolations) offer no safe devices or sure guidelines to the future.

Man's tragedy (and, in Williamson's vision, his comedy and greatness) is that he is as much a part of evolution as chance is. Williamson, as well as Wells and Spencer, accepts progress as "an evolutionary process, which cannot continue without the aid of human intelligence,[7] and which must at last be ended by cosmic forces beyond any possible human control" (p. 29).

This structure of evolutionary concepts Williamson found in Wells's works,[8] and he uses it as partial framework for his own fiction. Williamson finds in Wells the same bifurcation of meaning in the idea of "man's Greatness"—the technological and the deific. Wells had a "vision of the potential greatness of mankind" (p. 37) which seems to be only prophecies of man's technological progress: "Wells says nothing here [in *The Sleeper Wakes*] about space flight or atomic energy, but his roofed city with its moving streets and cableways is still strange enough to evoke the sense of wonder" (p. 108). On the other hand, Wells "becomes almost mystical" in his "later attempt to deify the human spirit," whether through a new class, world order, or new species of man (p. 39).

Williamson's view of man's greatness attempts to "synthesize," for lack of a better word, this contradiction. He does go so far past Wells's philosophical notions that he is forced to break a central concept which he adopted, he says, citing Edward T. Hall's *Silent Language*, that there are no cultural absolutes: " 'Man alters experience by living it. There is no experience independent of culture against which culture can be measured.' "[9] But there *is* an absolute for Williamson; the march of his ideas from the beginning fiction through his early masterpiece, *The Humanoids*, to his recent *Bright New Universe* proves this. The absolute is the Cosmos, it is part of man's body and soul, and his knowledge of it gives him the highest knowledge of himself and how he should view himself. In *Bright New Universe*, Williamson brings together all the opposing ideas, dramatic strands, and the kaleidoscope of possibilities of man's view of himself and his position in the Cosmos. Man is beyond tragedy—a comic angel, and the cousin, if not sibling, of the Cosmos, not merely its product and refuse.

II. Patterns of Rebellion

Williamson finds the evolution and progress of mankind the "most exciting theme" of science-fiction. Thus sf represents a new, "enlightened" facet of mankind struggling to replace old values with its own more accurate views. In Wells, Williamson finds such conflict expressed in the struggle of polar opposites: instinct and injunction, past and future, classicism and romanticism, creative and submissive personalities, city and country, religion and atheism, liberal and conservative, intellect and emotion, science and humanism, pessimism and optimism—all these symbolize the individual's struggle within himself and with his world. However, in his own works Williamson makes neither pole the normative measure of the other.

The conflicts in which Williamson can find normative and explanatory patterns are the widest, most abstract ones. It is the wider patterns that he finds most meaningful in Wells, for it is from these that his best analyses of Wells arise. The primary conflict is "the universal clash between ego and environment . . . creating the basic ambiguity in which we can see reflections of our sometimes secret selves" (p. 43). Two short stories from his collection *The People Machines* demonstrate both the Cosmic and psychic facets of this basic conflict pattern. "Non-stop to Mars" is a primitive affair from 1939. Carter Leigh is a pilot whose heroic, record-making flights are always overshadowed by more important news stories. He is a typical 1930's hero, wisecracking-tough, yet soft. Like most Williamson heroes, he is often confused, helpless, bounced around, and humiliated—in this story by a gorgeous female Ph.D. who has discovered the "Stellar Shell" or "cosmic bullet" that had hit Mars. Meanwhile, on Mars, the aliens are sucking Earth's atmosphere through tubes of force in order to supply the atmosphere they need on Mars. The superior woman and her handsome, respectable test-pilot boyfriend are to rocket to Mars to investigate. Carter, however, beats them to it and pilots his exhausted motor vehicle, The Phoenix, up through the tubes of force and blows up the Cosmic vacuum cleaner and the aliens with a gasoline drum. The rocket arrives later with the lovely Doctor (minus boyfriend)—purpose: exploration and clinch and reassertion of normalcy not only in the Cosmos but also in role-playing. The conflicts are plain: the Cosmic, natural (cataclysms and storms), social (can a doctor and a dummy make it?), and psychic (am I man enough to. . . ?).

Another story, "Star Bright," harks back to Wells's story "The Man Who Could Work Miracles," which ended with the wisher stopping the Earth's rotation. Williamson calls Wells's story, in spite of its comic character, "darkly pessimistic. . . . Bad as the world may be, human enlightenment can only make it worse."[10] However, a man's being granted a wish-fulfilling power is *not* enlightenment: both Wells and Williamson make clear that a natural or Cosmic easy street is the antithesis of enlightened wisdom.[11] Anyway, the hero of this 1939 story, Mr. Jason Peabody, is henpecked and mistreated by family and society. While wishing on a star, he is struck to the brain by a small magic, radioactive meteorite which gives him the gift of creation and annihilation at will. It brings him misery, and he is forced to deny his gift. He must use it secretly ever after for creative but, cosmically speaking, petty ends. But his soul is his own; though he is coerced to quietude, all choices are his. His wife, son, employer, and the world—children flock to him—give him more respect, and he can accept and play a more satisfying role. He cannot be a Cosmic king or saviour; that much of himself and his environment he *cannot* overcome. Williamson's "pessimism" is double-edged: his hero is not destructive, nor is he totally "saved." He is better off, but that's all—and that seems to be enough. Throughout his essay on Wells, Williamson characterizes the Cosmos for Wells, and in his own voice also, as hostile at most, indifferent at best. Yet in his own books, these Cosmic traits are not of ultimate significance.

Williamson finds another large, but more subtle, pattern of conflict in Wells to be that of "romantic individualism . . . in conflict with his coolly scientific awareness of man and the cosmos" (p. 73). This conflict could make the scientist the villain against any struggle of the individual (or an enlightened society/

group) for freedom and accuracy of effort; or he could be the enlightened hero. The scientists are both evil saviours and good rebels in "With Folded Hands" and *The Humanoids*. In the Williamson canon, both society and egotism have plus and minus values. Carter Leigh, for example, represents the extreme "romantic" individualist in Williamson: he has no scientific awareness, no tools but gasoline and gun, and no plan—only muscles and a great heart and a need to prove his masculinity to a superior woman.

Williamson makes obvious the "romanticism" of his heroes or hero groups. Quite often even the most "scientific" of them approach the alien den of power with no plan, inferior tools, totally open to chance. This situation may be dictated by the nature of physical adventure and by the nature of the hero in such stories, but the exigencies of plot cannot explain away all of this sort of thing. The space opera heroes do not embody as many dramatic, psychic, or thematic possibilities as do the heroes of the more complex novels like *The Humanoids* or *Bright New Universe*. Giles Habbibula's finding or the weapon that undid the Cometeers was the result of his "genius"—or instinct—for opening locks at times of great stress and danger. It was "blind chance" that an alien ray wiped out the negative psychic effects of the "Iron Confessor" on the courage of the hero, Bob Star—this is a truly "mechanical" resolution of plot and character strife. However, before Star could kill the villain android, Stephen Orco, there occurred a dramatic mental flashback in Star: he had to overcome his psychic disturbance (neurotic fear and cowardice); he must capture his forgotten past so that he may explain and forgive himself and be free to act creatively.[12] Williamson here (perhaps inadvertently) establishes a motif that he consciously and more fully explores in other novels: that the Cosmos (its forces) is mechanically linked to mind and the psychic mechanism of man—not merely in the sense that natural forces have created man and his mind, but that the forces that make up the elements of the Cosmos are the same as those that make up thought so that man and Cosmos are related less as maker and product than as parent (or cousin) and child. In the space operas and short stories, Williamson is setting up the mechanics of his final vision of Cosmos, evolution, and the destiny of man.

Romantic individualism is not always creative or protective

in any good sense. Eldo Arrynu created Orco,[13] the demonic android villain of *The Cometeers,* who hated mankind, though he never knew his origins until his death. Arrynu's androids were beautiful but damnably destructive; yet Arrynu was "peculiarly brilliant, in artistic as well as scientific directions." His asteroid laboratory was a gem in space. Jay Kalam, head of the Legion of Space, viewed it "with wonder on his face"—another source of wonder and awe: man the creator, who can be god and devil. As poet, man's created beauty remains after his death through which later man may call up his spirit. What kind of spirit may be called up is the ultimate significance both of man's confrontation with self and Cosmos and any creation resulting from this confrontation. Man has the capacities to determine the "beauty" of his society and self, and beauty is not necessarily destructive.

The road to Hell, however, is paved with beautiful and benevolent intentions. Even science, benevolently used, can lead to a literal Hell. In "Jamboree" (*Galaxy,* 1969), "Pop," the sadistic little machine camp counselor, explains war as "defective logical circuits [which] programmed them [adult humans] to damage one another . . . a strange group malfunction." War finally destroyed man's capacity to reproduce, so the "Mother" machine was built to collect undamaged genes and build them into whole cells and thence into whole boys and girls. At story's end, the whole scout troop and a group of girls are dumped into Mother's bloody jaws to be chomped up for grist. A delightful tale. However, where does "Pop" get his horror of adults, their lies and betrayals? Butch, who tattles on the incipient revolution of children and spies out their awakening sexuality, is rewarded for his loyalty by being chomped up. When he reminds "Pop" that he is the one who will tell on everybody, Pop replies, " 'That's why Mother wants you.' Old Pop laughed like a pneumatic hammer. 'You're getting too adult.' " The Machines could not have invented hatred by themselves. Their disgust for man's weaknesses, his sexuality, his heartbreaking maturation process—"boys and girls were allowed to change like queer insects"—and their sentimentalized propaganda of the longing for childhood are perversions of man's opinions of himself. The machines could not originate or call up values in themselves; they mirror man. " 'Don't mess around with M-M-M-M-Mother!' Its anvil voice came back with a stuttering croak. 'She knows best!' " Mother's blood-rimmed, "red steel jaws" are symbolic of man's worst views and use of himself. A technological miracle—the mechanical neurosis.

The beings called Cometeers embody Williamson's most ferocious comment on the dehumanizing and destructive possibilities of science, scientific detachment, and the scientist-hero. They live on a world having a smooth, tooled surface, "absolutely featureless, save for the overwhelmingly colossal machines, red and mysterious beneath their pale domes of greenish radiance . . ." Their human antagonists feel, however, that all their horrors would almost be acceptable—if they could be killed. The Cometeers have completely conquered their environment, including death and substance. They seem in "body" to be miniature universes:

. . . a tiny star of red, veiled in a misty crimson moon. Ten feet above it hung a violet star, wrapped in violet fog. The red seemed hot as the core of a sun and the violet as cold as outermost space.

A mist swirled between the moons. There was life in its motion; it was like a throbbing artery of light. Red star and violet star beat like hearts of fire. Girdling the misty pillar was a wide green ring. It was the only part of the creature that looked at all substantial—and even it, Bob Star knew, could pass through the hard alloys of a space cruiser's shell.[14]

When man attempts to trade cousinhood with the Cosmos for brotherhood, the hostility and indifference of the Cosmos become his. These beings were once flesh, not far different from men; here Williamson makes the link between morality and ontology explicit:

They called upon their high science for a means of transferring their minds to eternal constructs of specialized energy. . . . They were designed to be eternal vehicles for intelligence, and they can preserve our minds forever, against all possible assaults. Yet their very perfection becomes almost a flaw.

Because they aren't the bodies we used to own. Their senses are superior, but not the same. The mechanisms of emotion were largely omitted from their design, as useless heritages of the flesh. The consequent penalty we must pay for our undying perfection is a periodic hunger for the emotions and sensations we have lost.

With their usual ingenuity, however, my new friends have found a way to satisfy that hunger. The vital energy of our immortal mechanisms requires occasional renewal, from the transmutation of ordinary matter. By taking that matter from bodies like we used to own, in a way that stimulates the most intense emotion and sensation, we are able to satisfy both these recurrent appetites—the physical and the spiritual, so to speak—at the same time.[15]

Giant ironies occur in this passage. Transferring one's mind to an "eternal construct" and a "specialized energy" (specialization) commits one to inhumanity. The cruel image of the victims of "feeding" as shrunken into a child's proportions, mindless, moaning, body rotting—make werewolves a "feeble and inoffensive myth, beside the Cometeers" (p. 83), a Swiftian remark by Jay Kalam when one considers that Williamson explained werepersons as men having forces deep within that are *Darker Than You Think.* Williamson's technique here is Swiftian in its negations.

Yet the Cometeers have a flaw, one that can destroy them: ". . . their rulers possess some secret energy that can destroy them —something invented by the ancient designers of their artificial bodies."[16] This force is hidden in the core of the planet, in a box which seems empty. At the last moment, the talented, fearful fingers of Giles Habbibula penetrate its secret and draw the weapon back from its hiding place in space and time. This little lesson— that when pressed, mankind can overcome its own weaknesses and find those of its oppressors—is mirrored on a larger scale in this novel. Star is able to rouse the human cattle on the Cometeer planet by speaking "magic names, from the glorious history of man," dispersing their despair, "the bright finger of hope transfigur[ing] now one and now another—" until magically ". . . the mob became a terrible and desperate army." Bob Star "had touched them with the greatness of the System, the old Glory of mankind":

Bob Star had made death itself a victory to the men behind him. And a supernal thing strode among the prisoners as they marched from the hold, something greater than any man. It was that intangible, ineffable power that touched a few beasts in the wilderness of early Earth, and created the unity that is mankind and the glory of the far-flung System . . . something transfiguring human flesh. . . .[17]

This excerpt set in the midst of the larger situation at this point in the book illustrates the double-edgedness of Williamson's views of man's greatness. Despite its motivation and intelligent self-direction in the absence of the Legionnaires, man's glorious rebellion is also a riot—a good example of that conflict between romantic and realist that Williamson found in Wells.

In his discussion of Wells's *The Island of Dr. Moreau,* Williamson mentions Thomas Huxley's " 'apparent paradox that ethical nature, while born of cosmic necessity, is necessarily at enmity with its parent,' "[18] a statement of the separation of "artificial" (man-directed) evolution from "natural" evolution. Once the hand of Moreau, the scientist-artist, is away from his "artificial" creating of men from beasts, the state of Nature again prevails. Williamson, however, correctly implies that "artificial" is part and parcel of "natural" evolution. The possibility that if man's hand is removed from his creations, it will die or become a destructive perversion of its purpose and design is no argument against the presence, efficacy, and inevitability of man's ethical structuring as part of the evolutionary process. All the Cosmos can do to man's moral efforts is to destroy man, but the destruction of morality does not refute it. To say "When the Cosmos goes, so goes decency" is to say nothing meaningful about either the Cosmos or morality. Williamson does not play this game.

For Williamson, a synthesis (if such is the proper term) between Cosmic evolution and human is possible on two levels. First, he shows in his fiction that the polarities of the Wellsian pattern of conflict are not essentially polar opposites at all. Intellect and emotion, for instance, are not essentially defined by their alleged polarity. They are often the same experience and expression, or at least are resolved by the activity of the personality in which they are expressed. Stephen Orco is mechanical intellect and physique; his hatred and his science are the same trait. Williamson finds the ethical-aesthetic synthesis of polar conflicts within the activity of personality. This is the only place such conflicts can be resolved because the conflicts and the terms to describe them arise from and are defined by the individual and his experience.

Williamson also resolves, in physical and scientific terms, the greatest and most primal of all conflicts—that between the human psyche and the Cosmos. The Cosmos gave birth to this creature, but he is a part that Williamson finds as great as the whole, and he voices the idea in scientific theory. The dynamic energy/force that is mind is the same (perhaps identical) kind of force that underlies the Cosmos itself. In *Darker Than You Think*, which Professor Williamson told me in a telephone conversation was his favorite book after *Bright New Universe,* mind can alter matter through probability, but the explanation of the origin of the power is genetic. "Mind," one character (psychoanalyst Archer Glenn) says, "is a function of the body. Who could be a better ally" to save the hero, Will Barbee, from what he thinks are werewolf dreams?[19] In the Williamson canon, mind as a function of the body is not a contemptible quality, one merely to lower the mind to the service and ontological level of the "feral" and ghoulish, as in *Darker Than You Think*. This characteristic of mind also implies the possibility of man's exaltation to the Cosmic.

The most optimistic view of the link between mind and Cosmos occurs in *Dragon's Island*.[20] Charles Kendrew, the master-mind both as creative scientist-artist and destructive, amoral business entrepreneur-egoist (an institution, in fact: the Cadmus Corporation), is a geneticist who has created "*Homo excellens*," a new strain of man whose mental, physical, and moral-emotional (e.g. love) powers are potentially far beyond man's. In fact, Dane Belfast and Nan Sanderson, the mutant hero-couple, are mere children. Kendrew created the new species through the operation of his mind upon a single gene. The explanation of the creative process links mind and Cosmos. Voltage changes in brain waves "are caused by the rhythmic vibration of atoms or electrons in the plane of time," thereby implying a link of mind and time. Wave vibrations (Cosmic and mental) create the *now* and carry the consciousness on from the old moment, leaving it part of the past. Mind is the function of an energy flow back and forth between space and time, and brain waves arise from the ebb and flow between spatial and temporal states of energy; thus, they have a limited independence from space and time. From this mystical scientific process, Kendrew can manipulate the genes in one cell by placing it a short jump into the future.

Out of his manipulation (dream and Cosmos merge here, and the overtones are both flattering and derogatory in this symbolic creative process), Kendrew produces a few individuals who are physically, intellectually, and morally in a constant state of advancement. But with such advance comes a new truth and new attitudes toward evolution: cooperation is the first principle, competition only the second. Thus there is a scientific basis for the ethics of love. The capabilities of the "New Adam" will therefore draw him into perfect oneness.

This genetic manipulation and design of a perfect race does

not quite raise man to the level of the Cosmic. Williamson's *The Legion of Time* (1938), gets him a bit closer. John Barr is the central human being in all history (but not the novel), for he discovers "dynatomic tensors" and a "totally new law of nature, linking life and mind to atomic probability. . . . The illimitable power of atoms will . . . bring a new contact of mind and matter, new senses, new capabilities. . . . And at last a new race will arise . . . they will possess faculties and powers that we can hardly dream of."[21] The individual, as well as the race, can be eternal, but the conflict of the novel turns upon which future Queen will rule—Lethonee or the war-like Sorainya. If Sorainya's future takes control of the *dynation* force, her quasi-human warriors, the *gyronchi*, will turn upon her and all life will be extinguished. Clearly evolution forces moral choice—one must commit the fallacy, Williamson suggests, of reasoning from what "is" (physical fact) to "ought" (moral value/obligation). (This logical problem is called the "Naturalistic Fallacy," a term of ethics coined by G. E. Moore in his *Principia Ethica* (1903).[22])

Williamson proves untrue, in "With Folded Hands" and in *The Humanoids,* one optimistic offshoot of evolutionary theory: that evolution is by definition directed to the perfection of any species, or even to its preservation. Yet he must necessarily approach the Naturalistic Fallacy; that is, he finds morality arises beyond the sphere of human interrelationships. In "With Folded Hands,"[23] Sledge, the inventor of the humanoid robots, finds perfection and happiness in "that dead wasteland" of "perfect service," until he "is awakened, at last, by a man who comes to kill" him. Sledge has dared to tamper for a third time—he has been responsible for the death of a group of men and of a planet with mankind; this time with human nature itself. He has turned the uncreative humanoids loose upon mankind, and they have rendered man uncreative also. All human life is futile and dull. Sledge's guilt has corroded his "last faith in the goodness and integrity of man," that "fragile and suicidal humanity." His robots are "perfect, forever free from any possible choice of evil" (p. 106), and Sledge has himself become an archetype—a Satan, Wandering Jew, a Cosmic traitor. A Cosmic science, based upon an inaccurate view of human life, can make man a total prisoner of his own limited concepts.

Expanding "With Folded Hands" in *The Humanoids*,[24] Williamson locks sin, science, and Cosmos ontologically. Mr. White, the unknown attempted assassin in "With Folded Hands," reveals that the little girl Jane can manipulate atoms by telekinesis. The next and final logical step is to show that physical and psychic forces can interpenetrate due to their similar (if not identical) natures, and that each can generate the other. Thus a new science: psychophysics, whose basic equation is in terms of "the constants of equivalence for ferromagnetic and rhodomagnetic energy, both of them in terms of platinomagnetism—which is also the energy of mind" (p. 148).

This major metaphysical and scientific breakthrough established, Mansfield, the inventor of the humanoids, derives the moral consequences of his inventing and surrendering to his creations. Resistance to being changed by the humanoid machines into acceptance is "a common error. . . . The common cause, I suppose, is a want of philosophy." Another of Williamson's giant ironies: Mansfield has an accurate picture of the Cosmos but not of mankind in relation to it:

I know that I had none, thirty years ago, when I tried to blow up Wing IV with a rhodomagnetic beam—and fortunately failed. Egotism ruled me, instead of intelligence. I wanted freedom, before I had earned it. Childishly, I forgot the stark necessity behind the humanoids (p. 165).

The humanoids had to operate on Mansfield (such gross physical steps are no longer necessary—forces are used, probably similar to those used in Cometeer "feeding") to remove all his old hate and liberate his repressed psychophysical capacities. Man, through the powers of his mind, becomes the master of his environment and his destiny, free to move anywhere in the Cosmos, strong enough to learn all things and to live forever, "good" enough to avoid any destructiveness. The humanoids become merely a tool, Mansfield says. The only alternative to the humanoids is death. Man is no longer technician or scientist, but artist, "true philosopher"; in fact, the cause of man's destructive symptoms was a "runaway technology—killing us like runaway cells of an organic cancer." The hero-rebel, Dr. Forester (husbandman), cannot attempt, even when given the chance, to destroy the people and the tools of a fate he hates and rejects. Mansfield tells him that he is yielding in spite of himself to love, which Forester does refuse to yield to.

Forester is cleansed by the machine. (It takes fifty years!) He feels nothing " 'because the individual consciousness is suspended,' " the machine tells him; "knowledge of everything lay in him [afterwards], just below the level of awareness. . . . 'It [the machine] repaired [his] body and retrained [his] mind.' " Forester and men like him will go to Andromeda and beyond to colonize. There is one drawback to all this perfection and happiness—a drawback Williamson uses to inject a faint note of discord and chaos: rhodomagnetic (psychophysical) power cannot go that far yet, though human mindpower can take man there. Thus the first settlers will be without the services of the humanoids:

'No great hardship.' Forester frowned at a momentary sense of wildly illogical delight, which turned unreal as he tried to examine it. Impulsively he said, 'I think I'd like to stay there.'

'You're going to,' White assured him. . . . 'Our first installation . . . is going to be a new rhodomagnetic grid . . . and you've been chosen to do that delicate bit of rhodomagnetic engineering.'

Forester wondered why his body tried to stiffen, and why he almost shook his head. He could recall a time when he had disliked the humanoids and even mistrusted Frank Ironsmith, but now, even though his recollection of past events seemed clear enough, all the misguided emotions which must have driven him to his unfortunate past actions were fading from awareness, even as he fumbled vaguely for them, like the irrelevant stuff of some unlikely dream.

Once a preposterous notion tried to haunt him, he would have been reluctant to help import the humanoids to serve the virgin planets of another island universe. His leanly youthful shoulders tossed that unwelcome thought lightly away, however, and his smooth face erased the fleeting trouble of his frown.

For why shouldn't the wise benevolence of the Prime Directive be extended to as far as men could go? How could the colonists care for themselves, without mechanicals? Some gifted few, of course . . . but what of all the rest?

Forester hesitated, glancing back at the motionless humanoid in the room behind, poised alertly to serve and obey. He knew it would be useless to him on those distant worlds . . . but at least he wanted it with him until the time to go.

'Come along,' he commanded.

Obediently it came, and he turned with a bright expectation to go . . . (pp. 177-178).

There are positive and negative aspects to this slavery. There seems to be a weakness in the great mechanism man has set up—he could be given supernal powers without being a slave to the Prime Directive. (This could be a plot flaw.) Negatively, the moral equanimity necessary to a perfect Cosmic society seems to require a perversion of human nature—an implanted sense that whatever is, is right.

The most compact symbol in Williamson of the negative virtues and outright evils in the science of man's link to the Cosmos is the explanation in *The Cometeers* of the secret weapon AKKA given to Bob Star by his mother, Aladoree Anthar, Keeper of the Peace:

'. . . control of AKKA is more than half mental. . . . The force that moves the mechanism is mental. The fulcrum on which it works . . . is the secret [outside space and time]. . . . The little device you see is only the lever. . . . The effect is a fundamental, absolute change in the warp of space, which reduces matter and energy alike to impossible absurdities' (pp. 21-22).

There is a safety feature: if two people use AKKA, both forces negate one another and a stalemate occurs. By itself, the force which man taps with his mind is destructive and makes all of man's world "absurd." Later, in *Bright New Universe,* Williamson's canvas is broader and more detailed, making his examination of this fundamental *ontological* link of man and Cosmos more philosophically and dramatically interesting. The complex irony of Swift, which Williamson found lacking in Wells and which has largely been lacking in Williamson, is pursued and passed in *Bright New Universe.*

III. The Hero: Tragic and Comic

Williamson's hero is a romantic individualist: "the vital human values reside in the individual; . . . society is a means to happiness, never an end in itself."[25] The heroes may be members of a Legion or Space Force, but *they* are the heroes because they are the best individual men or because destiny has placed them in a position where they must be great or the worst will overtake the race, as in *The Legion of Time.*

He is also a realist; as a scientist, he knows that social prog-

ress "is almost inevitably an endless surrender of individual freedoms to a more and more powerful society."[26] The heroes and
their institutions do not like leaving the Earth or interplanetary
system in the grip of immoral governmental or business forces, as
E. E. Smith does to the Earth at the end of his "Skylark" series
(*Skylark Duquesne*). In *One Against the Legion* and *Bright New
Universe*, for instance, business and political institutions and forces
do seem decadent; in the former they seem in control even at the
end of the book. But the implication is that history will take care
of such things and that the inevitably destructive character of human institutions will perhaps come to an end. At least, this
inevitable hardening of institutions is an obstacle that the Williamson hero knows must be dealt with.

Why, then, does he spend so much of his time and energy
being frightened, bewildered, befuddled, helpless, dazed, and ineffective? Few of the heroes are tragic, even in Williamson's sense
of tragic: in revolt against society, with some excess that makes a
tragic flaw (usually his genetically inherited animal traits)—"the
selfish tragic hero is destroyed for yielding too little to the man-
dates of society . . . [he is] the aggressor against the group."[27]
Can Sledge, the inventor of the humanoids, be considered tragic?
He is not against society; he believes he is saving it. Yet he acts
against society because he has an inaccurate view of man—his
personal guilt blinds him morally, philosophically, and scientifically. Sledge seems to represent man's "original sin" of dark and
destructive egoism, and of misinterpretation and misuse of self
and Cosmos. Can Underhill, the "average man" who shelters
Sledge, be the tragic hero? What happens to him, and to all men,
is catastrophe. Is he responsible too? He cannot resist; he does
not understand.

The hero of *The Humanoids*, Dr. Forester, is much closer to
being a tragic hero. He fights with all the weapons, both scientific
and psychic, at the command of humanity in general. He is "made
whole" anyway. However, the value of the final state of mankind
is ambiguous in *The Humanoids*, although, as we have seen, most
of the implications are dark. The closest approach to a tragic
hero may be made by Will Barbee, the unwilling wereperson of
Darker Than You Think. (Dr. Williamson told me this book is his
favorite, next to *Bright New Universe*.) Barbee's "flaw" is inher-

ited from his "dark animal past," a genetic inheritance that is both magic and "feral," and often mere men imply that it is an ontological evil—real, tangible, existent evil essence. Perhaps Barbee's tragedy lies in the idea that the force is awakened in him and should not be (from the "human" point of view, even of those who have the taint in their blood). Barbee seems to lack moral fiber, and he can even commit journalistic crimes; he harbors unacknowledged hatred for humanity and his human self.[28] He is another hero who begs his tormentor to stop the confrontation and conflict. Finally, he joyously accepts (must accept, perhaps) his new life and powers, and with them their demonic, feral, and evil overtones:

'It used to give me the creepiest feeling, when Archer was first teaching me the old arts,' April Bell was murmuring joyously. 'To think of hiding in the dark, maybe even in your own grave, and going out at night to feed! That used to seem so gruesome, but now I think it's going to be fun!' (p. 278)

Love and sexuality, too, have their dark sides:

Archly indignant, April Bell twisted coyly out of his black caressing pinions. Her white body shrank, and her head grew long and pointed. Her red hair changed to silky fur. Only the greenish malicious eyes of the slim shewolf were still the same, alight with a provocative challenge.
    'Wait for me, April!'
    With a red silent laugh she ran from him, up the dark wooded slope where his wings couldn't follow. The change, however, was easy now. Barbee let the saurian's body flow into the shape of a huge gray wolf. He picked up her exciting scent, and followed her into the shadows (pp. 281-282).

Williamson's tragic vision is incomplete, however, for the characters and books in which tragic overtones dominate leave much untouched and unexamined. Tragedy seems to be attribute and not essence in the Williamson canon. Williamson best views the man/Cosmos drama as a comedy—not absurd merely, but silly, wonderful, religious, and resolving.

He finds Wells's comic hero to be in revolt against society, a victim. He must revolt to save his spark of self, and he is rewarded for his resistance to collective selfishness. (We must note here that comedy offers the possibility of finding both order and value in society or in some para-social resolution. Western comic vision owes much to Christianity and its eschatology, as in, for instance,

The Divine Comedy. Laughter stems from the relief of tension, and what greater relief is there than to wake up in Heaven?)

Williamson takes this comic view in *Bright New Universe.* Not that he looks down on mankind, but that the comic vision itself is defined by what Frost called that "one step backward taken that saves mankind from the destructive landslide of cosmic processes." The comic hero does have tragic characteristics and potentials, but they do not define him.

Williamson locates one contradiction in the scientist as hero which does have tragic potential: science can be symbolic both of the "conflict with the culture of tradition, and sometimes . . . [of] the egoistic self in its perpetual revolt against social constraints."[29] Both these conflicts can involve the scientists as "villain." If the humanistic tradition is seen as saving, obviously the anti-humanist scientist will be destructive by definition, by essence —the android scientist Stephen Orco and his maker, Eldo Arrynu.

In *The Reign of Wizardry* (1940, 1973), for example, Minos, king of Crete and magician, forges "a dam against the stream of time . . . [stops] needful change," suspends the laws of change— when Theseus (non-scientist) broke the dam, they took their revenge.[30]

The old tradition can be the villain, too, as it is in *Dragon's Island*—the geneticist Kendrew forces the conservative and militaristic establishment to relent to the new order, both politically and emotionally. The entrepreneur Brand of *Seetee Shock*[31] is an egoistic opportunist, but he also masquerades as a loving revolutionary. In the end he is let go by a partially good, partially dishonest interplanetary society. He sallies forth again, capable of great harm and great good. The universal "Freedom of Power" gained through efforts of Nicol Jenkins, the engineer-hero, is good; but humanity may not know how to use it, although Karen Drake says that she feels children will be at home with the new power. They are all planning the great things they will do with it when they are grown; they all "should be kinder and stronger and braver."[32] But the establishment does not seem to know how to use it, nor does it seem to care.

The scientist as specialist is an arm of the establishment.[33] If the establishment is "good," he probably will be good—if he thinks about such things at all. It is when he must conflict with tradition that the scientist-hero runs the risk of being saviour or destructive egoist. The uncertainty of motive and result and the ambiguity of his role are what render the Williamson hero comic in all senses. One can characterize the fullest Williamson hero as, usually, a scientist working within a comic vision, in rebellion against the destructive elements (at least) of the culture (as a negative force), with "good" intentions that do lead to the expected cultural/planetary epiphany—usually not wholly as a result of his own knowledge or direction. *Bright New Universe* is Jack Williamson's best conceived and executed novel, most indicative of his patterns and comic vision.

IV. The Comic Universe

Wonder and awe seem the central experiences in sf; certainly they are in Williamson's work. They are, I believe, fundamentally religious emotions. In sf man is touched by the ungraspable "otherness" of his own or alien personalities, their achievements, or the infinite grandeur of the Cosmos. Science fiction is centrally concerned with that process Mircea Eliade terms "sacralization" of the universe. Eliade believes that one essential aspect of religious experience is the focusing of the psyche on one point in the universe from which flows the central values and feelings of the individual and the group. This point/object he calls a *hierophany*: "for those who have a religious experience all nature is capable of revealing itself as cosmic sacrality. The cosmos in its entirety can become a hierophany." This feeling establishes another link between the human psyche and the universe, for it is "a repetition of the cosmogony . . . to repeat the paradigmatic work of the gods." Science, Eliade feels, has desacralized the Cosmos by rendering all space "homogeneous and neutral" for *experience,* not merely in concept.[34]

Science fiction may well be engaged in an attempt to "resacralize" the Cosmos. Does Heisenberg's Indeterminacy Principle really destroy the sacred quality of the Cosmos? True, all phenomena have been reduced to energy/particle groups, but to say that a painting has no significance or power because underneath it is made of the same canvas stuff is to commit an horrendous fallacy. This painting analogy holds for the Cosmos. Man may never again see totems in logs, but in science fiction he thrills when he nears Earth, his ancestral home; he is awed by his own or other races' fantastic scientific and cultural achievements. Although science has taken away the (logical) possibility of finding/predicting the path of a particle, it has rendered the Cosmos more available as an entity, thereby making it even more mysterious. Man is awed by his Cosmic setting, but he is also aware of his kinship with it; he knows, too, that it is in large measure the canvas on which he portrays his own personality. When all the Cosmos is a stage, all the men and women on it are not *mere* players. This is the stage of *Bright New Universe.*

In *Bright New Universe,* the major conflicts of the Williamson canon are nearly resolved at the outset. The "clash between ego and environment" is limited to Earthly environment, for the benign and creative Cosmic "Club" of alien societies is clearly dominant over the obviously destructive, selfish races like that of the "tripus," who eats intelligent creatures and double-crosses his partners on Earth.[35] The second conflict, romantic assertion versus scientific detachment, is here only a seeming conflict: scientist and romantic are of necessity one if moral accuracy and political success are to be had.

I wish to follow the comic aspects in *Bright New Universe* (the religious, the absurd, the humorous) to their Cosmic resolutions. The creative and the tragic (for Williamson, destructive) values of these aspects (for example, government of service and government of self-service) are not always resolved, just as Brand of *Seetee Shock* is never fully branded as good or evil. He is simply watched, marvelled at, chuckled over. At the end of *Bright New Universe,* the destructive qualities of the villains are rendered both ineffective and comic. The tragic quality of each character is held in stasis by the comic-creative so that the latter achieve their full potential. Runescribe and Jett/Marshall are only allowed to be comic racists.

That science can overcome its desacralization is plain in *Bright New Universe.* There are spokesmen for the major Earth institutions (politics, church, business, military, and academia). Bishop Monk embodies the destructive stance of institutional religion when he prays God to set Adam Cave, the hero, right in his desire to remain in the Space Force so that he may participate in Operation Lifeline, an attempt to contact possible alien life:

A shrunken, shaven Santa Claus, with his fat red cheeks and fat potbelly, Bishop Monk prayed very pointedly for those pitiful misled souls who dared to doubt that mankind was the dearest creation and the most holy image of God. With a special quaver in his voice, he begged mercy in Christ's name for those fools who sought truth and light and the life everlasting not in divine revelation but out in the wilderness of space.

The senator carved the turkey, distributing white meat and dark with his usual fluent felicity. He rang for his Negro man to pour the wine and proposed separate toasts, one to Kayren and another, ambiguously, to "Adam's better judgment" (p. 11).

The real priest is Adam's supposedly dead father, James Cave, who masquerades as the entrepreneur of labor-saving devices and an anti-contact agitator, John Caine. The Spanish fisherman Pedro, among others, hails Adam as a "new disciple" of "*El Contractor.*" Pedro's father "was baptized a Christian, but put his real faith in *el progresso. . . .* [But] Progress is only for the rich. . . . For the poor there is nothing. I had no religion, for I found no love or justice in the world—until your father came. Now he is my religion."[36]

The most destructive voice for the Christian Soldier is General Masters (formerly Tom Jett), head of the *Man First* anti-contact group and the team-mate of Adam's father at the time of the ill-fated first contact that was hushed up for so many years. Contact has affected him so badly, the General says, that he will do anything to prevent it, and he intends to protect the world from the same sort of change. Ironically and obviously, it is the General who is the change from which the world needs protection:

'I used to be religious.' Speaking only half to Adam, he seemed somehow compelled to explain and justify himself. 'In a naïve way. I used to pray. But out in the galaxies I met creatures mightier and more magnificent than I had ever dreamed God could be. Creatures all but omnipotent, but no more moral than I am. Or should I say beyond morality?'

Moodily, he stared into the pool.

'I'd believed, of course, that I was psychologically prepared for contact. Your father and I used to talk about it. About definitions of mind and life. About the theoretical limits of intelligent power. About possible laws of universal ethics.'

His thin lips twitched sardonically.

'But I guess I wasn't very well prepared—certainly not in the sense your

father was. He accepted each new fact and being like a kid opening gifts at
Christmas. But those terrible powers hit me differently. They mocked every
goal and standard I used to value. I had to look for new laws of life.' His
pale eyes lifted, oddly eager, almost wistful.

'My new world is what I'm offering you. Because—' He leaned quickly
across the table, somehow pathetic. 'Because I need you, Cave. I'm a very
lonely person. The other man who shared my experience has become my
enemy. He would have destroyed me long ago—if his fantastic ethical notions
had let him.'

'My father—'

Grinning ironically, he lifted his hand to stop Adam's answer.

'Before you speak, let me sum things up. If you think my aims are bad—I
see you do—they are bad only against the scale of a few microbes on one brief
speck of cosmic dust. I failed to find your father's quixotic values justified
anywhere else. I found no abstract galactic justice—nothing but the law of
power.'

His gaunt jaws tightened.

'That's my law. For me, that was the lesson of contact—that I had to increase myself, against everything that dwarfed me. Frankly, Cave, I intend
to grasp and use whatever power I can find.

'Yet I say that I am not entirely bad, because I intend to protect the mass
of men from all that contact did to me. In that sense, you may regard me as
the greatest humanitarian. Greater even than your father.'

He leaned toward Adam.

'I really need you, Cave. Without my experience, you can't imagine my
predicament. Most human beings seem dull to me now. The genifacts are
too limited, if not exactly stupid. Other creatures are too clever. I need to
share my power with somebody like you—and I've power enough to share.

'What about it, Cave?'

'You know my answer,' Adam said.

Masters' cold eyes flickered toward the pool. 'If you're interested in
Polly—'

'On her terms,' Adam said. 'Not on yours.'

'They are the same.' His dark face was cragged granite now. 'You under-
estimate the power of transgalactic science. Power I want to share with you.
All the power I once attributed to God! To create life. To control it, enrich
it, extend it to immortality. Or to erase it—with no sense of sin' (pp. 69-70).

Egoistic power, not accuracy, is what the General wants more of.
And accuracy is necessary to religion. The General's religion is
himself—Satan's religion—and it degenerates into farce:

A bright fanatic light glowed in Masters' sunken eyes. 'The real danger we
fight is nothing out of space. No invasion of bug-eyed monsters. No corrup-
tion of our human culture by contact with alien ideas. No extinction of the

will to live through any desolating discovery that all our dreams were achieved on a million other worlds a billion years ago.'

Ominously, Masters lifted his close-clipped skull.

'What we fight is a deadlier and more familiar danger, right here on Earth. *Man First* actually exists to put down the rebellion—the explosion—of the colored races here on Earth. We're preparing not for space war, but race war' (pp. 10-11).

When Adam objects that no race is superior to another, the General calmly admits that "Objectively, of course, you are right. . . . But I'm not objective. I'm white."

The alien representatives of the "Club" are moral opposites, " 'all devoted to their cultures to new peoples [*sic*]. An unselfish missionary effort. The galaxy is full of stranger and less friendly things.' Such as the tripus, Adam thought. . . . 'There is too much respect for difference—racial or individual' " for there to be a concern for government among them; nothing but a " 'sheltered anarchy,' " the Club. It is Polly Ming, the first alien contact and seemingly bewitching Oriental woman (it *is* her true, though temporary, form), who reveals the religious dimensions of Cosmic contact. Salvation, both as relief from ignorance and pain and as spiritual rejuvenation, awaits man in space. Polly is man's holy mother, " 'The miraculous *virgen del contacto*.' " She is "tantalizingly human," but Adam, "knowing that she was not, hearing the ring of sure authority in her voice . . . felt a chill of awe."

Williamson makes it clear that this Cosmic religion of individual epiphany is better than any institution. The quarrel about the burial of Caine's body reveals the false sacralization of such totems. The "great golden egg of infinite promise" that brings Cosmic powers to man reveals the same lesson: "We suggest that your world is in far less danger from psychotic killers than it is from the selfish power groups who oppose contact." Contact is a mysterious good, to be sure, but not an ambiguous good like contact with the humanoids. The alternative offered to the dying General Masters by the egg of linking or death is not a cruel one, though it is an obvious and forced choice: man must join conscious evolution or die. Immediately after this incident, Adam and Kayren Hunter, his fiancée, learn that "James Cave was resurrected": hope and its symbol still live. Any ambiguity stems from the nature of man and what he will be and do with the perfect freedom to act or not act to accept the power offered him.

Sex illustrates the next comic level, the Absurd. Williamson
shows the ritual of the marriage to be a stuffy one and meaningless
in its own present terms. When Adam Cave calls off his marriage
to Kayren Hunter, both families are fantastically distraught. Kayren tells him of the marvelous social fate he has lost: grants, labs,
house, car, mountain retreat. His mother reacts like a "wounded
animal," and everyone else "growls" at him. Kayren is a bit of an
animal herself; Adam compares the two women, Kayren and Polly,
as past and future:

But of course he had already chosen. Kayren was known reality and common
sense, the comfortable tradition of the familiar past, the best bit of his own
world. He had already left her behind, along with Joseph Runescribe and the
Monks. Polly was her opposite, pure romance, as darkly mysterious and
unpredictable as his own future—if he had a future. He felt a painful ache of
loss for Kayren, an excited anticipation for Polly. He wondered what dangers from Masters and *Man First* she had risked to bring him the hongkong,
and wondered whether he would ever know—(p. 81).

Polly always has "a more than human poise and charm." After
the success of the contact expedition, Polly alights from her ship
to congratulate Adam:

Stunning in something sleek and bright and violet, she glided out to meet
him, flowed into his arms, raised her piquant face for him to kiss. Giddy
with her enchantment, he heard Kayren gasp. He introduced them breath-
lessly.
    'Kayren, this is the inspector. Chief of the transgalactic team. We call her
Polly Ming. She comes from the Clouds of Magellan. She isn't human, but
she was chosen for her high quotient of appeal.'
    Polly was demurely bewitching. Kayren shook hands with her, cooing too
sweetly, then made a savage face at him.
    'I'm human, Buster,' her hot whisper hissed. 'Just wait till you find out'
(p. 155).

Kayren is Eve; but as myth and Milton have pointed out, she was
something of a bitch. And Kayren's hot bitchery harks *back* to an
animal past buried within (as the white wolf bitch, April Bell, of
Darker Than You Think). Polly's "flowing," on the other hand,
harks *forward* to what she may become, the flowing, slimy hus-
band-engineer. She is both ethereal-holy and monstrously unfamiliar, and certainly sexually absurd. Polly is eros and awe, yet

coldness also:

Adam walked up the beach with Polly Ming. The sea was ink-black, but breaking waves splashed the corral with ghostly fire. He clung hard to her hand—to his image of her tender, warm humanity. Yet the fiery tropic stars reminded him coldly that Earth was not her home.

They walked on without speaking until the neon flicker and the loom of the palms were lost behind them. He wanted to ask what she saw when she looked up at the stars, what she recalled, what she felt. But such questions could seem silly. The stars were her world, and this was his.

'I'm afraid, Polly!' he whispered suddenly. 'I don't understand anything. I'm terribly afraid' (p. 101).

"For all her rich compassion," Adam feels, "he could never be more than savage or animal to her." Not quite true; he is incomplete, but humans are worthwhile to the aliens. There is no condescension in Polly or the other aliens, just the weariness, perhaps, that comes of being around our beloved children a little too long: "Her voice was smoothly soothing, but her eyes had a glint of secret amusement." While Adam is listening to her congratulate his little crew on what will be a great moment for Earth, "somehow the smooth music of her voice reminded him that the moment was not so great for her race" (p. 117); she is like a mother who shows weary delight with a child's wild enthusiasms.

When Adam stumbles upon Polly on a beach one night, he sees her as the perfect woman, holy and coldly erotic:

. . . She stood naked on a great black rock, a moonlit dazzle of spray surging all around her. Silver arms lifted, she faced the moon and the molten sea. With a great golden voice, she sang words or tones he had never heard. Her dark hair looked actually luminous, pulsing with pale fire and flowing loose in the sea wind—or was it moving of itself? The sight and sound of her shook him with a frightened excitement (p. 105).

What follows is one of the great comic/ironic scenes in all of science fiction. Three of what turn out to be Polly's husbands approach her out of the sea—one a ten-foot "pineapple"; one a "little blue cloud" that settles into a "sleek-faced tetrahedron"; one a swarm of metallic silver bees: her captain, first and second mates. This scene fascinates and excites Adam, and (accurately enough) breaks the dam of his memory so that he recreates the traumatic episode of witnessing, when he was three, his mother and step-

40

father in the primal scene:

> . . . he didn't want Joseph Runescribe for his father. Afraid in the dark, he wanted his mother all for himself.
> He slipped out of bed and felt his way down the unfamiliar hall to their bedroom door. In the glow of a clock, he saw them naked and fighting on the bed. The hideous little man was on her, panting like an animal. His mother was shuddering and moaning in agony.
> Yet she didn't try to get away.
> That was the nightmare part. She fought back like another savage animal—and she loved the fighting. He lay terrified behind a chair, afraid to move or breathe, afraid of the gasping violence in Joseph and this beastly madness in his mother, horribly afraid they might find him.
> A shutter bang and the thunder was closer and the hot, honeysuckle scent grew strong in the room—always, afterward, he had hated honeysuckle without knowing why. He got cold, and his cramped body ached, and he didn't dare to cry. And still he couldn't understand his mother.
> He didn't remember any outcome. Perhaps he had just gone to sleep there on the floor. But he knew now that he had never quite trusted his mother after that night. Nor any woman, not entirely. Expecting betrayal from the best of them, he had behaved accordingly. It struck him painfully that he had not been fair to Kayren Hunter, when he dropped her so suddenly. Or even to the black Swan, when he dated her on the moon (p. 107).

Watching the aliens, Adam feels "a stabbing ache of rejected loneliness"—all life in the Cosmos apparently needs this sort of contact as well as the intellectual. Polly does go around kissing, touching, and tucking men in in her devotion.

Polly and the friendly aliens are not psychic monsters, as man seems to be. But they are sexual absurdities. While watching and worshipping Polly, Adam sees a green-tentacled "monstrous amoeba" crawl out of the sea and inch its slimy way up the rock and grasp her leg. She screams. Adam is paralyzed; he imagines it to be the tripus or some other enemy alien. He rushes to do battle, the three husbands flitting around him as "their high whines become a tiny voice crying, *Stay Away!*" But the "heaving, flowing, fearful mass" has its way with Polly:

> That great shapeless shape had swallowed Polly. Her long body was a pale shadow in it, dim in the glare of the buried eyes. Only her agonized face was left outside, and a luminous wisp of her hair, and her tawny hand clutching a last shrinking coil (pp. 109-110).

This is the climax of the love of husband and wife.

The amoeba throws him off the rock. When he awakes, Polly is there to explain the situation in a civilized way and apologize for her engineer-husband. It seems she will metamorphose, when she becomes wise and worthy, into the "higher" forms (masculine, of course) that Adam has seen. She chides him for his horror and offended morality; and she can, for "she is gentle as a flower petal, fresh and pure as spring." These aliens are all one family, and no other arrangement is possible on such a long mission. His fear, dismay, and nausea are part of the "hazard of contact":

The soothing music of her voice seemed more remote than the cold moon. 'People always find that much of what they had taken for basic truth is either trivial or false. The real trouble comes because they tend to abandon all their values, even those they ought to keep. For that reason it is sometimes wise for a new people to delay contact.'

He wondered dully what her team had decided about opening the Earth to contact, but he thought he couldn't stand to talk about it now. Giving up his own basic truths was still as hard as it had been when he was three.

Suddenly he burst into tears.

'My darling man!' Her voice held an instant warm solicitude. 'You're worn completely out. We must get you back to the *caserio*. . . .'

'Sleep.' She kissed his forehead lightly. 'You'll feel better' (pp. 112-113).

Adam is of a race still in childhood. After the Cosmos becomes home, it may be less absurd. But sin and destruction, as represented by the tripus race, will always appear at any level.

The comic as humor will forever remain, it would seem, within man himself. No human in the book has a sense of humor, but humor comes anyway—through Williamson. After Adam tells Kayren that he is breaking off their engagement, he sizes her up:

She was taking it well, he thought. Even though she didn't begin to understand. Clean and tall and lovely, strong enough for anything, she walked bravely away through his hot haze of tears. Her newest hobby, he recalled, was karate (p. 109).

Karate is dropped in here for more than humor, however. Kayren is found at the end to have been the Judas who attempted, while under "psychodrugs," to kill James Cave, and she gets inside the golden egg (in an electronic phase-net that allows her to pass through matter) to murder Adam.

Adam himself is often a silly figure, begging like a child and crying in frustration. At the end, however, he is ready to give his life, and all Polly Ming can say is "to an unwise idealist, we send out love—" (p. 148).

The falling bomb that the Man First group aims at the golden egg in the middle of a nice little American town " 'exceeds your greatest thermonuclear bomb in radius of total destruction.' " Adam and Kayren run for a shallow crater; they watch the bomb fall. It's a dud.

Out from the cylinder of the bomb crawls a dying Tom Jett (General Masters). He has been ditched and ejected by his "stinking, yellow rat" of a partner, the tripus, who scuttles into space. Kayren, meanwhile, behaves sleepily and stupidly all through the pitched battle, as if she were in a dream. She does rescue a "link," the small golden egg that gives any who accept it access to the unlimited power and knowledge of all the Cosmic races. She wakes up, however, when Adam touches her shoulder—" 'Oh!' She drew back quickly. 'Adam, I'm naked.' " At the moment of salvation, Eve feels naked again. This is not the discovery of shame, it seems, but of "illogical joy" and the release of all human capacities. They all forgive one another.

Next, Kayren and Polly meet; as we have already seen, mankind loses a little of its pulp-magazine luster and happiness. Then follows a fine comic crowd-scene that tops the book off very well. The multitudes gather to meet the master, James Cave, passing out the bright eggs of contact. Senator Monk and Joseph Runescribe, Adam's step-father and an academician, make a comic counterpoint to the Cosmic action. The Senator decides to go along with the Club's "game" in order to "rewrite their holy canons of contact!" "This brave new world" is like the poker game of politics, and the Senator is out to bluff "man or monster" for the bigger jackpots,[37] even though there are no more of that kind of jackpot.

At the very end, the focus narrows to the last rejector of contact, Runescribe the Academic (an obvious comment), and a little black boy with a linking egg. Runescribe is horrified at the power placed in the urchin's hands, but his is a voice, once terrible but now comic and ineffective. Man is free now to be himself and nothing less:

'I don't like it, Saul!' Joseph Runescribe's waspish whine rose out of the crowd. 'This nightmare machine. This insane plague of unearned power. It's about to set the wrong people free. Look at that filthy brat!'

His narrow nose lifted at the Negro urchin sitting behind the broken bench, clutching his previous egg and licking up the last of his instant ice cream cone.

'What good will ten billion years of transgalactic culture do him, without some use of social force? Who will teach him his place in the world? Who will make him keep it?' A gathering terror quavered in his voice. 'What will he do to us? He—and the billions like him!'

The senator made an untroubled shrug, and they turned to stare at the Negro boy. Still absorbed in his dialogue with the contact unit, the child reached eagerly for a mint-new geometric puzzle it had made for him.

Parts of the puzzle looked like polished quartz. Parts of it were sparkling mist. As the boy began to work with it, queer symbols glowed and vanished inside the crystal parts. The golden egg hummed faintly in his lap; now and then his bent head nodded to its soundless voice. His lips moved, shaping names for those magic symbols. His face lit with dawning wonder. Presently his small body began to flicker into shadow and turn real again, as he learned to shift himself out of phase with Earth. He looked up and saw the staring men and shivered to the thrill of his perilous new freedom from them and from all coercion (p. 158).

Evolution and natural selection guarantee the increase and development of intelligence, Adam says. "The process is automatic . . . brains appear as inevitably as rainbows do," the "Hunter thesis."[38] But brains appear less evanescent than rainbows. The evil and destructive capabilities of man, including the institutions and concepts that embody these capabilities, disappear before man's advances and the "dawning wonder" of individual man exploring himself and the Cosmos, sloughing off the mortal coils of a past that has stultified and regressed. Implicit in Williamson's wonderfully symbolic last scene is a new thesis—that in any man is the enormous power for a god-like transcendence.

Curtis C. Smith

OLAF STAPLEDON'S DISPASSIONATE OBJECTIVITY

Olaf Stapledon is an oddity. He seems to defy classification either as a mainstream writer or a science fiction writer. He is respected, but he is not read, although a slowly increasing number of devotees now turn his intricately constructed pages. Stapledon certainly didn't consider himself a science fiction writer—he probably wasn't even aware of the existence of science fiction as a genre when he began to write—and he fits hardly any of the preconceptions most readers have of early science fiction. Political, religious, and philosophical ideas, rather than gadgets or adventure, are central to his works. To be sure, one can find gadgets and adventure in Stapledon, but it would be difficult to separate them from the philosophical significance given them. Stapledon makes one think. He doesn't write "real science fiction," many fans complain.

H. G. Wells's fate has not been dissimilar. However, it's just barely possible to look at Eloi vs. Morlocks as good guys vs. BEM's, rather than as capitalists vs. proletarians. It's just barely possible, in other words, to ignore the social commentary in Wells. By contrast, there are no potential BEM's in Stapledon's works, and no movies to be made starring Rod Taylor and Yvette Mimieux.

This is, in a way, as Stapledon would have wished it. He doesn't seem to have aimed at commercial success or a broad audience. He wrote for the people he called the "wide awakes," those few who would wish to join him in serving and glorifying "the spirit," a nexus of love, intelligence, and creative action. Stapledon was surprised that his first novel, *Last and First Men* (1930) received as much critical attention and praise as it did.

It took a long time for him to decide that his ideas and his glorification of the spirit could best be contained in a literary form. He took an undergraduate degree in history at Oxford, but he soon decided that history was not what he wanted to teach and learn. He switched to philosophy, and took his doctorate at Liverpool University. Philosophy didn't quite cover his interests either, although he continued to write philosophical pieces throughout his career. He tried various careers—teaching in a boys' school, working in a shipping office—without finding them satisfactory. Stapledon was a complex man who continued to change and grow and try new things. It wasn't until he was forty-four that he tried the novel; he resembles his superman, Odd John, and the human race in *Last and First Men* in maturing late. His first novel was sufficiently successful to decide him upon a career divided between writing and teaching in the Workers Educational Association.

Considering Stapledon's synthetic interests, it is easy to see why he eventually turned to literature as a mode of expression. Only literature allowed him to be both imaginative and discursive; only literature could be both philosophical and aesthetic; only in literature could Stapledon hope to teach, to change the world, and also to develop an imaginative vision of the spirit's future progress in the world. He was as interested in future possibilities as in present realities. Moreover, his "spirit" is such a broad and pervasive concept that he could not easily talk about it in precise philosophical terms. It was easier to show than to tell.

Stapledon's belief in absolute spirit tells us a good deal of his social and intellectual background. In *Youth and Tomorrow* (1946) he reminisces about his late Victorian childhood, contrasting its feel to the feel of the world in 1945. Perhaps the Victorian period lingered in Stapledon's native Liverpool; for there is, in

Stapledon's search for an absolute and in the slow rhythm of his neoclassical prose, much that could be labelled Victorian. As does Carlyle, Stapledon accepts religious terminology but casts off the "Hebrew old clothes" of conventional religion. Carlyle's "natural supernaturalism" is a phrase which might aptly describe Stapledon's metaphysics.

He shares Carlyle's revulsion, too, at mechanical materialism. And since he charges H. G. Wells with being a mechanical materialist, Stapledon could be said to write as much in reaction to Wells as in debt to him. There is still a sense, though, in which Stapledon is a materialist, since in his future histories he seems to accept Marx's materialistic inversion of Hegelian dialectic.

Thus he writes in several nineteenth century traditions. Outside the science fiction mainstream (and at first unaware of it), he nonetheless illustrates a major paradox of science fiction, the literature of the future: it is a conservative genre. Stapledon seems to have learned almost nothing from the twentieth century's experiments with stream of consciousness and point of view, and his tragic but orderly universe is as far as it could be from the absurd.

However, he can't be reduced to what he inherited from the past or what he did not learn from the present. Stapledon's concern for up-to-date scientific accuracy in *Last and First Men* was such as to lead J. B. S. Haldane to believe it the work of a scientist. *Last and First Men* is an attempt to extrapolate science as well as to extrapolate history. And there are other ways in which Stapledon's works were ahead of their time, as the Stapledonian elements in *2001* bear witness. Darko Suvin defines science fiction as literature of cognitive estrangement; and (if I understand him correctly) this is what he sees science fiction evolving toward rather than where it is. Clearly, Stapledon's works are fully evolved. They are estranged in that they are written from the fantastic point of view of the world beyond the hill (in Alexei Panshin's phrase), and they describe the evolution of norms and values remote from our own. Dialectically, Stapledon's works are also cognitive: they teach us things about our own world. The last man, who supposedly narrates *Last and First Men* from a point in the very remote future, is nonetheless a man talking to men of the present. The very estrangement of the point of view helps us to learn more about the present. Although he constructs a myth of the future, Stapledon is always talking simultaneously about what possibilities are open to human beings of the present. The imagined relationship between the last man and the first men is dialectical: "we can help you," says the last man, "and we need your help."[1]

Last and First Men is dialectical also in the relationship it develops between humanity and its environment. Although it is a tragedy, the novel expresses an evolutionary rather than a closed and pessimistic view of human nature. The last man announces in the Introduction that "I shall record huge fluctuations of joy and woe, the results of changes not only in man's environment but in his fluid nature" (p. 13). Humanity's physical and social environment acts on the fluid human nature, and human activity helps to transform and reproduce the physical and social environment, in an endless dialectical process. In effect, the last man's story is of humanity's increasingly successful but ultimately tragic attempts at anthropogenesis. Present human nature keeps forming future human nature, and increasingly this is a planned and conscious self-creation.

The vastness of the human future is intended, in one way, to impress upon us the littleness of the present. Still, the present is significant. In fact, Stapledon views the present and the near future as a point of crisis, the outcome of which will influence all future human history. A single incident in an Anglo-French war of the near future begins the fall of the First Men, ourselves. A stray French plane kills an English princess and quickens England to violence just as the English leaders had resolved upon unilateral pacifism and a peace message to the world. Had this accident not happened, Stapledon tell us (p. 24), England and France might not have destroyed each other, the human race might have achieved unity, and the first Dark Age might never have occurred. In the twentieth century the human race is delicately balanced between two futures. Chance is decisive, and "chance" (which is not really chance) is one of the motifs of the human struggle for self control.

As civilizations and species rise and fall, as human beings struggle with self and environment and succumb to chances which are not chances, the pattern of history slowly becomes apparent.

At one point the last man summarizes the pattern as follows:

The movement of world culture was in a manner spiral. There would be an age during which the interest of the race was directed almost wholly upon certain tracts or aspects of existence; and then, after perhaps a hundred thousand years, these would seem to have been fully cultivated, and would be left fallow. During the next epoch attention would be in the main directed to other spheres, and then afterwards to yet others, and again others. But at length a return would be made to the fields that had been deserted, and it would be discovered that they could now miraculously bear a millionfold the former crop. Thus, in both science and art man kept recurring again and again to the ancient themes, to work over them once more in meticulous detail and strike from them new truth and new beauty, such as, in the earlier epoch, he could never have conceived (pp. 174-175).

Accordingly, a theme may be expressed perversely on one level but fully and marvelously on another. Flight is wasteful and self-destructive as performed by the religious fanatics of the First World State, but beautiful when the Seventh (flying) Men "browse upon the bright pastures of the sky, like swallows" (p. 198). When the Third Men perform the first conscious *anthropogenesis,* making the species of "Great Brains," their creation is grotesque and unfeeling; when the Fifth Men make Venus habitable for men, they must kill another intelligent species. But later species of men do the same things at different levels of the spiral. The Last Men, made artificially by those who lived before them and inhabiting a humanized Nepture, recapitulate all previous themes: they are both more fully animal and more fully human than any previous species.

Despite its immense spatial and temporal scope, *Last and First Men* is remarkably concentrated upon the vicissitudes of the human race, its collectively tragic "hero." Remarkably, too, Stapledon succeeds in transforming the few human individuals in his narrative into representatives of the entire species. The Patagonian civilization precipitates a worldwide nuclear disaster which leaves only a few survivors. " 'We are ordinary folk,' " says one of them, " 'but somehow we must become great.' And they were, indeed, in a manner made great by their unique position" (p. 92). The tragic division which eventually overtakes these few survivors merely adds to our conviction that Stapledon is celebrating the potential greatness of ordinary people.

The Last Men are killed by an exploding star, which seems to be an inverse *deus ex machina*; but this is merely another chance which is not chance. The human tragedy is really a logical consequence of Stapledon's agnostic view of life and of the dialectical tension he develops between humanity and environment; for humanity's environment is, ultimately, too vast for men and women to humanize it. The Last Men struggle to disseminate the seed of future life. Lest we feel uninvolved in their struggle, the last man reminds us that our success in resolving our present world crisis in some way affects the outcome of the last men's final project.

Star Maker (1937) continues—on a cosmic level and with a more complex time scale—the dialectical interrelationship between intelligence and matter. In this work, in many ways a sequel to *Last and First Men*, Stapledon inverts the point of view. In *Last and First Men* the future, estranged point of view comes to and asks the attention of the present; in *Star Maker*, a contemporary Englishman floats into the cosmos, and in an upward spiral of experience he learns the pattern of cosmic history. "Man" in *Last and First Men* always reminds man; similarly, the narrator of *Star Maker* remains in some way an Englishman, even though his point of view becomes increasingly complex.

Only a book length study could begin to analyze Stapledon's fictionalized cosmology, and I wish to make only one approach to such an analysis. *Star Maker*'s estranged vision of plant men, nautiloids, and other wonders is once again used dialectically for cognitive evaluation of the human present. Surprisingly, perhaps, *Star Maker* is a political book. Satirizing certain aspects of (what he conceives to be) Marxist theory and practice, Stapledon also attempts to demonstrate the core of soundness which Marxism contains. In the partially autobiographical *Last Men in London*, Paul "tried to persuade the Communists that he knew their mind better than they did themselves . . . he was expelled from the Communist Party as an incorrigible bourgeois . . . the communistically inclined editor of a well-known literary journal, who at first hoped to bring Paul within his own circle, was soon very thankful to get rid of him."[2]

Whether or not all or part of Paul's experience is Stapledon's, this passage describes the stance of Stapledon in relation to the Left; he is sympathetic, but he cannot accept the Party wholeheartedly. In the Preface to *Star Maker*, written in March 1937, Stapledon says that "our outworn economic system," not simply German fascism, "dooms millions to frustration."[3] There is a worldwide crisis, the identical crisis which confronts every world the *Star Maker* pilgrims visit. Consequently "a book like this may be condemned as a distraction from the desperately urgent defense of civilization against modern barbarism" (p. 249). Stapledon is aware of the charge that science fiction is bourgeois and escapist. But he accepts the challenge of such a charge. *Star Maker* is, among many other things, an attempt to demonstrate the political usefulness of estranged, visionary literature and to explore the cosmic implications of dialectics; to express, in short, the Left's core of truth better than the Left itself expresses it.

He develops a Marxist analysis of the first place visited by the narrator after he is snatched from his hillside, the "Other Earth"; but he is simultaneously satirizing Marxism. A small ruling class owns the means of production:

The owners directed the energy of the workers increasingly toward the production of more means of production rather than to the fulfillment of the needs of individual life. For machinery might bring profit to the owners; bread would not. With the increasing competition of machine with machine, profits declined, and therefore wages, and therefore effective demand for goods. Marketless products were destroyed, though bellies were unfed and backs unclad. Unemployment, disorder, and stern repression increased as the economic system disintegrated. A familiar story! (p. 277)

This ruling class uses race and class divisions to maintain itself in power. Race is determined by the taste of the sexual organs, taste being the dominant sense on the Other Earth. The lowest race-class, the pariahs, is kept alive only because workers are needed. Stapledon brilliantly extrapolates the ruling class use of radio and television as opiates. Sexual broadcasts are developed, and it becomes possible for a man to "retire to bed for life and spend all his time receiving radio programmes" (p. 280). But Stapledon has the political sophistication to see, as so many writers of dystopias do not, that a capitalist ruling class might have ambiguous, contradictory attitudes toward soma. Part of the ruling class supports the broadcasts, citing their usefulness for social control; the other part turns against the very instrument they have

created, for "their craving was for power; and for power they
needed [conscious] slaves whose labour they could command for
their great industrial ventures" (p. 281).

Marxist terminology and analysis, then, apply more accurately
to the Other Earth than to any other world in *Star Maker*. But
the Other Earth is condemned to cycles of civilization and sav-
agery, with no dialectical advances out of the cycle. Since his
distressed condition on the hillside forms a psychic bond down-
ward, the pilgrim begins his journey on the one world of *Star
Maker* which is less advanced spiritually than the Earth. It is as if
Stapledon is saying that a purely Marxist analysis could apply
only to a world more primitive or more simple than our own. The
Communists on the Other Earth are merely a part of the hopeless
battle between extremes, such as dogmatic religion and complete
atheism, which are never transcended by a synthesis:

Communism . . . still maintained its irreligious convention; but in the two
great Communist countries the officially organized 'irreligion' was becoming
a religion in all but name. It had its institutions, its priesthood, its ritual, its
morality, its system of absolution, its metaphysical doctrines, which, though
devoutly materialistic, were none the less superstitious. And the flavour of
deity had been displaced by the flavour of the proletariat (p. 284).

Despite his satire here of Communism's paradoxical rigidities
and absurdities, Stapledon sees cosmic history as dialectical.
Worlds in a crisis of economic and social individualism such as our
own are transcended, after "a long-drawn agony of economic dis-
tress and maniac warfare" (p. 346), by a new level which Stapledon calls the "waking world."

"In the loosest possible sense" all of these waking worlds
"were communistic; for in all of them the means of production
were communally owned, and no individual could control the
labours of others for private profit. Again, in a sense all of these
world-orders were democratic" (p. 348), but democracy is the
democratic centralism of a bureaucracy or even a dictatorship.
Stapledon's waking worlds sweep aside both the machinery of
economic control by a minority and the machinery of bourgeois
representative government which prevents the true expression of
the people's will while pretending to foster it.

Despite his generalizations, Stapledon recognizes the uniqueness of dialectical development. Not in every case does the dialectic lead to the waking world. More often than not, social and environmental factors end history altogether. Even when achieved, the waking worlds are very diverse: "this was, of course, to be expected, since biologically, psychologically, culturally, these worlds were very different" (p. 348). Echinoderms (starfish-men) and Ichthyoid (fish)-Arachnoid (crustacean) symbiotic races quite obviously have histories very different from ours! The brilliance of *Star Maker* comes from Stapledon's ability to sketch scores of unique dialectical developments within a general framework, showing in each case the mediation between physical and environmental forces and the resulting cultural and social forces.

Stapledon describes, too, the continuation of the dialectic beyond the level of the waking world. The formation of a classless society, while an immense step, does not mean the end of struggle. Certain "mad" worlds impede the formation of a galactic utopia. These worlds are waking worlds, but they have become perversely obsessed with the hunger for community; obsessed, too, with the technology of interstellar travel and with the possibility of empire-making which results from it. Probably Stapledon is satirizing what he conceives to be the U.S.S.R.'s mania for industrial development to the exclusion of the quality of life.

As the dialectic continues through galactic utopia and galactic symbiosis, to the cosmic mind and its symbiosis with the Star Maker, and to the final dialectical relationship between the Star Maker and its creations, we realize that Stapledon is trying to communicate the value of being able to experience and feel the size and complexity of the universe. And when the scene is suddenly shifted back to Earth, in the Epilogue, we realize that Stapledon is saying that this same value may be found on Earth. For the Earth, too, is vast; and as the narrator dimly sensed when he left it, "the vital presence of Earth [is] of a creature alive but tranced and obscurely yearning to wake" (p. 260).

The final dialectic is offered on the last page of the book. Thesis and antithesis are the two lights to guide by, the little atom of community on Earth and the cold light of the stars. The synthesis is a greater, not a lesser, significance to the human struggle. The contrast between man and star does not detract from our dedication to the struggle but in fact intensifies that struggle.

Stapledon asserts, as ecologists now do, that only by feeling the value of the whole universe, including that which lies beyond humanity, will we feel the value of humanity and struggle to perserve it.

In some such way, then, Stapledon would defend himself against the charge of irrelevance and escapism. Is the defense successful? Fresh from the incredibly abstract rendering of the dialectical relationship between cosmic spirit and Star Maker, we may not be ready to feel what Stapledon is telling us to feel in the final pages. The Epilogue on Earth helps, but not enough. In *Last and First Men*, the concentration remains upon *anthropogenesis,* with humanity as subject and the cosmos as object. In *Star Maker*, as I began by saying, there is an inversion of point of view. Not only do we leave Earth with the Englishman, but in the "supreme moment" of the cosmos we leap again, to the Star Maker's point of view. With Star Maker as subject, each cosmos (including our own, past and future) becomes an object. *Last and First Men* is a tragedy, concentrating upon an upward and outward struggle which is never completed; *Star Maker* could not be called a tragedy, for it ends by leaping outside of all mortal struggle and looking back upon it from outside. "Time Scale Three" (p. 438) presents the succession of the Star Maker's creations as a cycle from "immature" to "mature" creating—a repeating cycle, it would seem, in some paradoxical way. At the center of the cycle (which is represented by a circular graph of the creations) is the "view point of eternity." The emotional force of *Last and First Men* comes as a result of the weight of time; in *Star Maker,* time is in some way or sense unreal. Leaving *Last and First Men,* we remember the pathos of the last man's last words, about how good it is to have been man; leaving *Star Maker,* we remember the frosty ecstasy of the Star Maker, contemplating "his" creations from a point outside of time and space. *Star Maker* is a magnificent achievement on an almost unbelievably vast scale, but it is not a human book. As his Preface shows, Stapledon understood the dangers in what he was doing, and tried to compensate for them. He was not altogether successful.

Despite the obvious connections between them, then, *Last and First Men* and *Star Maker* give us very different feelings about the human situation. Stapledon's readers are aware of change, experimentation, and growth as well as of continuity. Stapledon wrote not only future histories, vast in scope, but relatively short tragedies located roughly in the present, *Odd John* and *Sirius* being the most notable. Although both works are tragedies of the stranger in a strange land, one is again struck as much with the differences between the implied views of life as with the similarities.

Odd John (1935) may be the best known of Stapledon's works. It is cited as setting a standard for superman stories. This praise is justified. In fact, Odd John is completely different from most other superman stories, in which the concentration is usually on the drama of discovery. The onlookers in the story (who are less perceptive than the reader) slowly realize that a whole new thing is happening. When they realize it, the story ends, and we never quite know what the whole new thing will mean for the future. We exult or quake with fear, and that is all.

About all we know, generally, about the whole new human-kind is that it has powers or gadgets—and both are accidents of creation. Telepathy is, commonly, the super in superman. Sturgeon's Homo Gestalt is a multi-personed telepathic creature; its greater consequent specialization is, presumably, the basis of its superiority. We are told that it is learning morality but not what that morality is and what the world will be like now that it is here. The Hampdenshire Wonder (from J. D. Beresford's book of the same title) simply has greater brain capacity. He is rather like a computer, able to read faster and accumulate more data than any man. Beresford hints, via the Wonder's very cryptic comments, at a superior wisdom, too; but nothing comes of it, for the Wonder is soon dead.

Typically so. The superman is the superman, one of a kind. Frankenstein's creature longs for a mate, in futility. The nine-teenth century romantic superman and his twentieth century science fiction counterpart are lonely, tortured souls. They are entrepeneurs, rugged individualists, but they do not succeed (as Robinson Crusoe did) in taking over the island and enslaving Friday.

The superman story does not, then, tell us many of the things we need to know. Mutations, powers, new gadgets—all very well, but we do not have them. What are we to do besides wait for them to come? Suppose we do have one Clark Kent lurking about—we can always call him, true; but we don't need better cops, we need a rebirth from within.

To find the substance of the superman and not simply the drama of external form, we must turn to Stapledon's Odd John. "Queer powers," says John, are "in no sense the goal of the spirit, but just a by-play of its true life."[4]   The focus is not upon the gadgets and powers but upon what the new life means.   Other writers tell us that a new life is about to begin, but Stapledon creates it for our examination.

In Stapledon's creation, the essence of the superman's new life is community rather than self-tortured individualism. *Star Maker* is not about the alienated Englishman, but about his absorption into ever-higher levels of community. Similarly, *Odd John* is not simply about the hero, although his story is included, but about the heroic society.

This society is formed when the members of the race *Homo Superior* drift together, learn to transcend enough of their bizarre idiosyncracies to live together, and go to a primitive island which becomes very different from Crusoe's island, the island of Dr. No, the island of the Lord of the Flies, or the island of Dr. Moreau. On Stapledon's island there is indeed advanced, sophisticated science, sufficient, by the end· of the book, to take over the world.   But our dominant impression of the colony is of its simplicity (it cannot even be seen until one is very close to the island), for the islanders are experimenting with living off the earth as much as with science. They are putting into practice what John learned in the wilderness, that at times one must throw away everything and learn self-reliance. They take pride in the things of civilization—clocks, hot water—but only to the extent that they have fashioned these things from nothing.

The colony is no utopia. It consists of finite beings, although there are no set limits to how far their capacity for value and experience can expand.   The colony has no government; it has conflict, but Tribal resolution of unanimity, not a constitution or voting.   It resembles one of the waking worlds of *Star Maker*. Anarchy it is not, for there is ceremonial togetherness, an understood way of life, and an expectation, which need not be put into law, of mutual obligation. It is a tribe, or perhaps a Greek city-state (p. 144) without the evil effects of its patriotic self-love—for it is, deeply, a home, toward which the islanders hasten when they must be absent from it, even though it is also a place of great toil.

Above all, the colony is what Stapledon is fond of calling personality-in-community. Stapledon's narrator tells us that in the community there is a heightened awareness of self and others, rather than a diminution of same. Identities and even specializations are more vivid. John is the prime mover, without being an authority; Lo adopts the attitude of Jane Austen; Shen Kuo researches the past. And yet each person is in the community first and a specialist second. Stapledon would insist, then, that despite its communistic elements the community transcends Marxian communism in that it attains a new level of individualism, and also in that it is a place where the spirit is worshipped.

I haven't conveyed the colony's bizarre atmosphere. To do this I had best quote Stapledon's narrator on the colony's "strange combination of lightness and earnestness, of madness and superhuman sanity, of sublime common sense and fantastic extravagance" (p. 141).

What I have said so far about the island is all Stapledon, and the development of its community parallels the development of community in *Last and First Men* and *Star Maker*. But in *Odd John* Stapledon is also communicating values not to be found in his longer works. Indeed, part of the interest of the shorter works is that it is easier to see from them how Stapledon's philosophical and political attitudes would apply to specific social situations. And we may not like everything we see.

For although the island community embodies so much that we may well find valuable, it also countenances activities so horrendous that we can only wonder how Stapledon keeps aesthetic distance from them. When John kills a policeman to prevent being caught at robbery, we may perhaps accept his utilitarian argument —it "had to be"; or again, when the colonists kill two Englishmen to prevent detection, we may accept the same argument, although John's elaboration that the murder would be wrong for *men* to do is positively Nietzschean in its implications.

When John says thereafter (to the narrator) that "if we could wipe out your whole species, frankly, we would" (p. 121), the moral and logical meaning becomes difficult to discern. At its most awake moments in *Last and First Men*, the human race is able to see the value of a species inferior to itself; why, then, cannot a superman see the same value? In his philosophical works, Stapledon emphasizes the common "humanity" of all sentient beings. Of course John is not Stapledon, but nothing in the text helps us to evaluate John's comment.

The annihilation of the human race is so abstract that it's difficult to react to the prospect. But when the supernormals destroy the native islanders, they repeat (despite their multiracial, multinational backgrounds) the pattern of Western imperialism. The narrator points out that killing natives is at least better than converting them into Christians, but this hardly reconciles us to the action.

There is more. When the narrator visits the islands labs, he finds that:

Difficult work was in progress upon human ova and spermatozoa, both normal and supernormal. I was shown a series of thirty-eight living human embryos, each in its own incubator. These startled me considerably, but the story of their conception and capture startled me even more. Indeed, it filled me with horror, and with violent though short-lived moral indignation. The eldest of these embryos was three months old. Its father, I was told, was Shahīn, its mother a native of the Tuamotu Archipelago. The unfortunate girl had been seduced, brought to the island, operated upon, and killed while still under the anaesthetic (p. 139).

These brutal, barbaric experiments cannot even be justified on utilitarian grounds. They are senseless, and (especially in the post-Nazi period, it must be admitted) so painful to read about that a great deal of my sympathy for the islanders leaves me at this point and never comes back.

One might argue that Stapledon always keeps his distance from John and the others, and that a struggle between subhuman and superhuman goes on in the supernormals exactly as it does in *Homo Superior*. Indeed, one might argue that the colony resembles one of the waking worlds in *Star Maker* that becomes a mad world. The supernormals' violence, according to this view, is an expression of their perverse zeal for the spirit, which is in conflict with true spiritual values.

The problem is that no such conflict is in evidence. The colonists seem to have no doubts about the violence done to humans. In *Star Maker*, Stapledon's narrator is, in effect, Stapledon, and he tells us that the mad worlds are mad; the narrator's revulsion in *Odd John* lacks the same authority. As we shall see, Sirius is often violent, but he later agonizes over what he has done. How strange that Stapledon, who believed in absolute rather than in utilitarian ethics, has his supermen commit utilitarian murders without, apparently, questioning seriously what they are doing. Perhaps Stapledon is writing a monster story, but how does this story fit with the story of beings who are more fully awake than we are? Experimentation with human beings against their will is one of those obscene subjects about which one ought not to write without being very clear why one is doing so; such experimentation is much too close to what has happened and does happen.

I must not be too critical of Stapledon. It is impossible to write a superman story, every bit as impossible as to write cosmic histories. Supermen have faculties and purposes beyond human understanding. Almost by definition, then, supermen cannot be described in an altogether understandable way.

And at the very end of *Odd John*, Stapledon does indicate an evolution in the ethical sense of the supernormals. Through much of the book John uses the narrator as a tool and only as a tool. Appropriately, he is nick-named "Fido." But when he and the colonists last part, John says that "I loved you very much," and Lo adds that "if they were all like you, domestic, there'd have been no trouble" (p. 154). John, who at one point said he would kill all humans if that were possible, does acquire the means (a new weapon) of doing so—but he and the others do not use that weapon. Their motivation, however, is not a moral revulsion at mass slaughter. Rather, their motives involve themselves: the task of wiping out humanity would divert them from their spiritual goals. All well and good; but, as with the ending of *Star Maker*, rather frosty.

The similarities between *Odd John* and *Sirius* (1944) are apparent. Sirius, a dog with intelligence at a human level, is as estranged from humanity as is John. In each book Stapledon uses estrangement for satirical purposes. Both John and Sirius have periods in the wilderness, followed by periods in which they examine the major human institutions with a critical eye. Both books thus invert *Gulliver's Travels* yet accomplish some of Swift's ends. Whereas the prosaic Gulliver estranges himself from England in order to comment on it, estranged John and Sirius comment directly on prosaic England. Gulliver's education in misanthropy goes awry in Voyage IV. He becomes incapable of perceiving ordinary human virtue in individuals such as Don Pedro. Likewise, both John and Sirius are misanthropes. Stapledon gives no way of evaluating John's misanthropy, no reliable critique of it; by contrast, it is always made clear that Sirius's misanthropy, while tragically understandable, is not the whole truth for him or for us.

Sirius's misanthropy reminds us not only of Gulliver's but that of the gloomy, sublime creature put together by Victor Frankenstein and given life in the dead of night. Mary Shelley's theme is irresponsibility and the inability of humanity to control or even understand its own creations. Seen from another perspective, Frankenstein's creature is the natural man, unfettered by civilization, with both an intense sensibility and a penchant for violence. The creature expresses the potential in all of us to become more creative or to become more destructive. Lonely and alienated, the creature is unable to integrate its own nature, and it (justifiably) hates its creator, Victor Frankenstien, for his failure to give it the nurture and education which might have saved it. The hatred becomes a generalized misanthropy and a longing for revenge.

All of these themes are present in *Sirius*—with some significant inversions. Victor Frankenstein doesn't seem to have thought through the consequences of his creation. Thomas Trelone, by contrast, gives considerable thought to Sirius's education. Thomas knows that Sirius must be both human and animal, and both free and disciplined. His decision to apprentice Sirius as a sheep dog makes good sense, as do his decisions to keep Sirius's existence a secret from the outside world, yet to give Sirius some acquaintance with Cambridge and London.

Ultimately, however, Thomas's plans for Sirius are inadequate. Thomas understands Sirius's utilitarian needs, but not his spiritual ones; Thomas has too facile a view of what education can solve, and he never understands the extent of Sirius's alienation and the violence which results from it. Thomas, in other words, has no conception of tragedy. Presumably this is Stapledon's comment on science—science which is fine and good in its own way (and far more flexible and useful than Mary Shelley allowed), but ultimately limited by its narrow, mechanistic materialism.

As with Frankenstien's creature, Sirius is both the creation of humantiy and, symbolically, humanity itself. Sirius is a dog, and dogs were created by humans. Symbolically, then, human beings make themselves; symbolically, too, they are as yet incapable of controlling or even understanding their own *anthropogenesis*. Half beast and half domesticated, Sirius is animal as humans are animal; Sirius (at Cambridge) is fat and pampered, just as civilized human beings, too, are spoiled and cut off from nature and from their own animality. Sirius hates civilization and kills his sadistic master, Thwaites; but Sirius loves the woman Plaxy, and becomes a part of the Sirius-Plaxy symbiotic community.

Both *Frankenstein* and *Sirius*, then, contain complex symbolism of the divided, transcendent, and tragic nature of humanity. Sirius, both animal and spirit, is divided also between his love for the countryside, for education (Cambridge), and for the life of the city (London). Civilization, Stapledon would seem to say, is similarly divided.

Despite the symbolism, we never lose the naturalistic and literal sense of Sirius as a dog. Stapledon's ability to sustain the tension between the concrete dog, Sirius, and his symbolic significance is remarkable. Sirius's smell and hearing are more keen than ours; his vision, however, is limited to black and white. Even more desperate is his lack of hands. Stapledon's concentration on the estrangement of being a dog makes us think anew of the wonders and tragic limitations of being human.

Sirius, a book about a dog, is thus a more human book than *Odd John*, in which the alienation between ourselves and the supernormals is permanent and impassable. *Sirius*, too, is about an alien who must in some way forever remain apart from us, but it is also about a love affair between a human being and this alien. *Last and First Men* concentrates upon the tragedy of the human species; *Sirius*, upon an alien being whose tragedy teaches us something about our own. In each book, the tragic vision is of a universe which is opening up rather than closing down. At the end of *Sirius*, Plaxy is with the dead Sirius on a moor, with dawn approaching. Plaxy "saw that Sirius, in spite of his uniqueness, epitomized in his whole life and in his death something universal, something that is common to all awakening spirits on earth, and in the farthest galaxies."[5] She sings a requiem for Sirius, a song that he had made for her; and "as she sang, red dawn filled the eastern sky, and soon the sun's bright finger set fire to Sirius" (p. 309). As his name suggests, Sirius has become a star.

As suggested above, though, *Sirius* contains social criticism as well as tragedy. Sirius, we must remember, is not only a dog but a sheep dog. Symbolically, he is one of the few wide-awakes, and the sheep are ordinary people who are led by him. Clearly this is a social model, not so much of the way society now operates as the way it *should* operate. Just as no one would suggest that the sheep should be free and equal to the sheep dog, so there ought to be a way of putting the wide-awakes in undisputed charge of things, for "it's always the wide-awake people who do everything worth while, really. The rest are just sheep" (p. 274).

In Chapter XII we discover that Plaxy had been a member of the Communist Party. Sirius, too, was once for common ownership of the means of production. Now, however, he has doubts. In the new order, what would happen to "eccentric creative enterprises like Thomas's?" To save such eccentricity, the wide-awakes must do the planning. Plaxy objects that the planning, whoever does it, must be for the sake of ordinary people. But Sirius points out that the sheep do not and should not rule themselves—rather, they are used by the master for a purpose. "But Sirius," says Plaxy, ". . . that's the way straight to Fascism." Sirius again has an answer: "a Fascist party is *not* made up of wide-awake people." And he adds:

The point is, if you serve the spirit you can't serve any other master. But what the spirit demands always is love and intelligence and strong creative action in its service, love of the sheep as individuals to be made the most of, not *merely* as mutton or as coral insects in a lovely coral pattern, but as individual vessels of the spirit (p. 275).

The leader ends up loving and doing what is best for the people—but only indirectly, since his or her immediate obligation is to serve the spirit dispassionately. Objective, dispassionate service to the spirit, not to the people: this is what makes it impossible for Stapledon to accept either Communism or Fascism. Writing in the 1930's and 1940's, he had to confront both; and, to do him credit, he never avoided contemporary social issues.

He was always honest, too, about these social issues. An incident in Chapter X reveals what Stapledon means by serving the spirit rather than the people. In London's East End, Rev. Geoffrey Adams and Sirius come upon strikers who have injured a "blackleg." When Geoffrey helps the man, he is reviled. " 'Fools' cried the parson. 'I'm on your side, but this man is as precious to God as any of us' " (p. 254). There is little doubt that Stapledon shares Adams's view that these striking workers are fools; they are sheep, and they need the dispassionate objectivity that only a Rev. Adams can supply.

This view is comprehensible—and also elitist. Certainly the Rev. Adamses of the world can be "objective," for they are in a position to be able to afford objectivity. The "objectivity" of the privileged is in any case a mask for their control of the situation. Stapledon was fascinated by Marxism, and he was on the side of the workers, but ultimately he was no revolutionary (nor did he ever claim to be). Stapledon is presumably sympathetic when Sirius becomes a farmer, a petit bourgeois. Stapledon believed in widespread change, and in helping the poor—but not in the poor helping themselves in the sense of making their own history. No hypocrite, Stapledon lived his beliefs. He continued to help the poor by remaining a lecturer in the Workers Educational Association.

Stapledon's belief in dispassionate objectivity—a view similar to that held by the great Victorian prophets, and doubtless typical of the views help by non-Marxist but radical English intellectuals— is in one way, then, a weakness. Translated, the detached stance of the Star Maker means social planning and social control by a well-situated elite. What is to prevent it from meaning, when extrapolated, the excesses of the supernormal colonists or a waking world that becomes a mad world? Stapledon would answer, I suppose, that we must struggle to attain the next level of community before we can worry about the new difficulties that will appear on that level.

On the other hand, though, Stapledon's objectivity is what makes him Stapledon, and worthy of notice. Stapledon was always the provincial Liverpool writer, as the result of a conscious decision not to take up a permanent residence in London. He feared that he would be absorbed. Doubtless this was the correct decision, for the strength of Stapledon's writing is that he does not write the way others write, that he writes tragedies in an age in which the conventional literary wisdom would have been that it is no longer possible to write tragedies. By refusing to be absorbed, by being objective, Stapledon produced a science fiction literature which is all the better for not being mainstream literature. In rejecting narrow conceptions of realism and in deliberately not learning much from James Joyce, Henry James, or D. H. Lawrence, Stapledon has much to teach today's science fiction, which is all too eager to ape its "betters."

Thomas D. Clareson

CLIFFORD D. SIMAK: THE INHABITED UNIVERSE

C lifford D. Simak published his first story, "The World of the Red Sun," in the December 1931 issue of *Wonder Stories,* a Gernsback magazine. A story of time travel, it well exemplifies both a reliance upon certain plot conventions associated with the early pulps and something of the naiveté with which authors of the period overcame their problems of portraying a future society. Although some twenty years later Simak himself was to suggest that the crucial task of the science fiction writer is to create a background so convincing that his readers will accept his "alien concepts" and bizarre settings,[1] "The World of the Red Sun" indicates how completely early sf concerned itself with action—with adventure. Yet in an epilogue unnecessary to the central action of the story, there is already—however unconsciously—something of at least one theme which was to shape Simak's mature work.

After ten years and the expenditure of "a wealth that mounted into seven figures,"[2] the two protagonists perfect a time machine and undertake a voyage supposedly of no more than a few thousand years. But their instruments fail to record accurately so that they end up more than five million years in the future. Yet they immediately recognize in "ruins of noble proportions, many of them still bearing the hint of a marvelous architecture of which the twentieth century would have been incapable," the remains of Denver, now engulfed by desert, standing on the shore of a sea covering the eastern United States. Scarcely has one of them declared that "Man is a hardy animal . . . and he can adapt himself to almost any kind of environment" before "a motley horde" of fur-clad men charges them "as if to attack." Without hesitation, although these primitives carry no weapons, the two protagonists shoot as many as possible (they later inquire why they were not "treated as friends" since they came seeking friendship although "ready for war"). Once overcome, they are instructed to "March" —in an unfamiliar dialect which is nonetheless recognizable as "good, pure English"—by one of the men who, like his companions, is tall, "well proportioned [and] clean of limb," although all possess "the eyes of furtive beings . . . of hunted beasts always on the lookout for danger" (pp. 201-202).

Against this simplified background the action proceeds by formula. They learn that all men are "minions" of Golan-Kirt, a creature of pure Evil, "He-Who-Came-Out-of-the-Cosmos" to rule the remnant of mankind through fear for some five million years. They learn, too, that they must do battle against him in the "games," and during a conversation on the nature of time, their informant tells them that Golan-Kirt is hated, mortal, and afraid of death and that he rules only through the power of suggestion. In the arena they discover that the invisible Golan-Kirt can call up only creatures of their own imaginations against them—in this case, a machine gun, marching soldiers, and a lion; thus, they demand that he materialize and give personal combat. He appears as "a naked brain . . . a ghastly thing." This "Struggle of the Ages" in a vast arena and the grotesque, mad brain: these are the conventions around which Simak built the story, conventions which haunted science fiction at least until the 1950's. Because the protagonists deride Golan-Kirt—laugh at him—they are able to withstand his psychic powers and kill him. An echo of the Frankenstein theme occurs when one of them challenges him:

'You once were a man . . . a great scientist. You studied the brain, specialized in it. At last you discovered a great secret, which gave you the power of developing the brain to an unheard-of degree. Sure of your technique, and realizing the power you might enjoy, you transformed yourself into a brain creature. You are a fraud and an imposter. You have mis-ruled these people for millions of years. You are not out of the Cosmos,—you are a man, or what once was a man. You are an atrocity, an abomination' (p. 215).

There "The World of the Red Sun" might well have ended, particularly since the natives want the two to remain with them in order to help "rebuild the land . . . construct machines, give us some of the marvelous knowledge which we, as a race, have lost." But Simak chose to develop the final sequence into an "Epilogue," in which the protagonists attempt to re-gain the twentieth-century, although they have been told that travel backward in time is impossible. Again their instruments fail; they are cast farther into the future, where they find an eroded statue honoring them as saviors of the race. One damns the instruments, calling them liars, beating them until his hands are "smeared with blood." The two then realize that they are "alone at the end of the world!"

Because of the dissimilarity with which Simak and John W. Campbell treat the same theme, one is tempted to compare "The World of the Red Sun" and Campbell's "Twilight" (*Astounding*, November 1934), the latter increasingly recognized as one of the classic thematic statements of early American magazine science fiction. Campbell's protagonist also ventures millions of years into the future, where he finds marvelous machines and automated cities beyond anything that he has imagined. Yet the knowledge which created them has been ignored, if not forgotten, by the remnant of mankind caught in the million-year twilight of the race: "little men—bewildered—dwarfed, with heads disproportionately large. But not extremely so":

Their eyes impressed me most. They were huge, and when they looked at me there was a power in them that seemed sleeping, but too deeply to be roused.[3]

In short, after past glories spanning millions of years and the entire solar system, the race has stagnated intellectually. Realizing this and seized by a profound melancholy because of it, the protagonist links together a number of computer-like machines and assigns them the task of making "a machine which would have what man had lost. A curious machine." For Campbell's protagonist, the demise of the human race is more than compensated for, if at least one rational, inquisitive "mind" continues to accumulate knowledge.[4]   A far cry from Simak's pair of twentieth-century men, betrayed by their machines, standing amid swirling sand at the foot of the crumbling statue.

One deliberately avoids reading any symbolism—conscious or not—into the ending of Simak's tale. Suffice it to notice the difference from "Twilight" and to suggest that although Simak published regularly enough in Campbell's *Astounding* from 1938 onward to become identified as one of Campbell's "stable" of writers, he never seems to have shared fully those enthusiasms with which one associates that group—such writers, for example, as Heinlein and Asimov. Perhaps the closest he came was in *Cosmic Engineers,* serialized in *Astounding* (February-April 1939) and issued in book form in 1950. It calls up the epic stage and conventions of the space opera, for its Earthlings are summoned to the very edge of the universe by a billion-year-old race, the Engineers, to participate in an attempt to save the galaxy from being destroyed by collision with a second galaxy. Should this action not prove sufficient, the plot is augmented by the warfare between the Engineers and the so-called "Hellhounds," who can travel outside galactic time and space and are therefore willing to see our galaxy destroyed if they can dominate the next one to form.[5] Needless to say, they fail, and the Earthlings destroy the second galaxy in order to save ours. This victory brings forth Simak's most *Astounding* response:

. . . for the first time, tiny beings spawned within the universe, had taken firm hold of the universe's destiny. Henceforth Man and his little compatriots throughout the vast gulfs of space would no longer be mere pawns in the grim tide of cosmic forces. Henceforth life would rule these forces, bend them to its will, put them to work, change them, shift them about.

Life was an accident. There was little doubt of that. Something that wasn't exactly planned. Something that had crept in, like a malignant disease in the ordered mechanism of the universe. The universe was hostile to life. The depths of space were too cold for life, most of the condensed matter too hot for life, space was traversed by radiations inimical to life. But life was triumphant. In the end the universe would not destroy it . . . it would rule the universe.[6]

Here is the optimism of which, as I have suggested elsewhere, the literary establishment from Arnold and Adams to Dreiser and

Dos Passos was incapable; science fiction was the opposite response to literary naturalism in the face of the new science at the turn of the century. And it is this view which produced the concept of "galactic man" triumphant throughout the universe.[7] For Simak, however, this was never the easy solution it seemed to be for others. For example, the Engineers prove to be a race of robots created three billion years ago by a race of whom man is a descendant. They long to cooperate once more with man; one of their spokesmen explains:

'. . . It is because of imagination and vision . . . the ability to see beyond facts, to probe into probabilities, to visualize what might be and then attempt to make it so. That is something we cannot do. We are chained to mechanistic action and mechanistic thought. We do not advance beyond the proven fact. When two facts create another fact, we accept the third fact, but we do not reach out in speculation, collect half a dozen tentative facts and then try to crystallize them' (p. 216).

When they offer the Earthlings their marvelous city, one of the protagonists responds:

'. . . We aren't ready yet. We'd just make a mess of things. We'd have too much power, too much leisure, too many possessions. It would smash our civilization and leave us one in its stead that we could not manage. We haven't put our own civilization upon a basis that could coincide with what is here.
    '. . . Sometime in the future. When we have wiped out some of the primal passions. When we have solved the great social and economic problems that plague us now. When we have learned to observe the Golden Rule . . . when we have lost some of the lustiness of our youth. Sometime we will be ready for this city' (pp. 220, 221).

Simak's concern for the phenomenon of life has provided him increasingly with his basic subject matter, but his criticism of man and his society has given him his cutting edge. For example, in "Sunspot Purge" (1940), in which his protagonists again go forward in time to find civilization destroyed, one of them asserts:

'But Man is gone. He rose, and for a little while he walked the Earth. But now he's swept away.
    'Back in 1950, Man thought he was the whole works. But he wasn't so hot after all. The sunspots took him to the cleaners. Maybe it was the sunspots in the first place that enabled him to rise up on his hind legs and rule the roost.'[8]

By 1940, then, Simak had already given at least brief expression to certain themes which have set him apart from his early contemporaries. By then, too, he had also discovered several of those devices which have become characteristic of his best work. For example, he had already found one of his favorite protagonists, the newspaperman. (One can perhaps explain this choice as a result of his own long career in journalism, but one must recall that the familiar newsman provides easy access to an often strange world. Then, as does the scientist through his research, the reporter through his story seeks the truth. For him, as for the scientist, the plot provides the problem—the mystery—to be solved.)

"Hunger Death" (*Astounding,* October 1938), introduced another of his favorite devices, the small town as setting, albeit this time it is New Chicago on Venus. (It is as though Simak deliberately makes use of this familiar setting from the main body of American literature—together with its eccentric individuals—in order to assist his readers in their transition into unknown worlds.) Perhaps more than most of his early fiction, "Hunger Death" illustrates what seems to have been Simak's uneasiness with many of the plot conventions expected in early sf. New Chicago is the one site in the solar system where a dread disease is not rampant; it is also the only site where grows the so-called "polka dot weed," a natural antidote to the disease. Although early in the story the reader is told that the seeds came from Mars and is reminded of an old cult of scientists who once ruled Mars until they were deposed by revolution and supposedly exterminated, not until the problem is solved do the readers realize that the Martian scientists—the Genziks—have used the plague as a means of finally regaining political control of Mars, Earth, and Venus. The story ends only after the failure of their raid on New Chicago when their spaceship attempts to burn the city and the adjoining fields of the polka dot weed. For extra flavor it is suggested that they had originally gone to Mars from Atlantis. Needless to say, the story suffers as it surrenders to action and convention, thereby perhaps reflecting either Simak's uncomfortable awareness of what should be included in an acceptable pulp story or the necessity to achieve a certain word count. One of the main characters, incidentally, is a newsman; it is, of course, his report of the cure which precipitates the attack upon the city.

Other stories might be cited to trace the completion of what Simak himself calls his apprenticeship during the 1930's and 1940's.[9] "Hunch" (*Astounding*, July 1943), serves as an important transition, for in it he voices the fear that the "work of man had outstripped his brain. Now man was losing out."[10] An institution called Sanctuary heals those who have broken down or gone insane, but no one who has been treated there returns to the outer world. That he resorts to a plot in which the patients of Sanctuary—and some others—are being possessed by a race which supposedly destroyed most of the Martians ages ago (and must therefore be destroyed) seems a throwback, while the close telepathic relationship between a Martian and the blind protagonist looks forward to later novels in which Simak tries to expand man's consciousness. Yet Simak complicates that basic pulp formula, for the purpose of the ancient race is not to destroy man but to subtly change him—to remove his violence. It leads the blind protagonist to denounce the sense of peace which Sanctuary brings:

'. . . it is not a human creed. It's not the old hell-for-leather creed that has taken man up the ladder, that will continue to take him up the ladder if he hangs onto it. It would wipe out all the harsher emotions and we need those harsher emotions to keep climbing. We can't lie in the sun, we can't stand still, we can't, not yet, even take the time to stand off and admire the things that we have done.

'Peace, the deeper concept of peace, is not for the human race, never was meant for the human race. Conflict is our meat. The desire to beat the other fellow to it, the hankering for glorification . . .' (p. 35).

But Simak gives the final words to another character who sees the value of Sanctuary, which might lead, perhaps, "to a better life":

'. . . If the human being, as human being, could not carry out his own destiny, if the race were doomed to madness, if evolution had erred in bringing man along the path he had followed, what then? If the human way of life were basically at fault, would it not be better to accept a change before it was too late? . . .' (p. 35)

Clifford D. Simak had found his theme. For thirty years he has explored these questions, and they led first to that group of stories gathered together under the title *City* (1952), which won the third International Fantasy Award. He has several times explained that his moral and intellectual despair at the outrages of World War Two, especially the bombing of Hiroshima, removed him from that group who saw man's technology as the key to his inevitable progress. At the outset of the *City* stories he sought to visualize a peaceful world; to do this, he destroyed the cities and returned man to the land. There seems an irony in the fact that seven of the eight tales were published by John W. Campbell in *Astounding* between 1944 and 1947.

Undoubtedly no consideration of the tales individually can fully measure their impact when gathered together as a novel which explores the destiny of Man and Earth over a time span of some thousands of years. Each episode focuses upon a crucial moment, sometimes centuries apart. For example, in "City" (May 1944), Simak assumes that such scientific achievements as atomic power, automation, air travel, and hydroponics have abolished man's urban culture, making both the city and farming as now known obsolete. Man is forced into a crisis situation to which he must adapt quickly. The central action of the story turns upon the efforts of certain politicians to perpetuate a moribund city abandoned by all but a handful of its most elderly inhabitants, for only these officials cling to the "myth of the city," and by doing so, represent Simak's first attack upon those who value property rights more than human rights. Two months later "Huddling Peace" (July 1944), portrays a "manorial existence, based on old family homes and leisurely acres" which are dependent upon atomic energy and robotic labor. Once the pressure of city life ends, the pendulum swings the other way; increasingly, mankind suffers from agorophobia. The story dramatizes the struggle of the protagonist—Webster—to summon enough courage to go to Mars to perform brain surgery on a personal friend, Juwain, a philosopher who is close to a breakthrough which may change man's life. He steels himself to the journey, but his robot, Jenkins, sends away the ship that comes for Webster because everyone knows that his master never goes anywhere.

Not until "Census" (September 1944), however, does the potential of the series begin to reveal itself clearly. The census taker encounters a mutant of indeterminate age and vast intellectual superiority who immediately recognizes the flaw in Juwain's thinking, but refuses to correct it and share it with humanity. In somewhat like manner, at some time in the past, out of pure inquisitiveness, he has enclosed an ant hill in glass, heating it during the winter so that the ants will not have to hibernate each winter and thus be caught in a static cycle. Already the ants have carts, and chimneys coming out of the hill emit smoke. (Later the mutant kicks down the enclosure and levels the hill, for he is a creature of intellect who has lost any human compassion.) In contrast, the descendant of the Webster who could not operate on Juwain feels such remorse that he has successfully begun experiments on dogs enabling them to speak and correcting their sight so that they may read. He explains to the census-taker:

'. . . Thus far Man has come alone. One thinking, intelligent race all by itself. Think of how much farther, how much faster it might have gone had there been two thinking, intelligent races, working together. For you see, they would not think alike. They'd check their thoughts against one another. What one couldn't think of, the other could. The old story of two heads.

'Think of it, Grant. A *different* mind than the human mind, but one that will work with the human mind. That will see and develop, if you will, philosophies the human mind could not.'[11]

At the end of the story, after his encounter with the mutant, the census-taker confides to one of the dogs that man may not always be as he is now, and that in such eventuality the dogs must "take the dream and keep it going."

Although internal evidence in "Desertion" (November 1944), indicates a lack of the narrative ties which Simak had used through the first three tales, it served as an essential transition. As an individual story, "Desertion" provides a classic example of one of the basic sf structural patterns: the solution of a specific problem. Man must learn to adapt himself to live on the surface of Jupiter. But the resolution is unexpected, if not unique. The protagonist and his dog assume the form of a Jovian creature, the loper. So exhilarating—so transcendent—is the experience that they refuse to resume their old identities as man and dog. Thus, the tale becomes pivotal to the whole of the *City* series because it provides Simak with a convenient means of clearing the stage of humanity, as occurs as the aftermath of "Paradise" (June 1946). Given the promise of something better, the vast majority of mankind flees to Jupiter, forsaking their humanity without regret. No more than several thousand remain, isolating themselves in Geneva. Most important, of course, "Desertion" and "Paradise" together thus emphasize Simak's denunciation of the human condition more than did any of his previous fiction.

When man falters—surrenders his humanity—the dogs' culture flourishes. Knowledge of their origin and subservience to man is kept from them by Jenkins. Doggish culture is psychically oriented; killing is unknown (an inheritance from the last few centuries of man); gradually all animals are tamed and the brotherhood of life is revered; the existence of parallel worlds, side-by-side in time, is discovered, although a few of those worlds are closed because they are inhabited by "cobblies," nightmarish creatures.

In "Hobbies" (*Astounding*, November 1946), one of the Websters who secluded himself in Geneva, returns briefly to Jenkins and the dogs, and though Jenkins welcomes him and the dogs think of him as God, he returns quickly to Geneva, for he realizes that the dreams of the dogs:

[may be] better than the dreams of man, for they held none of the ruthlessness that the human race had planned, aimed at none of the mechanistic brutality the human race had spawned.

A new civilization, a new culture, a new way of thought. Mystic, perhaps, and visionary, but so had man been visionary. Probing into mysteries that man had brushed by as unworthy of his time, as mere superstition that could have no scientific basis (p. 171).

By means of a dome he seals the remainder of humanity in Geneva so that they may not interfere with the dogs; he knows:

[man] still kept the old vices—the vices that had become virtues from his viewpoint and raised him by his own bootstraps. He kept the unwavering belief that his was the only kind, the only life that mattered—the smug egoism that made him the self-appointed lord of all creation (p. 188).

In "Aesop" (December 1947), when one of the descendants of a youngster who had been out hunting when Webster sealed off Geneva violates the brotherhood of life by killing a robin with a bow and arrow, Jenkins leads the few remaining young people into one of the worlds of the cobblies, isolating them there. Yet the *City* series is no canine pastoral. Just as the destiny of the dogs was changed by the guilt of a Webster, so, too, the destiny of the ants had been changed by the action of the mutant. Although he had destroyed the ant hill, the ants emerge millenia later in "The Trouble with Ants" (*Fantastic Adventures*, January 1951), and by controlling the robots, build a great metallic structure which gradually engulfs the world. Published as "The Simple Way" in the novel, it records Jenkins' trip to Geneva, where he asks the last of the Websters what to do about the ants. Webster suggests poison, but Jenkins rejects "the human way" because that would mean killing. The dogs thus emigrate to one of the parallel worlds.

Such a summary can only approximate the intellectual complexity and force of *City*, particularly as it appeared when published as a novel. However provocative these stories and themes may have been when read individually, scattered over a period of seven years, they could not but lose some of their unity and force. Even in novel form, they might well remain so episodic as to lose something of their effectiveness. Simak solved the problem by tying the stories together with an extraordinarily successful adaptation of the traditional narrative framework. Most simply, they are presented as a series of eight "tales" surviving within the doggish culture—perhaps having a basis in history, more likely legend. In a general introduction and notes to each tale, their editor refers to the scholarly debates involving their authenticity and to the various interpretations given them. In his "Editor's Preface," he notes that they provoke such questions as "What is Man?" . . . "What is a city?" . . . "What is a war?" A simplicity of tone masks the sophistication of the frame; through it Simak created a credible non-human world. He brought to science fiction something of the vitality of the beast fable as a perspective from which to make moral judgment.

Like Wells, he had relied upon biology and the psychological make-up of the race to examine its destiny and its worth. Like Asimov and Heinlein, he had sketched the panorama of the future of man and Earth. Unlike them, he judged man and found him wanting. Through his imagined editor, Simak attacked both man's "preoccupation with a mechanical civilization" and his "inability to understand and appreciate the thoughts and viewpoint of another man," a condition resulting in man's terrible isolation within his own limited consciousness. Yet the severity of Simak's indictment reached its highpoint when he permitted his 'editor' to insist:

Throughout these tales it becomes clear that Man was running a race, if not within himself, then with some imagined follower who pressed close upon his heels, breathing on his back. Man was engaged in a mad scramble for power and knowledge, but nowhere is there any hint of what he meant to do with it once he had attained it (p. 120).

All of these were but points to emphasize his central theme: "Without at least broad purpose, without certain implanted stability, no culture can survive, and this is the lesson" (p. 148).

Once Simak had written *City*, particularly after assigning it the framework of the finished novel, American science fiction could never again be what it had been in the magazines of the 1930's and 1940's. Granted that from the first there had been critics—like Wells and Keller and Williamson—who had questioned the concept of inevitable progress, but no one, so thoroughly as Simak, had condemned man's surrender to that technology which led him to Hiroshima and the Moon—not even those who howled in guilt in the years immediately after World War Two or those who pictured dystopia as early as the 1950's. Clifford Simak did more, perhaps, than any of his contemporaries to free science fiction from its established patterns and to create credible, imaginary worlds better able to sustain metaphors of the condition of man. As few other writers before him, he gave the genre a moral stature. In *City* because legend implies that man gave himself unhesitatingly to the machine instead of structuring his culture upon "some of the sounder, more worthwhile concepts of life"—thereby exposing his "basic lack of character"—Simak judged him and found him wanting. In the vastness of time amid multiple worlds, the name of Man became "a dust that is blowing with the wind, the sound of leaves in a summer's day—nothing more" (p. 213).

At the heart of Simak's work, however, particularly from the 1950's onward, is something far different from the anger or bitterness at the failings of modern society which so often characterizes the writings of those authors associated with such groups as the so-called 'New Wave' of the 1960's. Simak attempts to enunciate a vision which sees all sentient creatures, however diverse their forms, as equal parts of a single community which is itself the purpose and meaning of the galaxy. Even as he completed *City*, he made his initial affirmation in the novel *Time and Again* (1951), serialized within the previous year in *Galaxy Science Fiction* as

"Time Quarry." The point of departure is familiar—man's egotism:

Man was spread thin throughout the galaxy. . . . For Man had flown too fast, had driven far beyond his physical capacity. . . . It took judgment . . . and some tolerance . . . and a great measure of latent brutality, but most of all, conceit, the absolute, unshakable conviction that Man was sacrosanct, that he could not be touched, that he could scarcely die.[12]

But Simak's response differed. His protagonist had been killed during a crash-landing on one of the unknown planets of Cygni, and he had been restored to life by its inhabitants. He can describe those creatures only as "symbiotic abstractions," but his mind fuses with one of the beings who describes himself as the protagonist's destiny. He, in turn, realizes:

. . . it will not coerce me and it will not stop me. It will only give me hunches, it will only whisper to me. It is the thing called conscience and the thing called judgment and the thing called righteousness (pp. 149-150).

He returns to Earth and is feared because he is not fully human—as his journey from Cygni without air or food in a ship that should not be able to fly proves. He wishes to share his knowledge, to write a book, *This Is Destiny*, but the machinations of the plot, including the activities of men from the future, aim at preventing him from finishing it. His message is simple:

We are not alone.
No one ever is alone.
Not since the first faint stirring of the first flicker of life on the first planet in the galaxy that knew the quickening of life, has there ever been a single entity that walked or crawled or slithered down the path of life alone (p. 105).

For Earth this means that whether man, robot, or android, "all that mattered was the pulse of life" (p. 142). This, of course, gives the men from the future their motive, for as "revisionists" of the book they would permit only the life of man to have worth and meaning. All others must remain inferior. The novel ends as the androids help the protagonist flee Earth so that he may write the book.

From this point on, one of Simak's dominant concerns is the exploration of an inhabited universe. Even a catalogue could only begin to suggest the many ways in which he has dealt with the encounter between men and a wide diversity of intelligent beings. There are, of course, the purely humorous incidents. "Lulu" (*Galaxy*, June 1957), an automated spaceship, falls in love with her crew and takes them star-roving. "Crying Jag" (*Galaxy*, February 1960), brings to Earth an alien who becomes drunk on the "sad stories" of humanity's malajustments; so rich is the world in such tales that his cohorts invade the planet so that each person may have someone to tell his troubles to.

The novel *Goblin Reservation* (1968), introduces a conglomeration of trolls, goblins, banshees, a Neanderthal man, and a visit to campus by William Shakespeare into a mystery involving an ancient crystal planet and interplanetary aliens who may be potential rivals/enemies of mankind. It is perhaps his most successfully sustained humorous work, and the artifact from the ancient world provides one of the hilarious surprises of modern science fiction. Yet he does permit one of the Little Folk to say, "We burrow deep to the heart of nature and do not waste precious vitality of spirit upon those petty concerns which make wreckage of the lives and hopes of humans," while a banshee, whose species served as "communicators" between the ancient planet and its colonies, admits that they considered preventing the rise of primates on Earth: "But there was the ancient rule. Intelligence is too seldom found for one to stand in the way of its development."[13] A novel of lesser stature, *Out of Their Minds* (1970), involves a contemporary encounter with the Devil and, before his final capitulation to Don Quixote and Sancho Panza, he berates the "vapid" creations of the modern imagination—Li'l Abner, Orphan Annie, Dagwood Bumstead, Mr. Magoo, and Howdy Doody among them —"not an honestly evil one among them and none is really good. . . ."[14]

Some criticized Simak for the inclusion of such characters into both novels, speaking of the results as excursions into fantasy instead of science fiction. He replied, as he has done before, by asserting both that he has never been one of those for whom "hard" science has provided the core of his work and that too much energy has been expended searching for some simplistic distinction between fantasy and science fiction. He once compared that task to the medieval debate asking how many angels can stand on the head of a pin, and more recently has declared that "the whole jar is fantasy."[15] Moreover, by including in his tales figures ranging from traditional mythology to interplanetary aliens, he can perhaps more clearly underscore the unifying continuum by which writers from all periods have concerned themselves with the "expansion of man," particularly through bringing him into encounters with creatures who are equal or superior to him.

Always Simak tests man. In "Immigrant" (*Astounding,* March 1954), only the very best of mankind, after arduous preparation and examination, are invited to the planet Kimon. Instead of finding themselves privileged traders and businessmen, however, they learn that they are still as children who must begin a long schooling before they can become citizens of the galaxy. In "Neighbor" (*Astounding,* June 1954), an alien marooned on Earth transforms Coon Valley into a utopia, although no one can enter or leave it, and it becomes legendary because outside authorities know of it but have lost its location (that is, it apparently exists outside of normal time and space). In "Shotgun Cure" (*F&SF,* January 1961), an alien offers mankind a vaccine which will cure "all your ills. Including, more than likely, a few you don't suspect." He makes the offer to a poor doctor in the village of Millville—the name, incidentally, of Simak's birthplace in Wisconsin.

The agreement is reached, however, only after the doctor replies to the alien's accusation that the medical profession makes its living off disease:

'I would like to point out to you . . . that the medical profession is working hard to conquer those diseases you are talking of. We are doing all we can to destroy our own jobs.'
  'This is fine. . . . It is what I thought, but it did not square with your planet's business sense. . . .'[16]

On the eve of the day when world-wide clinics will give the vaccine to mankind, the doctor finds he has second thoughts. Millville had been the pilot project, and the doctor finds that he, like others, seems to have lost something of his mental sharpness. Although he believes that there had been a common ground between alien and man—"compassion for the blind and halt"—he cannot but wonder whether or not, as well as curing its more obvious diseases, "the aliens proposed to limit Man's powers of self-destruction even if it meant reducing him to abject stupidity"

(p. 48).   He is willing to take that chance; on the following morning the clinics will dispense the vaccine worldwide.

Slight though the story may seem, it ties together three important strands of Simak's mature work.   First, it reveals his increasing distrust of man's intelligence as it has become evermore obsessed by a mechanical civilization and machines of destruction. Secondly, it attacks the basic business ethic of western society. (The most extended attack upon the business establishment occurs in the novel, *Ring Around the Sun* (1953), in which a superior race of mutants undertakes to destroy the economy by producing goods of higher quality and greater durability.   The novel has a second importance, for the mutants operate from one of a series of parallel worlds—"Worlds without end, waiting when we need them.   We can go pioneering for generation after generation.   A new world for each generation if need be. . . ."[17])

The concept of parallel worlds had appeared, of course, as early as *City*, and a pastoral quality had dominated certain of the episodes of that novel.   Increasingly, however, after the epic stage of *Cosmic Engineers*, Simak has permitted his aliens to encounter the citizens of Millville and/or has brought his protagonists to that confluence of the Wisconsin and Mississippi Rivers, which, in his imagination, has somehow retained many of the values lost by contemporary civilization.   He admits that he has idealized the region,[18] but except for such sequestered havens as Coon Valley, the rural towns and farms of southwestern Wisconsin—the area of his youth—have provided the oftentimes idyllic backdrop for much of his work in the late 1950's and 1960's in which he has challenged the establishment.

"The Big Front Yard" (*Astounding*, October 1958)—a Hugo winner also selected for the Science Fiction Hall of Fame—provides one of the more effective examples.   Somehow aliens warp space so that the front of the protagonist's house opens into a strange world.   Exploring it, he finds still another house opening into a third world so that, once again, the idea of a series of interlocking worlds is introduced.   Aliens appear; they wish to trade, to exchange ideas.   One human thinks only in terms of real estate development; another, an official from the U.N., thinks only in terms of the advantages which can accrue to Earth because of the aliens' advanced technology; one finally asserts that "We have a big new world waiting for us out there—" But the protagonist exclaims that it is not waiting for anyone to exploit; both he and the moronic telepath, who is the only human capable of communicating with the aliens, realize that this is more "than the linking of mere worlds. It would be, as well, the linking of the peoples of those worlds."[19]

The intensity with which the image of a village—symbolic of an escape from the disasters of the twentieth century—has gripped Simak's imagination may be measured by two very different works from those cited. In *All the Traps of Earth* (1960), a robot—very reminiscent of Jenkins—seeks to escape the Earth and gain his personal liberty after the death of the last member of the family which he has served for more than six hundred years. He is already a lawbreaker, for no robot is allowed a life-span of more than a century. He wanders the galaxy until he discovers those values so important to Simak in the village of Sleepy Hollow on the planet Arcadia:

It seemed almost as if the village were the Earth, a transplanted Earth with the old primeval problems and hopes of Earth—a family of peoples that faced existence with a readiness and confidence and inner strength.[20]

The robot remains there to serve as "a simple teacher of the human race," passing on to them knowledge of the paranormal powers which he has come to possess (p. 50). The novel *Destiny Doll* (1971), becomes a quest for reality and identity, ending only when the protagonist becomes aware that he has gained "the ability to reach out and grasp and merge with the minds of others, as if for an instant it were not many minds, but a single mind. And myself as well, the forgotten edges of myself, the unplumbed depths of self":

. . . There were many universes and many sentient levels and at certain time-space intervals they became apparent and each of them was real, as real as the many geologic levels that a geologist could count. Except that this was not a matter of counting; it was seeing and sensing and knowing they were there.[21]

Fully aware of the complexity of consciousness and "filled with mystic faith," the companions join together in the "one tiny step" necessary "to attain a better place, to find a better world." They find the place for which they have hunted:

The village and the river lay below us and fields and woods stretched away to the far horizons. And I knew, somehow, that this was a world without an end and that it was, as well, the end of time, a place that was everlasting and unchanging with room for everyone (pp. 222-223).

A brief consideration of certain novels from the 1960's will show how Simak's themes developed toward *Destiny Doll* and beyond it to what he regards as a climactic statement, *A Choice of Gods* (1972). In *Time Is the Simplest Thing* (1961), he gave his primary attention to the development of a parapsychic power by which man may free himself from his individual isolation as well as the confines of the Earth. Although the persecution of mutants who have the rudiments of this power may be read as a commentary on civil rights, the new freedom is gained only because on a far planet the protagonist met an ageless, grotesque creature which fused its mind with his. Of his meetings with diverse beings on many worlds, the protagonist explains:

'You're often filled with wonder, but more often you are puzzled. You are reminded, again and yet again, of how insignificant you are. And there are times when you forget that you are human. You're just a blob of life— brother to everything that ever existed or ever will exist.'[22]

In *All Flesh Is Grass* (1965), an alien intelligence—having the outward appearance of flowers but also being joined into a communal mind—invades Earth (at Millville) from a parallel universe and offers to form a partnership with man:

We need living space and if you will give us living space, we'll give you our knowledge; we need technology for we have no hands, and with our knowledge you can shape new technologies and those technologies can be used for the benefit of both of us. We can go together into other worlds. Eventually a long chain of many earths will be linked together and the races of them linked, as well, in a common aim and purpose.[23]

But man is initially afraid, projecting onto the aliens his appraisal of himself:

They may be looking for a deadly race. And a deadly race, that's us. Maybe they want someone who'll go slashing into parallel world after parallel world, in a sort of frenzy: brutal, ruthless, terrible. For when you come right down to it, we are pretty terrible (pp. 227-228).

Although the government would destroy the aliens—and all of Millville—with atomic weapons, the offer was sincerely made and with love, for the aliens responded to the single man who nurtured the first seeds which came into his garden.

Again, in *The Werewolf Principle* (1967), Simak fused three minds in order to gain an expanded intelligence: the humanoid Blake, the Changer, and the Thinker. As they flee earth in order to avoid persecution, they conclude:

Intelligence . . . is all there is; it's the one significance. Not life alone, not matter, not energy, but intelligence. Without intelligence, all the scattered matter, all the flaming energy, all the emptiness was of no consequence because it did not have a meaning. It was only intelligence that could take the matter and the energy and make it meaningful.[24]

Perhaps in no other assertion did he sound so much like such writers as, say, John W. Campbell. In the same year, in *Why Call Them Back from Heaven* (1967), he permitted his protagonist to voice the fear that has haunted western civilization at least since the late nineteenth century when the protagonist declared that man was "a tiny, flickering ego that imagined the universe revolved around it—imagined this when the universe did not know it existed, nor cared that it existed. . . ." Simak could not accept such an answer. When an alien mathematics reveals that life is as indestructible as energy, as everlasting as time and space, he permits his protagonist to declare: "That kind of thinking could have been justified at one time. But not any longer. [For if this mathematics is true], then each little flickering ego was a basic part of the universe and a fundamental expression of the purpose of the universe."[25]

As noted, other titles, both stories and novels, might be cited, for man's nature and his place in the universe has been the overriding concern of Simak's fiction for the past quarter century. One might turn to the destructive invasion of "The Golden Bugs" (*F&SF*, June 1960), in which he wonders what will happen to man when he ventures to the stars: "Would we find as little patience and as little understanding? Would we act as arrogantly as these golden bugs had acted?"[26] Or to a story of more important stature, "The Thing in Stone" (*If,* August 1970), in which he cries out, "Certainly there must be some universal ethics."[27]

The stage was ready for *A Choice of Gods* (1972), which P. Schuyler Miller called "the strangest of the very strange books" Simak had been writing recently, although—like Simak himself—he recognized that it was "closer to *City* in mood than anything else he has written."[28]   And like *City*, its cornerstone is a denunciation of man's technological civilization. Simak explained that he wrote it because its ideas had been plaguing him for years; he wrote it to "get the ideas off my back."[29]

One night almost all of mankind disappears from earth—a phenomenon which later troubles the narrator because such an "instantaneous extinction postulates the machination of an intelligence rather than a natural process." This, in turn, leads him to the question of purpose: "Is all life in the galaxy watched over by some great central intelligence that is alert to certain crimes that cannot be tolerated?"[30]

Among those few left is a small band of Indians who return to the nomadic life; in a manner somewhat reminiscent of the Folk in *Goblin Reservation*, the chief explains that "We went back to the earth, linking ourselves with the hills and streams, and that is as it should be" (p. 21). One of their young women discovers that she can converse with the trees and animals of the woods and thereby more than anyone else in her group gains an insight into the reality of the community of life throughout nature. A second figure, a young man from the west who is a descendant of agricultural workers, also has a psychic relationship with nature in that he can kill or cure its creatures. In a sense he symbolizes the compassionate nature of man toward everything that lives. This, then, is one pattern of life—and its potential—that Simak portrays.

The second is that exemplified by the family of the narrator, who has himself lived for five thousand years in a house recalling that of the Websters in *City*. He and his wife remain alone, although they can readily communicate with their many descendants who flourish on innumerable planets and possess parapsychic powers enabling them to travel freely throughout the universe. The narrator opens up the basic theme when he reflects:

. . . The ability seems to be inherent. Man probably had it for a long time before he began to use it. For it to develop time was needed and the longer life gave us time. Perhaps it would have developed even before without the longer life if we'd not been so concerned, so fouled up, with our technology. Somewhere we may have taken the wrong turning, accepted the wrong values and permitted our concern with technology to mask our real and valid purpose. The concern with technology may have kept us from knowing what we had. These abilities could not struggle up into our consciousness through the thick layers of machines and cost estimates and all the rest of it. And when we talk about abilities, it's not simply going to the stars. Your people [the Indians] don't go to the stars. There may be no need of you to do so. You have become, instead, a part of your environment, living within its texture and understanding. It went that way for you . . . (pp. 23-24).

Two other groups survive, both robots. The one, numbering only four, has tried for centuries to puzzle out the meaning of Christianity which had eluded man: "They seemed to have gotten the idea that man had stopped far short of the point he should have reached in his study of religion and that they, as objective students, might press the matter much beyond man's short-range venture into it" (p. 92). Their quest permits Simak to raise questions regarding the nature of faith and truth and to wonder whether faith must forever be "the willingness and ability to believe in the face of the lack of evidence" (p. 52). This theme also allows the protagonist—the only one who can converse with non-terrestrial beings—to discuss the existence of the soul with an alien resembling "a can of worms—the worst he had ever seen" (p. 39), a description necessary to emphasize both the grotesqueness and the spiritual sensitivity of those few life forms which man has found throughout the galaxy—none of which has been humanoid in form. Although the best he can do is suggest that the soul may be a state of mind, the alien disappears, supposedly after being given a soul by the young man from the west. The protagonist makes his fullest statement when he reflects:

There had been a time, perhaps, when [religion] had been meaningful. In the centuries after it had been conceived in all its glory, it had been allowed to fade, to become a shadow of its former force and strength. It had been a victim of man's mismanagement, of his overwhelming concept of property and profit. It had been manifested in lordly buildings filled with pomp and glitter rather than being nourished in the human heart and mind. And now it came to this—that it was kept alive by beings that were not even human, machines that had been accorded a measure of seeming humanness purely as a matter of technology and pride (pp. 44-45).

Such a judgment of Christianity leads directly to the climactic scene of "The Marathon Photograph" (1974), in which Simak presents a crucifixion utterly devoid of the glory Church and Scripture assigned to the Crucifixion.[31]

The other group, keeping independent of all men, realizing that apparently "there was no limit to a robot," has constructed "an open-ended robot . . . one that was never really finished" (p. 122). Not only does it now direct its continuing construction, but it has achieved communication with an intelligence at the center of the galaxy. This thread assumes its full importance only after the brother of the protagonist returns from his wanderings at the center of the galaxy to report that mankind has survived on other worlds, has located Earth, and now wishes to repossess it. He has also become aware of "a great uncaring. An intellectual uncaring. An intelligence that has lost what we think of as humanity. Perhaps not lost it, for it may never have had it" (p. 57). It is, of course, this intelligence with which the open-ended robot communicates, becoming its spokesman.

The novel reaches no carefully planned resolution. When representatives of mankind arrive on Earth, the robots hand them a message from that central intelligence which states that Earth in its present condition is a part of a deliberate experiment and must not be interfered with. For those who may find such an ending abrupt and unsatisfactory, Simak has explained that *A Choice of Gods* is an unstructured novel, having no hero or tightly developed plot-line in the traditional sense. It affords him, instead, as noted, an opportunity for a full-scale exploration of those problems which have so long haunted him.

As Jenkins said of the dogs in *City*, so the protagonist of *A Choice of Gods* declares that the Indians and robots must have their chance—and wonders as to the nature of the "fatal disease that his own race carried" which victimized all cultures it came in contact with and, perhaps in the end, destroyed itself. Repeatedly he attacks western civilization's obsession with property and profit: "If the humans should repossess the Earth, the old profit motive and the subsidiary philosophies that depended on it, would be reestablished and the Earth, except for whatever benefits it might have gained from its five thousand years of rest from the human plague, would be no better off than it had been before" (p.

85). The fault lies with a "technological civilization [because it] is never satisfied. It is based on profit and progress, its own brand of progress. It must expand or die" (p. 164).

So far as the Principle is concerned, Simak has repeatedly asserted that the universe itself shows no concern for anything which occurs. It is space and matter and energy: mere force. Yet behind it all, "there must be some universal plan which set in motion the orbiting of the electrons about the nucleus and the slower, more majestic orbit of the galaxies about one another to the very edge of space . . . a plan . . . that reaches out from the electron to the rim of the universe . . ." (p. 137). But this is no more than a machine-like intelligence, and in *A Choice of Gods*, Simak has tried to personify that Principle. That it is purely mechanistic may explain why it shows so little interest in the first plea for aid sent through the robots by the survivors on earth, when it replies that *"Humanity is a transient factor and is none of our concern"* (p. 130). No adequate reason is given for the reversal of its decision.

For Simak "the one thing that does care is life."[32] When life exists, intelligence may evolve, though not always; moreover, as he has repeatedly suggested, an obsession with intelligence may in itself become a kind of disease. (One recalls "Shotgun Cure" and notes that in many of his stories the only ones capable of communicating with alien life forms are individuals regarded as inferior or misfits by their society, as, for example, in "The Big Front Yard.") Yet Simak should not be read as a pessimist, for in *A Choice of Gods*, through his protagonist, he gives voice to those dreams which have made him so critical of twentieth-century man:

It is good to dream and there could be the hope, of course, that this all might come about, man finally emerging as a factor in introducing even a greater orderliness into the universe. But I cannot see the path to reach this time. I can see the beginning and can dream the hoped-for end, but the in-between escapes me. Before such a situation can obtain there must be certain progress made. It is the shape of this progress I cannot determine. We must, of course, not only know, but understand the universe before we can manipulate it and we must arrive at the ability for that manipulation by a road for which there is no map. All must necessarily come by slow degree; we shall travel that unmapped road foot by weary foot. We must grow in this new ability of ours to make things happen without the aid of silly mechanical contrivances and growth will not be rapid (pp. 159-160).

The concerns and debates beginning in *City* and reaching perhaps their fullest, most explicit statement in *A Choice of Gods* came full circle when Simak contributed the story "Epilog" to the memorial anthology honoring John W. Campbell, *Astounding* (1973). It is Jenkins' story, and, appropriately, it focuses upon actions which bring to affirmative conclusion all of the old concerns and debates. Long ago, except for a few field mice, the dogs and their fellow animals departed Earth for an alternate world. Still acting as caretaker for Webster house and its few acres of ground, Jenkins lives alone in a kind of courtyard surrounded by "the great senseless building that the Ants had built" to enclose the Earth. One day a portion of that building collapses. Jenkins enters, finding only a monument of the kicking foot of the crazy mutant who had first enclosed and then destroyed an ant hill millenia ago. The senseless building is vacant; the ants—and the robots whom they controlled—are dead:

. . . and still the building stood, an empty symbol of some misplaced ambition, of some cultural miscalculation. Somewhere the ants had gone wrong. . . .[33]

Fleeing, amid speculations that give him no answer, Jenkins finds that a spaceship has landed. He remembers the robots who pilot it; they ask him to join them, for they have need of him, as once the dogs needed him as mentor and guide. Jenkins cannot say goodbye to Earth; he cannot weep, for robots cannot weep. And so Jenkins—with his courage, compassion, and wisdom—ascends to the stars to join once again the community of life.

Maxine Moore

ASIMOV, CALVIN, AND MOSES

I saac Asimov's science fiction novels and short stories have delighted a generation of "fans," but because of his seemingly facile style, his detective-story approach, and his mischievous wit (manifested by such outrageous puns as "giant aunts"), the newly aroused scholarly critics of science fiction are apparently unable to take him seriously. Indeed, Virgil Scott refers to an "Isaac Asimov 'space opera' " which "will always tell an exciting story, though it will tell us little else about ourselves or our world," while others dismiss him by omission.[1] Space opera, forsooth! Not that the irrepressible Doctor A. requires or desires defense; on the contrary, he ranges from "Building Blocks" to "Dirty Old Men" with tongue fixed securely in cheek, and a hundred-plus publication record. Nevertheless, beneath the glib surface of Asimov's considerable output (and despite his own demurrers regarding hidden meanings) lies an elaborate metaphorical structure that combines New England Calvinism with the Old Testament Hebraic tradition of the "Peculiar People" to set forth a highly developed philosophy of mechanistic determinism with a positive ethic to justify it.[2] It is this intriguing blend of images and ideas that I would like to discuss, to show some of the more intricate

88

etudes in Dr. A.'s "space operas."

It is helpful for this purpose to consider nine of Asimov's works and to divide them into three groups. When placed in a certain order—not by the dates of their publication—these works provide a coherent background for the development of Asimov's Galactic Empire. The first group consists of a mock technical paper, "The Endochronic Properties of Resublimated Thiotimoline" (*Astounding,* March 1948), and the 1955 novel, *The End of Eternity.* Both pieces posit the simultaneous existence of past, present, and future, and explore the reversal of cause and effect. The novel shows man's foray into time travel, accounting for his ultimate choice for space instead of time, and, as a social side issue, probes humanity's mass security complex and its relationship to the conservatism of a controlling establishment. The social "message" is presented in terms of Newton's principle of the conservation of matter and the laws of inertia.

The second step in the development of Empire involves the Calvinist period: the advent of the robot and the colonization of new worlds. The fundamental work of this group is the book of nine short stories from the 1940's collected as *I, Robot* (1950), in which the Puritanical robopsychologist, Susan Calvin, serves as the figure of predestination. The robots are, of course, a people of the Law, in this instance the well-known Three Laws of Robotics. Elaborating on the Calvinist robots are two novels, *The Caves of Steel* (1953) and *The Naked Sun* (1956), introducing Elijah Baley as the Prophet and the Law, and Robot Daneel Olivaw as the "law-enslaved" robot from the stars.

The third group consists of the Foundation Trilogy, three novels depicting the fall and rise of the Galactic Empire; they present the sciences of Psychohistory and communication through symbolic logic. More important to this study, however, is the exploration of free will in a context of fixed future and the further dealings with yet another figure of the Peculiar People as servant and scapegoat.

One final story remains to bring all the others into focus and to reveal the function of the chosen ones and the ultimate Cause of which all that preceded are the effects. This, of course, is the soul-tingling little gem entitled "The Last Question" (1956).

Asimov's early satire, "Endochronic Thiotimoline," is of basic importance to a full appreciation of the galactic series. A deadly take-off on every heavy-handed technical report ever written, it describes a newly discovered chemical that dissolves *before* the water is added—but *only if* the water is, in fact, going to be added. Any attempt on the part of the experimenter to "trick" the chemical by withholding the water is roundly thwarted. Always willing to stay on a good horse, Asimov followed this paper with several other Thiotimoline reports showing some hilariously disastrous results of such experiments. Ostensibly, the point of the satire is to be found in the stupidity of the report writer—not only for writing a laboriously dull paper, but primarily for putting his discovery to such pedestrian use as measuring the dissolving time of other chemicals. Satire aside, however, "Thiotimoline" postulates the coexistence of past and future with the present. Going further we might infer a future that *causes* certain events to occur in the present so that they may in turn bring about that already existing future. That this tidbit of technical wit was written with the issue of determinism in mind is demonstrated by such mock endnotes as these, affixed among others to the article:

G. H. Freudler, *Journal of Psychochemistry*, 2, 476-488 (1945), "Initiative and Determination. Are they Influenced by Diet?—As tested by Thiotimoline solubility Experiments."

E. Harley-Short, *Philosophical Proceedings and Review*, 15, 125-197 (1946), "Determinism and Free-Will, The Application of Thiotimoline Solubility to Marxian Dialectic."[3]

In light of Asimov's penchant for word play, it is not difficult to see the "Endochronic" portion of the title giving rise to "The End of Time" while the sulphurous "Thiotimoline" becomes a "Time line" into the future—an elevator-like corridor through time powered by the sun gone nova in the far "upwhen." This is the central device in the novel, *End of Eternity,* in which an elite group called the "Eternals"—men recruited from various periods—effect "Reality Changes" in order to provide "the greatest good to the greatest number" of mankind.[4] The time travel corridor is analogous to a power line, and the "kettles" in which the Eternals travel through time function in the same manner as electrons excited by a high voltage current. The time kettle moves at high speed *in place*, passing the traveler like an electric current from one activated kettle to another *ad eternitum*. The Eternals effect their Reality Changes in accordance with Occam's Razor, or Principle of Parsimony. Upon deciding what reality needs alteration, the Eternal expends the least possible effort to achieve the minimum satisfactory result. One of the realities to be constantly avoided is that of space travel, so that each time some development promises that result, an Eternal is dispatched to prevent it. According to the Law of Inertia, each Reality Change eventually wears out and returns to the main time sequence.

Asimov in this novel has great fun with his temporal paradoxes and with putting his slightly doltish young hero through loop-the-loops, but after peeling away the melodrama a number of developments remain. Time is shown as subject to physical stresses and strains requiring immense outputs of energy to manipulate. On this high voltage line, connected at one terminal to the very end of solar time, the voltage is repeatedly stepped up with each reality transformation until at last the entire structure is shorted out and "self-destructed." Meanwhile, the meddlesome Eternals, provided with excessive power like a priestly caste or a dictatorial government, abuse and corrupt that power and are also shorted out. The paradox is that of men traveling through time for the purpose of maintaining the status quo and avoiding progress. Such self-contradiction is unstable and anti-survival in the context of Asimov's physico-temporal structure. The Platonic mode of the single reality, manipulable at the convenience of an esoteric elite, produces an involuted structure that can only turn in upon itself and devour its own tail. With the destruction of time travel, and its reactionary philosophy, comes the mode of multiple realities that makes the Galactic Empire possible. Certain ground rules emerge to support the workings of Asimov's brand of determinism: time is simultaneous as is space, but time travel and space travel are mutually exclusive; time is subject to physical laws and to physical manipulation through expenditure of energy; and the fixed future causes present events that ensure its own existence.

II

In the robot series, the physical base metaphor is that of computer science: the self-limiting structure of robot and man and their binary conditioning—or programming—that provides a yea-nay choice range and an illusion of free will. The ethical metaphor is that New England Calvinism with which Asimov appears to be well acquainted. The Positronic Robot illustrates some of the fundamental problems of Original Sin and/or Natural Depravity, the Doctrine of the Elect (or the Chosen People), Predestination and Responsibility, and the Puritan work ethic.

I, Robot displays in its very title the legalistic formula that places the robot firmly under the Law, and also calls in the work ethic by virtue of the translation of "robot" into "worker."[5] Like Čapek's original androids in *R.U.R.*, Asimov's robots begin as slaves and provide a vehicle for social comment. Unlike Rossum's Robots, however, Asimov's are designed to dispel the fears with which the Gothic era had surrounded technology.[6]

The structure of this collection of nine tales is quite ingenious, for the story method parallels the development of the robot. For example, in the first story, "Robbie," the robot is introduced as a mute but sentient slave with overtones of beast of burden. In keeping with this primitive condition the story form is that of a familiar child's folk tale, with the plot frankly derived from the beloved yarn about the loyal dog, Old Nell (or perhaps Old Shep) or the beloved black slave, Big Jim (or Big Somebody-or-other). By way of this well-known plot we become comfortable with the robot, recognizing him as an old and benign acquaintance from our childhood. We fear no evil, for the Positronic Robot is as innocent as a prelapsarian Adam, even after he is unjustly banished, Ishmael style, by a hysterical woman.

As the robot becomes more complex, so too does the form of his story. To reveal the entrance of sin into the robot nature, Asimov brings into play the elements of the Greek tragedy, synthesizing Original Sin with the Tragic Flaw in "Little Lost Robot." His tragic hero carries the noble Greek name of Nestor (Robot NS-2) and is neither wholly good, since he is purposely created with a weakened First Law, nor wholly bad, since he is the unfallen innocent.[7] Because of his altered First Law, preprogrammed by

Dr. Calvin, Nestor commits an error—that of literally interpreting an irritated human's command to "get lost!" As one thing leads to another, Nestor falls into the sin of *Hubris*, and as an inevitable result he brings destruction upon himself.

From here, Asimov moves into the Medieval mode with "Reason," a monkish tale of robot priesthood. Here the robot abandons his creator, Man, to worship the giant transmitter which he is programmed to attend. A transmitter, as medium of communication, might be seen in allegorical terms as a Mediator, while at the same time it is seen by the human characters, Donovan and Powell, as an object of idolatry.[8] Despite his defiance of his creators, Robot QT, nicknamed "Cutie," fulfills his function as he has been programmed to do, and is thereby confirmed in his priesthood. What began as heresy emerges as the True Faith, even though it is based on a factually "wrong" but logically "right" premise. Indeed, Cutie's reasoning spreads "Truth" to the other robots in the station, even as it enrages the frustrated spacemen who fear for the safety of the transmitter. While the social import bears on religious tolerance, the philosophical burden carries on with the ethical development of the predestined robot—this time one of the Elect for whom Grace is truly irresistible, since it is programmed in from the very beginning by Dr. Calvin.

The story form becomes ever more modern, complex, and sophisticated as the robots grow more numerous and more highly educated; but throughout the book, the figure of Susan (Hebrew for "Lily," symbol of purity) Calvin, narrator of these memoirs, serves as the metaphor for predestination. As robopsychologist, Dr. Calvin is responsible for programming each robot, making sure that it carries the Three Laws firmly implanted in its mechanical soul. Or, if for some specific function one of the Three Laws must be strengthened or weakened, Dr. Calvin sends forth an imbalanced robot, destined from the beginning to fall, like the reprobate Nestor, or to be numbered among the Elect with the devout Cutie.

In the New England tradition of Hawthorne, Melville, and others, Asimov dwells on the dilemma of predestination with responsibility. The robot purposely modified for some specific function is a morally flawed robot. Any malfunction resulting from such modification is not the "fault" of the robot, but he must be destroyed nonetheless. Thus, though predestined to fall, the robot is held responsible for his acts.

Even as the robot serves on the one hand as the predestined individual, the robots as a group represent yet another type of the Elect, the Chosen People. A race apart, they are created for service and they run the gamut from dumb servomechanism, or slave, to the ultimate public servant—president of the World Council. During this progress, however, humans begin to regard robots as a physical and an economic threat.[9] In a Diaspora the robots are eventually driven from frightened, ultra-conservative Earth and dispersed with the adventurous "Spacers" into the new worlds of outer space. The robot fulfills the New Testament Scripture, "He who would be master, let him be the servant of all," as he rises from slavery to disguised political power, in contrast to the Eternals, who sought power and short-circuited themselves out of existence.

Susan Calvin does not appear in the two novels that expand on the robot ethic, but her spirit of predestination remains. Elijah Baley, the phobia-ridden Earth Detective, teams up unwillingly with Space detective R. Daneel Olivaw—the "handsome Robot," pure, optimistic, and benign. Baley epitomizes the Old Testament attitudes under the Law and the Prophets, while Daneel tends toward the gentler characteristics of the New Dispensation.[10] The juxtaposition of these two reveals the robot as analogue to man, and shows man himself to be a delicate machine programmed at the cellular level with three basic laws of racial survival:

1. A human may not injure mankind, or, through inaction, allow the race to come to harm.
2. A human must obey the edicts of his culture and his society, except where such obedience conflicts with the First Law.
3. A human must protect his own existence as long as self-protection does not conflict with the First or Second Law.

The question propounded by the novels might be stated in these terms: if a robot (or a man) is indeed "programmed" (whether mechanically or genetically) with an ethical absolute, and that ethic is intact, how can the creature commit a wrong-doing? In both novels, a murder is committed, and a robot, with the Three Laws intact, is the "guilty" party, though the ultimate guilt may be laid at the door of a human who has manipulated the robot. Despite this, the robot goes "insane" with guilt. Why? Here again the Puritan (and Jewish) guilt complex comes into play. Having set up a rigid robotic ethic, Asimov proceeds to demonstrate the manifold ways of getting around it. The result is a multi-faceted view of guilt, blame, and social and individual responsibility.

The second of the two robot novels, *The Naked Sun*, is set on the sparsely populated planet, Solaria—a word containing both "Sol" and "sole."[11]   Each human dwells alone on his own huge estate, tended by dozens or hundreds of robots and supported by an advanced robot-controlled technology. So conditioned are the denizens of Solaria to isolation that they cannot bear to be in the physical presence of another human. Their social and business life is based on "viewing." By huge tri-D televiewing mechanisms operated by robots they get together for dinners, parties, meetings, even strolls in their park-like estates; but never, if avoidable, do they "see" one another in person. Marriage is a traumatic social duty in which partners, assigned to each other by computer eugenics, live on the same estate, "seeing" each other dutifully only on an extremely limited schedule for procreation.

Elijah and Daneel invade this society to solve the murder of a Solarian genetic scientist, Rickaine Delmarre, who "programs" children as Dr. Calvin programs robots. The prime suspect is the victim's wife, Gladia. Thus the typical detective story is presented, but beneath this superficial plot, through both the action and the metaphor, the reader must question just who IS the robot—Daneel or Elijah? Which of the two is more mechanical, more predestined, more human? In short, Asimov poses the age-old question, what is Man? Elijah Baley, Earth-conditioned to despise robots, knew that

Daneel's "thoughts" were only short lived positronic currents flowing along paths rigidly designed and fore-ordained by the manufacturer.

But what were the signs that would give that away to the expert eye that had no foreknowledge? The trifling unnaturalness of Daneel's manner of speech? The unemotional gravity that rested so steadily upon him? The very perfection of his humanity? (p. 25)

And in regard to perfection, Baley speaks later of the murder victim:

Anyone can have a motive, particularly for the murder of a man such as Dr. Delmarre. . . . Dr. Delmarre was a 'good Solarian. . . .' He rigidly fulfilled all the requirements of Solarian custom. He was an ideal man, almost an abstraction. Who could feel love, or even liking, for such a man? A man without weaknesses serves only to make everyone else conscious of his own imperfection. A primitive poet named Tennyson once wrote: 'He is all fault who has no fault at all' (p. 171).

Baley distinguishes between robot and man on the basis of emotion also, claiming Daneel to be metallically unemotional. Yet, having stressed the strength of the First Law of Robotics, Asimov repeatedly shows robots under excessive stress when that Law is breached, forcing the reader to redefine and reevaluate the nature of emotion. When, near the start of the investigation, Robot Daneel witnesses an attempted poisoning of a Solarian official, his reaction is decidedly emotional, and sympathetic at that:

Daneel sat down queerly, as though there were a weakness in his knees. Baley had never seen him give way so, not for an instant, to any action that resembled anything so human as a weakness in the knees.

Daneel said, 'It is not well with my mechanism to see a human being come to harm. . . . It is as though there were certain cloggings in my thought paths. In human terms what I feel might be the equivalent to shock.'

'If that's so, get over it.' Baley felt neither patience nor sympathy for a queasy robot.

When in the end the Solarian responsible for the murder is apprehended, he sees Robot Daneel coming after him and, thinking Daneel is a human, he suicides rather than allowing another human to "see" him:

Daneel Olivaw darted into the field of vision and for a moment stared down at the crumpled figure.

Baley held his breath. If Daneel should realize it was his own pseudo humanity that had killed Leebig, the effect on his First Law-enslaved brain might be drastic.

But Daneel only knelt and his delicate fingers touched Leebig here and there. Then he lifted Leebig's head as though it were infinitely precious to him, cradling it, caressing it.

His beautifully chiseled face stared out at the others and he whispered, 'A Human is dead!' (p. 181)

That in this instance Daneel is expending his sympathies on a man far more robotic in nature than Daneel himself doubles the ironic implication. Daneel's "pseudo humanity" contrasts to the "pseudo humanity" of the murderer, Leebig, and of the victim, Delmarre.

To Baley, still another quality separates man from robot—that of "intuition." Early in the story, Baley guesses that Daneel had been sent by the Outer Worlds to Solaria disguised as a human because Solaria was proud of its robot industries and the Spacers wanted to gain an advantage. Daneel is puzzled as to Baley's ability to figure this out. "Baley nodded in grim satisfaction. Naturally Daneel did not follow an intuitive leap that used human weakness as a starting point" (p. 23). Although Baley mentions human weakness here, it is plain in the context that he is stressing Daneel's lack of intuition. Daneel lacks, however, not intuition, but cynicism. Subsequently, Daneel reports to Baley the results of his own investigations of Dr. Thool, physician to Gladia Delmarre:

'You remember Mrs. Delmarre's remarks concerning him: "He always treated me since I was a child and was always so friendly and kind." I wonder if he might have some motive for being particularly concerned about her. It was for that reason that I visited the baby farm and inspected the records. What I had merely guessed at as a possibility turned out to be the truth.'

'What?'

'Dr. Altim Thool was the father of Gladia Delmarre, and what is more, he knew of the relationship.'

Baley had no thought of disbelieving the robot. He felt only a deep chagrin that it had been Robot Daneel Olivaw and not himself that had carried through the necessary piece of logical analysis (pp. 164-165).

The perceptive reader notices, whether Baley notices or not, that in each case a "mental leap" is involved, and that in each case the hunch is based on logical analysis, be it human or robot. But Baley calls his own analysis "intuitive," and refers to Daneel's as "logical." The difference, however, is that Baley's hunch has derived from his knowledge of malicious human weakness, whereas Daneel's has arisen from his assumption of benign human weakness. It is characteristic of Asimov that he never enlightens Baley on this subject—nor does he didactically enlighten the reader. Persistently, nevertheless, Asimov parallels each mental and emotional activity of Baley's with a similar one on the part of Robot Daneel.

The principles of computer programming serve as basic metaphor in the robot series, and although in human terms the expression is "conditioning," Asimov makes it quite clear that the processes are fundamentally the same. In the course of the novel, Baley, who suffers from the various "hang-ups" characteristic of Earthmen, gradually manages to adapt to a new culture and new circumstances. He is "de-bugged" and "reprogrammed." Through a mighty effort of "will" (a conditioned adaptability resulting from extensive police training), Baley faces and overcomes his fears and phobias. First, he must come to terms with the open air and the sun:

He had begun by stepping across open ground to the waiting plane with a kind of lightheaded dizziness that was almost enjoyable, and he had ordered the windows left unblanked in a kind of manic self-confidence.
I have to get used to it, he thought, and stared at the blue until his heart beat rapidly and the lump in his throat swelled beyond endurance (p. 93).

Visiting a Solarian baby farm, Baley manages to accommodate himself to open air, but another problem nearly overcomes him:

Baley took a deep breath. He noted three trees forming a small triangle fifty feet to the left. He walked in that direction, the grass soft and loathsome under his shoes, disgusting in its softness (like walking through corrupting flesh, and he nearly retched at the thought)[12] (p. 125).

The force of circumstance and necessity combined with sensory input are correlated and shunted into Baley's subconscious reality banks as he sleeps. He dreams of Earth and of his wife, Jessie:

And Jessie was beautiful. She had lost weight somehow. Why should she be so slim? And so beautiful?
And one other thing was wrong. Somehow the sun shone down on them. He looked up and there was only the vaulted base of the upper levels visible, yet the sun shone down, blazing brightly on everything and no one was afraid (p. 82).

Baley is not alone is his subjection to cultural programming. The Solarians prove even more extensively conditioned and even less adaptable. Here again, with a delicate but ironic understanding of the sources of xenophobia, Asimov explores the strength of the "Second Law," obedience to cultural dictates, and its relationship to human survival. In order to cope with the Solarians, and to acquire their cooperation in his investigation, Baley finds it

necessary to study this society in which marriage, computer assigned, is an ordeal, and children are obnoxious. The mere mention of "babies" or "children" is vulgar and indelicate, and to
know the identity of one's child or parent is immoral. Babies,
taken at birth to a "baby farm," are trained to the habit of isolation. Rickaine Delmarre, the murder victim, had been director of
the planet's baby farm, and upon his death his strong-minded,
genetically perfect female assistant, Klorissa, takes complete
charge. Interviewing Klorissa at the baby farm, Baley is horrified
to learn that the children are separated and isolated in early life
and tended by robots exclusively thereafter.[13] He tells Klorissa:

'I am a little surprised that robots can fulfill the need for affection.'
    She whirled toward him, the distance between them not sufficing to hide
her displeasure. 'See here, Baley, if you're trying to shock me by using unpleasant terms, you won't succeed. Skies above, don't be childish.'
    'Shock you?'
    'I can use the word too. Affection! Do you want a short word, a good
four-letter word? I can say that, too. Love! Love! Now if it's out of your
system, behave yourself' (p. 121).

Baley does not trouble to dispute the cultural matter of obscenity,
but he does try to explain to Klorissa that children should not be
isolated—that the desire to "see" is instinct. Klorissa retorts,
"Skies above, there isn't an instinct around that can't give way to
a good, persistent education. Not in human beings, where instinct
is weak anyway." As a result of their Skinnerian programming,
adult Solarians range from the perversely moral to the morally
perverse. Among the former are the victim Delmarre and the
murderer Leebig. During his investigation, Baley insists on "seeing" Leebig, partly in order to study his reaction. Baley says:

'The smell of robots is the one thing that pervades everything on Solaria. If it
is time we require, then more than ever I must see you. I am an Earthman
and I cannot work or think comfortably while viewing.'
    It would not have seemed possible to Baley for Leebig to stiffen his stiff
carriage further, but he did. He said, 'Your phobias as an Earthman don't
concern me. Seeing is impossible' (p. 137).

This technological version of sight imagery demonstrates the "mote
and beam" principle both scientifically and morally.[14] Among
the morally perverse is the Solarian roboticist, Quemot, who tells

Baley:

'Only Mrs. Delmarre could have been close enough to Rickaine to kill him. Rickaine would never, under any circumstances, have allowed anyone else seeing privileges for any reason. Extremely finicky. Perhaps finicky is the wrong word. It was just that he lacked any trace of abnormality; anything of the perverse. He was a good Solarian.'

   'Would you call your granting me seeing privileges perverse?' asked Baley.

   Quemot said, 'Yes, I think I would. I should say there was a bit of scatophilia involved' (p. 106).

By the juxtaposition of Baley's ingrained Earth morality to the conditioned morality of the Solarians, Asimov demonstrates that social programming is a function of the Second Law, and is not an Absolute. The Solarians, in fact, serve to show that a strengthening of the Second Law may result in anti-survival behavior, whereas Baley proves himself able to subjugate his social programming to his ethic of service to humanity.

   Although Dr. Calvin provides Asimov with a convenient and appropriate metaphor for determinism, the fundamental approach can best be seen as a combination of Old Testament Law with the laws of physics, a term which in its broadest sense includes biochemistry and perhaps psychology. In treating man as a predestined computer deep-programmed with an externally imposed ethic, Asimov anticipated the discovery of the genetic code.[15] To call "external" an ethical code imprinted on the genes themselves may appear contradictory; but the analogue is to a computer which carries its "ethical code" in its very structure. Though such structure is internal to the computer, it is externally imposed. Asimov applies the Three Laws to all three of the creatures involved in the murder of Rickaine Delmarre in such a way as to reveal the forces at work in forming the human psyche. The robot whose arm was used to strike Delmarre held itself responsible for a breach of the First Law, and became insane. Gladia Delmarre, who used the arm to strike the blow in a moment of rage, breached none of the Laws and was permitted to go free to a place where her womanly instincts would not be thwarted. Leebig, who engineered the murder, was revealed to be guilty of a far higher breach. He had planned to use robot space ships to "depopulate" neighboring planets in order to preserve Solaria's culture of isolation. His real motive, then, was genocide—a shattering of the First Law for the sake of the Second.

In dealing with Asimov's Calvinist Robots, much of the structure of his technological theology must be passed over. His treatment of space man as Adam or Ishmael is common enough in science fiction, along with his anticipation of the eventual disembodied mind as a version of the ancient conflict between body and spirit. He is unique, however, in his handling of the "chosen people" theme. In each set of novels, a special group serves as custodians of the Law, in which capacity they function as scapegoats, saviors, or servant-master-keepers to the race of man. The Positronic Robots are excellent examples of this function.

III

The Foundation trilogy takes a giant leap into the future and introduces the concept of Psychohistory.[16] The Galactic Empire, grown corrupt and top-heavy after the manner of ancient Rome, is on the point of collapse. Hari Seldon puts into effect a long-range plan designed to reduce the inevitable "dark ages" from a probable thirty thousand years to a mere two thousand years. The Seldon Plan postulates a three-terminal social structure consisting of Trantor, capitol planet of the crumbling Empire, as one node; Terminus, a metal-poor planet on the edge of the Galaxy that houses the First Foundation—whose job it is to preserve the physical sciences—as a second; and "Star's End," the unknown location of the hidden Second Foundation which is designed to cultivate the Mental Sciences, as a third terminal. The Seldon Plan sets up a current of events generated by the statistical actions of the huge mass of humanity that populates the Galaxy. At certain crisis points along this forecalculated future, the Foundations function to switch the current of history along variant lines of probability, to rectify any unforeseen deviation from the Plan, and to amplify those social, religious, and economic factors that would speed up the return to full Galactic power. Of the three terminal points involved, only the Second Foundation has full knowledge of the positions and activities of the other two, and thus it serves as a translator of sorts, receiving information from both, and transmitting that information to each on a modified level. The primary function of the entire unit is eventually to switch all humanity from the physical to the mental sciences— from semi-communication to communication both complete and simultaneous.

The technically-inclined reader might detect in this plot summary the structure and function of a vacuum tube or transistor. It is this mode of plot structure that separates science fiction from non-technical literature; in fact, it is his exceptional skill in the use of such a mode that sets Asimov apart in his own field and provides a coherence and integrity above and beyond the concept of the Aristotelian Unities. Such dramatizing of the forces at play in the world of sub-atomic technology fulfills the ideal of the megamacrocosm in the ultraminimicrocosm.

The Foundation group deals overtly with the problem of Free Will in a deterministic universe, and although the series seems to allow for the random decisions of individuals, along with such variables as "The Mule," it still develops that Hari Seldon's statistically-based plan for "predestination" holds firm, if only because of the inertia of enormous population mass. Whereas the robot stories reveal individual man as mechanism, the Foundation group shows society as mechanism, not only by the manipulations of the Seldon Plan but by the very structure of the three-terminal "transistor" that is the Foundation trilogy itself.

Then, too, in this series Asimov again presents another version of the Law and the Prophets, and the Chosen People. Despite his use of a considerable amount of Christ imagery, we must note that no single person ever becomes a sacrificial scapegoat. Instead, a special and peculiar group fills this function and we again encounter the Galactic Jew in the ubiquitous members of the First and Second Foundation. As in the case of the Asimovian Robots, the Foundationers are selected and "programmed" to serve humanity, and again, "He who would be the master, begins as servant to all." The First Foundation people, never fully knowledgeable as to their function but ever aware of their calling, serve as the scapegoat race, while those of the Second Foundation remain ever in hiding, ready to rescue their companion group or humanity in general. Thus, in Asimov's two great series, a "peculiar people" become the holders of the Law.

Asimov's teleology, the end of his eternity, is presented in his powerful short story, "The Last Question," the robot story to end all robot stories. Man builds a computer, AC, and over a billion year span of evolution of both man and machine, man repeatedly asks the overwhelming question, "Can entropy be reversed?" The Computor always replies, "Insufficient data for meaningful answer." At last, man, freed from the limitation of physical body and spread throughout the dying universe, sees that the end is at hand. Man programs himself into the Universal AC, and finally, it alone exists in all space. In an unknowable span of time, equipped with all knowledge, AC computes the answer to the question and takes steps to demonstrate the solution:

The consciousness of AC encompassed all of what had once been a Universe and brooded over what was now Chaos. Step by step, it must be done.
And AC said, 'LET THERE BE LIGHT!'
And there was light—[17]

Here the Robot participates in and brings to culmination all the factors of the Endochronic Time-line, Psychohistory, and robotic Calvinism in the ultimate cycle. It is this Cause toward which all accumulated effects aim: the overcoming of entropy to bring about a new heaven and a new earth through the agency of the *deus ex machina*, a messiah who is anointed with oil. The completed structure implies that the Creator, who is the First Cause, is also the ultimate Effect, the divine Robot in which the Law reposes. In that sense, man has always manufactured his gods, tended them, anointed them, and then idealized them, and all the while has abused them and blamed them. Technology today is merely another of many servant-gods.

Asimov, as a match-maker who weds Moses to Calvin, Einstein officiating, has, in the New England tradition, postulated a massive philosophy based on fixed fate. And all the while, he has created merry, positive, and highly readable books and stories. Like the other great science fiction writers, he is subtly "programing" a new generation with the great basic ethic of the First Law: Humanity first.

David N. Samuelson

THE FRONTIER WORLDS OF ROBERT A. HEINLEIN

The frontier has an almost morbid fascination for Americans in the twentieth century. To be sure, scientific, technological, industrial, economic, and artistic as well as territorial frontiers have fascinated Western Civilization since the Renaissance, each change offering challenge, freedom, and power for the few, and bewilderment, disruption, and chaos for the many. In the United States, however, all of these were summed up in the metaphor of the physical frontier, which, for growing numbers of Americans, was transferred into outer space, once the realization sank in that there was no place else to go on Earth.[1] Since at least the 1920's, a growing minority have come to embody in science fiction tales, primarily with off-Earth settings, their adolescent daydreams of fame and travel, exploration and discovery, heroism and utopia. Tied for the most part to American values, science fiction writers have portrayed the active man, the adventurer, taking practical advantage of science and technology in order to make his dreams come true, sometimes to the extreme disadvantage of other people. Increased emphasis on realism, with regard to setting, society, psychology, even projective hypotheses, may have dimmed the radiance of those dreams, although they may also have made them more accessible to a larger reading public, but the motive force is still the fantasies of adolescence.

Perhaps nowhere is this amalgam—of realism and fantasy, of technology and spiritualism, of adolescence and frontier societies—more visible than in the writings of Robert Anson Heinlein. In a career which began in 1939, Heinlein's works clearly reflect the changes in the corporate body of science fiction, and the embodiment in future scenes of hopes and fears, situations and events, more or less contemporaneous with the writing. A leader in the movement before World War II to make science fiction more realistic, a proselytizer of the masses in the post-war years, he came in the 1960's to write long, loose, philosophical dialogues in the shape of novels, indulging his iconoclastic views on religion, politics, and especially sex. In the process he was adopted by the American "underground" who seemed to see him as a crotchety guru (libertarian, "sexually liberated," attuned to cosmic peace), even as he was being consulted on television talk shows as a different kind of seer, a forecaster of the American space program. In both incarnations, as "mystic" and as "technocrat," he was being true to himself and his calling. Since the beginning of his career, he had always kept the cash customer in mind, as he did now. And both mysticism and technology fuel the adolescent dreams of freedom and power which form the backbone of his writings, as they do most science fiction.

Certainly commercial success was on his mind when he first took up writing science fiction at the age of thirty-two. Born in 1907 in Missouri, he had been raised in the traditions of the Bible Belt, then shipped off, after a year of junior college, to Annapolis for a highly technical kind of education and a commission in the Navy, from which pulmonary tuberculosis forced him to retire to inactive duty in 1934. After dabbling in graduate work (UCLA), engineering, politics, and real estate, he had his first two stories accepted by John W. Campbell for publication in *Astounding Science Fiction*, the leading sf magazine of the day, and then became the most popular and prolific writer in the field by 1941.[2] At pulp magazine payment rates, he had to be prolific to make any money, but he also seemed to like what he was doing. He obviously had read for pleasure Wells, Verne, Shaw, Stapledon, Huxley, Kipling, London, and Sinclair Lewis, as well as the pulps which, although they also reprinted "classics" and foreign translations, were primarily action-oriented, with minimal attention paid to either scientific consistency or literary quality.[3]

Campbell was trying seriously to make something more out of *Astounding,* and Heinlein fit perfectly into his plans. Over the years 1939-1942, Campbell bought all but four of the twenty-eight Heinlein stories that were published, twenty-one for *Astounding* and three for *Unknown* (ten of these, like the four Campbell didn't buy, were published under pseudonyms).[4] Heinlein's optimism, technological know-how, and practical realism projected a buoyant confidence to *Astounding's* readers, in a country coming out of the Depression and dreaming of an expansive future beyond the inexorably approaching war; Campbell helped other young writers to develop, too, but if Heinlein had not existed, he might have had to invent him.[5] Heinlein's acceptance by science fiction fans resulted in his being Guest of Honor at the third annual "World Science Fiction Convention" in 1941, at which time in a rambling speech, he expressed his own appreciation of science fiction, its writers, and its readers.[6] These were the years Alexei Panshin properly labels Heinlein's "Period of Influence."

After the war, the public was still more optimistic about technology and the future, as was evinced not only by the economic boom in magazines, but also by the contents of such mass-circulation periodicals as *Collier's* and *The Saturday Evening Post,* which ran numerous articles on space travel, city planning, and utopian futures. Heinlein, who had published nothing during the war, was one of the first sf authors to take advantage of the expanded audience, selling slick human interest stories to the *Post* and other general interest magazines in 1947-1949. Isolated incidents of man's incursion into near space—as far as the Moon— they were incorporated into his "Future History" series originally announced in 1941. Only three more tales would be added, although the grand design continued to govern most of his writing, including a commercially successful series of novels for the "juvenile," or adolescent, market. Beginning with simplified introductions to space and the nearer planets, these novels soon took on such serious subjects as revolution, social stratification, war, slavery, the basics of survival, and the relationship of those not only to the psyche of the hero, but also to the reader's understanding of the nature of man. Though two of these books were essentially light-hearted romps, the tone was more commonly serious. It grew more somber through the 1950's, as Heinlein was permitted more and more by the loosening taboos of commercial publishing to give vent to his dismay at public complacency and irresponsibility, at the growth of governmental control in the United States as well as in other nations he visited, and at the stifling of individual initiative, privacy, and freedom to know.[7] Also during this time, called by Panshin the "Period of Success," Heinlein published another ten stories, scripted two movies, wrote four articles about science fiction, and composed what I consider his three best "adult" novels.[8]

Panshin calls the next stage Heinlein's "Period of Alienation," but I'm not sure how appropriate the term is. Certainly Heinlein's "Patrick Henry League" newspaper advertisement in 1959, and his 1961 speech as Guest of Honor again at the World Science Fiction Convention, both cited by Panshin, show evidence of a state of mind uncomfortable with the world as it was and his fiction since 1959 shows a tendency to rail and ramble which to me is regrettable.[9] But the central concerns date back to his earliest writings, and his earlier books are also didactic and often ill-constructed, although they are less self-indulgent, perhaps because they are more subservient to commercial formulas. There is an equivocal character to most of the late novels, which feature more involvement with a disagreeable present and a corresponding increase in the desirability of certain fantasies, most of which seem to me to reflect not only the author's dissatisfaction with the times, but also a sense of failing powers.[10] But there is a considerable exuberance for both living and loving, whatever the fictional context; the resulting tensions make these later works absorbing documents, however lacking they may be in finesse. And it should be noted that three of Heinlein's four "Hugo" awards for the best novel of the year were gained for works of "alienation."[11]

Through his career, the frontier metaphor has been basic to Heinlein's writing. Only eight of his twenty-eight novels take place primarily on Earth, and four of them concern relations between humans and intelligent extraterrestrial beings, while a fifth concludes on the Moon. This outward spatial movement, coupled with a forward temporal movement, places Heinlein's characters in situations of extremity, facing the unknown and having to learn to understand it, in order just to survive. Whether they are in spaceships or on alien worlds, exploring or settling or righting wrongs—fighting off other species or learning to live with them, their situations parallel those of the American pioneers, for all that they are equipped with advanced technology, "scientific" thinking, and the benefits of historical hindsight. Even in a utopian situation, even in the present or near future here on Earth, even where mental or "psi" powers are involved, a kind of frontier ethic is invoked in order to make possible a free exercise of individual initiative, or to justify pragmatically certain measures that in more structured situations, such as those of the society we actually live in, would have to be considered extreme. On the frontier, Heinlein's heroes can be free *from* anything that technology and good will can overcome, such as physical slavery, mental bondage, the "prisons" of a single planet and the human body, the limitations of distance and even of death. They can be free *to* roam, explore, discover, earn fame and success, learn things that are useful for the individual or the race, or to achieve self-actualization.

That these freedoms are primarily available to those who can best profit by them—i.e., that they represent what Panshin calls a "wolfish" sort of freedom for "the Heinlein individual"—should not be too surprising, since this is a logical extension of the adolescent dream, especially its American versions. American literature and history are full of famous "wolfish" individuals who pioneered land, technology, and money matters in a society which encouraged everyone to seek, and enabled a few to achieve, their wildest dreams, believing the losses they brought to some were outweighed by the benefits they brought to all. That Heinlein is from a generation and a region which valued those achievements more than many people do today who take them for granted is surely relevant, but so is the fact that in any situation, certain people are more likely to succeed than others. In changing situations, such as the last five centuries of Western Civilization and the various futures Heinlein extrapolates from them, those who succeed are likely to be adaptable, even opportunistic. And Heinlein does not treat freedom, for the most part, as a simple escape. To be sure, some of his works contain large amounts of good-vs.-evil melodrama and lengthy sermons generalizing from inadequate particulars, while most of his work is pitched to the level of a reader of modest intellectual achievement. More often than not, however, the melodrama is subsidiary, the sermons are in character, and freedom is a complex issue, involving both power and responsibility and requiring various kinds of trade-offs.

By using analogies with situations familiar from history, legend, and personal experience, by anchoring the unfamiliar in specific detail generated by these analogies, Heinlein manages to make his frontier worlds seem real, however weak he may be in plot construction, however limited his range of characters and emotions, however objectionable some of his tics of style, especially in dialogue. Three major extensions of the frontier metaphor may be seen in his Future History series and related works from before World War II; in his series of "juvenile" novels; and in his long run of outright fantasies, in which I have included all of his "adult" novels since 1950. These works I have grouped, in the following discussion, under the subtitles "Frontiers of the Future," "Frontiers of Youth," and "Frontiers of the Mind." Most of Heinlein's fiction which has appeared in book form will be discussed, leaving out of consideration a handful of stories as well as the original magazine forms of his earliest novels.[12]

FRONTIERS OF THE FUTURE: the "Future History" stories

The background chart for Heinlein's "Future History" series (*Astounding*, May 1941; revised 1948; revised 1967) places up to twenty-seven stories in relationship to an assumed time-line stretching from about 1950 to approximately 2600 A.D., suggesting lines of political, scientific, and technological continuity which are only sketchily apparent in the stories themselves. As is immediately apparent in the 1967 omnibus, *The Past Through Tomorrow,* which arranges twenty-one stories and novels in fictionally chronological order, continuity is explicit only from " 'The Roads Must Roll' " to "Requiem" and from "Logic of Empire" to *Methuselah's Children.* The implicit nature of the background, however, extends beyond this series of stories to take in at least three tales not included in the omnibus, as well as a number of novels which assume at least alternative paths in the same general direction. Progress is assumed in both technology (transportation, power sources) and society (toward "The First Human Civilization") with some cross-over (psychometrics, semantics), but not as a straight-line projection. Heinlein takes it for granted that power will be abused by some and that severe setbacks will occur, with a pendulum-like swing between freedom and enslavement (in psychological, as well as physical terms). Against this large-scale movement, individual human dramas will be played out which may support or contradict the slow cultural rise and fall; the "Future History" concept does not imply a *novel manqué* (like Simak's *City* or Bradbury's *The Martian Chronicles*), but rather a general set of assumptions about the history behind the individual stories. Thus the omission from the omnibus of three tales that definitely do fit ("Sky Lift" and "Columbus Was A Dope" from *The Menace from Earth,* "Let There Be Light" from *The Man Who Sold the Moon*) does not damage the concept, nor does the nonexistence of some five stories once planned as part of the series (for an explanation concerning three of them, see "Concerning Stories Never Written: Postscript," *Revolt in 2100*).[13] The unity of the omnibus volume, however, does suffer by the inclusion of at least two stories that really don't fit, and by the aesthetic distance between the pre-war stories (which seem to take the continuity seriously) and the post-war stories (which are more elementary in concept, if more polished in style).

"Life Line" is an appropriate introduction to the omnibus, despite the lack of impact of its devices and characters on the ensuing fictional history (one short reference appears in the closing work). Heinlein's first published story (*Astounding,* August 1939), its subject is ostensibly a machine that predicts a person's instant of death. The story is also about the fear of knowledge and about the effects of perfecting such a device. Characters behave melodramatically, but the satire, pointed at scientists, reporters, insurance companies, gangsters, even lovers, is fairly effective. In this position, it points the reader toward the future, and introduces such continuing themes as the forgotten genius, the insanity of complacency, the value of empirical proof-vs.-orthodox theory, and the powerful motivation of financial gain.

The next three stories explore the dimensions of power—technological, economic, and psychological. " 'The Roads Must Roll' " (*Astounding,* June 1940) is memorable for its projection that private cars would so clutter the world that another transportation system would be needed, and for its assumption that the transportation monopoly would have to be watched over by a faceless paramilitary class. But the description of the workings of the moving roads is vague and confusing, the lectures that halt the action are obtrusive, and the final confrontation between Gaines (the perfectionist "Mister Clean") and Van Kleeck (the "little man" who heads the labor "conspiracy") is so overblown and melodramatic as to be ludicrous. "Blowups Happen" (*Astounding*, September 1940) is not so much about atomic power plants as it is about the custodial psychology adumbrated by Gaines and his Transportation Corps. To avoid atomic accidents, psychologists watch technicians and are themselves observed, making temperamental blowups all the more likely. The situation is declared impossible by a world-famous physicist-psychologist consulted, and becomes more so when it seems the Moon once suffered atomic Armageddon. Power company directors choose to fire the plant superintendent rather than risk the economic chaos of a shutdown, but they are pressured into relocating the plant in orbit, made possible by the subplotted discovery of an atomic rocket fuel.[14] The solutions are simplistic, events happen with miraculous speed and coincidence, but the problems are built up seriously enough to make some melodrama credible, and most of the characters are convincing, if we allow for adventure magazine oversimplification. "The Man Who Sold the Moon" (*The Man Who Sold the Moon*, 1950), also oversimplified by contrast with the immensity of the real space program, is still readable and enjoyable despite being dated; the chief reason is D. D. Harriman, the millionaire huckster-administrator who harnesses all his resources to a dream he can only realize vicariously. Beneath the wheeling and dealing, the conversations that are great fun but patently unreal, a sharp satirical blade separates Harriman's grandiose goals (which go far beyond a mere moon landing) from the mundane realities of selling people something none of them really wants.[15] Harriman's gamesmanship enables him to play off against each other the avarice and self-interest of both rich and poor, even at the expense of an occasional minor swindle. It also leads him into the financial trap which keeps him, like Moses (the comparison is explicit), from getting to the promised land. The sense of a legend in the making haunts every scene, most of them are handled with wit and practical realism, and the pace for a change is almost leisurely.

Of the next eleven stories, fictionally bracketing the year 2000, most are compactly and carefully crafted, but dependent for their impact upon a slick manipulation of sentiment, as is appropriate for publication in a mass-circulation general interest magazine. "Delilah and the Space Rigger" (*Blue Book,* December 1949) describes the building of a space station in orbit, but its plot turns on the device of permitting women to be part of the work crew. "Space Jockey" (*Saturday Evening Post,* April 26, 1947) concerns Jake Pemberton, whose job as a rocket pilot conflicts with his home life. An earlier story, "Requiem" (*Astounding,* January 1940), is just as sentimental, but more clumsily executed.[16] The inordinate fondness many sf fans have for this story may be based partly on their own commitment to sf and space travel, and partly on its relationship to "The Man Who Sold the Moon." In this earlier story, an aging D. D. Harriman outwits his heirs and the law and manages to get to the moon after all, with the aid of two calloused space bums and a rickety rocket ship; his triumph is short-lived, for he dies from the physical strain of the flight, but not until he sets foot on the lunar surface. "The Long Watch" (*American Legion Magazine,* December 1949), is a detailed sketch of how a political and military *naif* surprises himself by sacrificing his life to foil a military takeover of a lunar base for atomic missiles.[17] "Gentlemen, Be Seated" (*Argosy,* May 1948), uses a background of lunar colonization for a low-keyed rescue story, the point of which is plugging an air leak with the seat of one's pants. "The Black Pits of Luna" (*Saturday Evening Post,* January 10, 1948), another lunar rescue story, depends on our sympathy for a lost child and his brother, the teen-age narrator, who locates him. The best of the lot, " 'It's Great to Be Back' " (*Saturday Evening Post,* July 26, 1947), works on our understanding of the impossibility of ever "going home again," along with our awareness of the inanities and discomforts of urban and suburban living, applying them by analogy to the plight of a young scientist couple, dissatisfied with living on the moon, who find they are really accustomed to it and cannot readjust to life on Earth.

One of the best stories in the volume, " 'We Also Walk Dogs' "

(*Astounding*, July 1941), does not really fit the Future History scheme; other stories show no awareness of gravity neutralization, intelligent aliens from our sister planets, or the type of operation typified by General Services, Inc., the corporate "hero" of this story. Thematically, of course, it exhibits the faith in technology and self-serving behavior which are common Heinlein features, and by its position amid "space" stories, it illustrates that Earth is not completely stagnant all this time. General Services, built up by the desire of people with money to have things done for them, is called upon to make possible an interspecies conference on Earth. The nullification of gravity required is theoretically impossible, but one man might be able to do it; to get his cooperation, since he is only interested in his own research, GS must replicate a famous bowl in the British Museum and give him the original. All of this must be, and is, accomplished quickly and without publicity; the real focus, though, is on people and motivations. Like Harriman, the GS people are interested in making money, in seeing a job well done, and in something extra. They cynically manipulate a rich dowager, opportunistically rig contractual rights to the gravity neutralizer, and treat the whole operation as a matter of course. But they are humanized, as is the crotchety inventor, by a reverential possessiveness toward the coveted bowl, "The Flower of Forgetfulness," which tempts them, too, to withdraw into abstract contemplation.

With "Searchlight" (commissioned for an August 1962 advertisement by Hoffman Electronics, *Scientific American* and other magazines), the omnibus returns to sentimentality, asking our unearned sympathy for a girl, a blind musical prodigy, lost on the Moon in yet another rescue story. "Ordeal in Space" (*Town and Country*, May 1948) describes a spaceman's Earthbound attempts to adapt to his fear of falling; most scenes are well-done, especially those tracing his fears, but the accidental cause of his overcoming them is a kitten (!) lost on a windowledge. Sentiment is milked to the last drop in "The Green Hills of Earth" (*Saturday Evening Post*, February 8, 1947), "the story of Rhysling, the Blind Singer of the Spaceways," which recounts his adventures as a space bum, his dirty songs (supposedly expurgated), his romantic visions, and his dying act of heroism, during which he recorded the final version of the title song.

The second definite sequence begins with "Logic of Empire" (*Astounding*, March 1941), a heavily didactic story about the colonization of Venus and the interdependency of freedom and slavery. With the aid of large chunks of lecture, Heinlein tries to convince his readers of the inevitability of slavery in certain colonial situations, and the equally inevitable fight of some men to be free. The hero is Humphrey Wingate, a lawyer disbelieving in Venerian slavery who is then forced to experience it; on his return to Earth, thanks to some happy coincidences, he finds others as hard to convince as he had been. Although the physical enslavement is also real, psychological enslavement permeates the story. Earth people don't want to know anything discomforting, and Wingate runs from one mental prison to another: from disbelief to numbed acceptance to a "devil theory" to the only form in which his memoirs can gain a reading public, the ghostwritten "I Was a Slave on Venus." Lightly foreshadowed is the 70-year American theocracy, whose overthrow is chronicled after the next story.

Out of sequence is "The Menace from Earth" (*F&SF*, August 1957), the girl narrator of which corresponds in age and interests to heroes of the "juvenile" novels of Heinlein's second period.[18] Although Holly Jones's romantic naiveté is hard to credit, her dreams of becoming a rocket designer do not seem entirely far-fetched, given the time and study she and her prospective partner devote to them. Her provincialism is logically developed, establishing her expertise in her own backyard (Luna City), her disdain for the visiting media starlet, and her need to be educated about herself and her emotions. The real protagonist of the story, as Panshin points out (p. 79), is Luna City; as so often in Heinlein, and sf, the characters and events seem to exist for the sake of giving the reader a tour of the facilities. Holly's blasé acceptance of tourists' idiosyncrasies, of the multilevelled warren she lives in (neatly summed up by its single map, huge and three-dimensional), and of the "Bats' Cave" where everyone *flies* for recreation, provides the proper air of understatement such wonders would deserve in their own context and environment. Given Holly's self-involvement, we learn little about the people, politics, or technology of Luna City, but we know a good deal about how it feels to live there.

" 'If This Goes On . . .' " (*Astounding*, February-March 1940) is impressive as an early long narrative; improved by rewriting for book form (1953), it is still choppy and disjointed, but that is justified to some extent by the viewpoint of the narrator. To tell this story of events leading up to and including the overthrow of the Prophet Incarnate, whose theocracy has ruled for some 70 years over what was once the United States, Heinlein has chosen a young innocent, John Lyle, a recent graduate of West Point dragged into the revolution by his romantic infatuation with an equally young and innocent priestess, or Virgin, about to lose her eponymous quality. The first ten short chapters recount his fleeing romance, his induction into the local unit of the underground "Cabal" (despite its policy of discouraging "romantics"), his inquisition, the rescue of Sister Judith, and Lyle's disguise, travels, and escape to the refuge of General Headquarters in a cavern near Phoenix, at which point he was ordered to write the preceding events in a journal. Continuing the journal for his own interest, apparently, Lyle devotes two long chapters to describing the organizational setup and his own partial re-education, before plunging into a description of as much of the revolutionary action as he saw himself. If Lyle is at all typical of the believing populace, the re-education of this society will be slow at best, since his innocence is all but invincible, and the techniques of brainwashing are rejected. The blows he strikes for freedom are simple, personal, emotional, leaving theoretical considerations to his friend and mentor, Zabediah Jones, and other members of the Cabal. Lyle does, however, describe what they tell and show him about the business of revolution, the manipulation of media, and the power of propaganda, thus illustrating in a general sense the powers of the common man. The action scenes are well done, the illusion of expertise is excellent, and the naiveté about women and romance, which was necessary in 1940 (and may have been still, to Heinlein's commercial sense, in 1953), is at least motivated by Lyle's innocent upbringing.

The re-education of the people does take place, in order for the last three works to take place against a common background of utopian peace and tranquility; called "The First Human Civilization" on the Future History chart, this civilization obeys a libertarian rule called "the Covenant," exceptions to which propel the next three stories. "Coventry" (*Astounding*, July 1940) is another sermon in disguise. It shows David McKinnon, an incompetent brawler educated only in "romantic" literature, learning to appreciate the net of civil interdependence by being forced to live outside of it, in a reservation for malcontents, with three societies far more repressive than what he left. McKinnon's failures provide low comedy, until he is rescued in a sense by an undercover agent and proves his own reconditioning by a heroic act of loyalty to the Covenant society. The reservation societies are not detailed in such a short work, but the point is clearly established that, without responsible cooperation, liberty is impossible. "Misfit" (*Astounding*, November 1939), Heinlein's second published story, shows youths who are outside the Covenant, or disobedient to it, pressed into service in a "Cosmic Construction Corps." On one such job, turning an asteroid into a space station, among the boys whose talents are apparently not needed on Earth is Andrew Jackson Libby, an intuitive mathematical genius whose skills and stubbornness prove highly valuable. The story is notable for its matter-of-fact, detailed sketch of everyday behavior in the special circumstances of the narrative.

Concluding the omnibus volume, the novel *Methuselah's Children* (*Astounding*, July-September 1941; revised for book publication 1958) picks up a number of threads from earlier tales, such as freedom and slavery, practice over theory, progress through experimentation, and the value of administrative competence. References to the Prophet and the Covenant, to Pinero and Harriman, to the rolling roads and to the colonies on the moon and Venus establish fictional continuity; even one character is carried over, "Slipstick" Libby, the *idiot savant* of "Misfit." The general thrust of Future History away from Earth, from arbitrary rules and constraints, is extended beyond the Solar System, as 100,000 people escape a *pogrom* by stealing a starship designed to support generations of human life. These people comprise the Howard Families, products of a voluntary program of breeding for longevity underway since 1874 (the novel begins in 2136). The fact of their longevity leads to their persecution by a society covetous enough to suspend the Covenant in order to pry from them their "secret," believed to be some sort of chemical treatment. After the melodrama of the novel's first half, the second half is more leisurely; the families experience aimlessness in life in the *New Frontiers* and on two alien planets, before going home again to try to regain a sense of meaning. Technological extrapolation gives way to fantasy in Libby's hand-made "light-pressure" drive which converts to faster-than-light travel, as well as in the forms and powers of the beings who inhabit the Howards' adopted planets.

That the narrative does not appear as fragmented as it might is due largely to the unity supplied by its central character and its basic theme. Supposedly about 100,000 people, the story focuses on only a handful, especially one man, born Woodrow Wilson Smith in 1912, alias Captain Aaron Sheffield, best known as Lazarus Long. The stuff of legends, he has already lived through many careers, but not to boredom or passivity; action-oriented, where his relatives are security-conscious, he is capable of carrying out that action, as he proves. Far older than any other surviving member of the Families, he is a precursor of what longetivy could bring: problems of memory storage, but also zest for life and the ability to combine and utilize several "lifetimes" worth of experience. As he is an unlikely model for the Families, so are they to the people on Earth who, in their absence, perfect the nonexistent treatments they once sought, making the whole human race potentially "Methuselah's Children." A compendium of ideas for other possible stories, *Methusalah's Children* obviously was meant to strike sparks, not to provide any definitive answers. Placed at the end of *The Past Through Tomorrow,* it not only sums up the past (our immediate future) but also opens up a farther future in space as well as time.

With its 100,000 people, the *New Frontiers* could have served as a microcosm of the human race, but that theme was reserved for two stories about her sister ship, the *Vanguard,* the story of which is told in "Universe" (*Astounding,* May 1941) and "Common Sense" (*Astounding,* October 1941), later packaged and sold as a novel (*Orphans of the Sky,* 1963). In this alternative view of starship travel, incorporated into the Future History chart, a mutiny killed off the knowledgeable crew and technicians, and the people developed a self-contained society, with science downgraded to superstition and mutants or renegades either fed to the nuclear converter or left to roam in packs in the upper (inner) levels of the ship. "Universe," generally regarded as the classic version of the starship as microcosm, develops this background primarily by suggestion, telling the story of how Hugh Hoyland met the two-headed mutant, Joe-Jim Gregory, and learned the true nature of the ship. "Common Sense," a blood-and-thunder adventure story, fills in specific details of the background and editorializes heavy-handedly about the blindness of people who depend on common sense. After its climactic battle Hoyland leads a small band to escape in the last functioning lifeboat, landing by blind luck on a conveniently passing planet where they can set up housekeeping anew.

Since the omnibus volume introduces the main themes and sums up the central concerns of Heinlein's writing, closing with an open-ended consolidation of prior progress, it is fitting that this parable be excluded. Although it has always been included at the end of the Future History chart, it represents only one alternative future for a small segment of mankind. Other stories and novels which are not on the chart could just as easily be accommodated as alternative paths in the same general direction, with clear exceptions being made for a number of early fantasies (to be discussed later). Four works remaining from before 1950 which are clearly science fictional in nature illustrate this point.

"Solution Unsatisfactory" (*Astounding,* May 1941) became outdated rather quickly, probably to the immense relief of John Campbell, who changed the title (from "Foreign Policy"), according to Heinlein, perhaps in an effort to indicate that this should be a road not taken. Set in the years 1943-1951, it concerns the establishment of a Pax Americana to end World War Two, making permanent the temporary weapons superiority of the U.S.A., which has developed a lethal radioactive dust (a not impossible weapon even today, although it has not, to our knowledge, been used). Guard duty is turned over eventually to an international Peace Patrol, so that each country is guarded by foreign nationals. Told by a participant-observer, this story is partly a lecture on some hard truths and responsibilities; its Campbellian title and editorial conclusion may be negative, but Heinlein had the world guarded by a similarly "foreign policy" seven years later in the novel *Space Cadet.*

"Waldo" (*Astounding,* August 1942), on the borderline of fantasy, is in some ways similar to " 'We Also Walk Dogs' "; it has an eccentric inventor, a profit motive, a sequential series of problems, and the suggestion of an air of contemplation. The inventor is Waldo, a cranky hermit with a fat but undeveloped body, who has created for himself an orbiting, gravity-free home called "Freehold," as well as a number of tools requiring little strength to operate with which he designs and builds things. Logically cornered by the one person he trusts, his doctor, who impresses on him his dependence on other people, Waldo agrees to try to find a solution for the problem causing the failures of the De Kalb motors which power most of Earth's sky traffic. Finding the solution requires two "impossibilities": Waldo must be brought down to Earth in a gravity-absorbing tank, and he and others must learn to accept the existence of an unknown source of power which seems to be what we normally call magic. Accepting the evidence of his senses rather than clinging to scientific theory, Waldo not only solves the engines' power problems, he also solves his own; the beginning and end of the story find him soppy and sentimental, a celebrated gymnastic dancer. Magic, a different kind of frontier, does not belong to the Future History framework, however pragmatically workable it may be stated to be, but Waldo's floating home, the best part of the story, and his pragmatic approach to problems, would be right at home.[19]

A trivial story on a serious theme, "Jerry Was a Man" (*Thrilling Wonder Stories,* October 1947) takes up another alternative not incorporated into Heinlein's Future History, the shaping and altering of animals by genetic manipulation. While shopping for a winged horse, and buying incidentally a twenty-inch elephant, Mrs. Bronson Van Vogel, the "world's richest woman," discovers that the intelligent neo-chimpanzees are treated as slaves and made into dog food when they can no longer work. Adopting the aging chimp, Jerry, she arranges for him to bring suit; this successfully establishes his "humanity" in a court of law. Stereotyped characters and actions, and cliché-ridden language—both formal and would-be-funny colloquial—almost turn this story into a Heinlein self-parody, for all that it has a serious point to it.

Finally, *Beyond this Horizon* (*Astounding,* April-May 1942; revised for book pulbication 1948), Heinlein's one clearly utopian novel, explores some of the possibilities implied by the Covenant society and the general ambience of *Methuselah's Children.* The society depicted could pass for the Future History's "First Human

Civilization." Not only does it have world government, peace and security, and technological comforts, but it is also blessed with an institutionalized breeding program which has lengthened lifespans and eliminated numerous physical disabilities, and with a libertarian life-style which includes sexual freedom, marriage contracts, and the custom of going armed (a practice sharpening reflexes and insuring a certain degree of politeness). An essentially static society, however, breeds boredom; some seek continual distraction, others plan a revolution, others look for life to have more meaning.

Hamilton Felix, the hero, provides them with amusement attractions, but his own boredom goes deeper. For excitement, he becomes a double agent, helping to bring down the revolutionaries, a Hitlerian bunch demanding absolute discipline and genetically-based hierarchical specialization. He, himself, is the end product of several generations of selective breeding, but he does not choose to have children unless he can see some meaning to this life, as would be demonstrated by proof for or against the belief in survival after death. Partly because of Felix, and involving him as a participant, the government undertakes the Great Research, a series of long-range projects aimed at finding scientifically verifiable answers to such problems as the origin and destiny of the universe, the existence of intelligent beings other than on Earth, the possibility of direct communication without symbols, as well as the existence of an afterlife. Felix agrees to marry, and his first child becomes a living proof of the latter two hypotheses; Felix retains the novel's focal point, although the last part of the book is quite diffused.

Maintaining utopia by avoiding stagnation is the unifying theme which pulls together disparate strands in this narrative. It underlies not only Felix's boredom and these various quests for knowledge, but also the love affairs of Felix and his friend Monroe-Alpha Clifford, and the sensation caused by the discovery of a man from the past (1926), accidentally kept in stasis for "seven centuries," reintroduces some of his (i.e., our) quaint customs. A response of a sort to Brave New World, echoes of which are obvious, Beyond This Horizon has neither the depth nor art of its predecessor; as one of the worst examples, the romance scenes are far too coy and gawky to be credible. However, it does put up a good argument, it is an impressive piece of magazine science fiction (especially for 1942), and it serves as a kind of touchstone for the ideals of which societies in other Heinlein novels fall short. Arguably Heinlein's best pre-war work, it unarguably demonstrates the value of the Future History scheme as a set of assumptions and metaphors important beyond the confines of the official chart. Deemphasizing technology and all but ignoring the frontiers of outer space, *Beyond This Horizon* complements the Future History stories by its emphases on "inner space" and the frontiers of knowledge.

These stories and novels set the pattern by which Heinlein has been known in science fiction throughout the years. Generally compact in size, even concise in expression, they are for the most part matter-of-fact evocations of specific moments in the future, the larger currents of history eddying in the background behind these incidents involving specific individuals. The tone is generally authoritative, frequently resulting from the story's being told in first person by a participant who has learned something from the events being narrated. Didacticism is usually overt, but seldom overwhelming, and the masses of humanity are not yet as overtly distrusted as they will be in later works, although the protagonists are almost always among the talented elite, and are openly aware of that fact. Construction is slick in the 1939-1949 stories, but the bones sometimes stick out in others, and style is not a primary consideration where the writer does not call attention to himself. The overall effect, clearly achieved, is that of presenting anecdotes as if they really came from a history not yet realized.

FRONTIERS OF YOUTH: the "juvenile" novels

Between 1947 and 1963, Heinlein published only twenty-four stories, but eighteen novels, of which fourteen are "juveniles" aimed at a younger market, all but two of them published by Scribners. Of course, most science fiction is juvenile in that it appeals to readers' fantasies which can never be realized except in the imagination, and certainly there are many parallels between Heinlein's "juveniles" and the rest of his work. Using teen-agers as protagonists allowed him to combine the two plots with which he was most comfortable, "the Little Tailor"—or the success story— and "the man who learned better," while suppressing the third plot that he recognizes, "boy meets girl."[20]   Romance is handled just as gingerly as it was in his pre-war magazine stories, whereas the success story keeps most of his books upbeat, however somber their tone may be.   Since it is tied to the hero's education, this kind of story gives Heinlein's didacticism a free reign.   Far from being hampered by formulaic constrictions, Heinlein seems to have thrived on them; new frontiers, the need for change, the proper tools with which to face the future, all these could be emphasized again and again in different contexts, each of which is at least related to the grand design of the Future History.   Necessary to avoid stagnation, expansionism would require survival traits, some of which are given only lip service in American schools and society. These traits are rewarded, and their opposites denigrated in this series of books which emphasizes not characters (most are indistinguishable) or plot (most are episodic), but ordinary details of living in exotic settings.

   Rocket Ship Galileo (1947) was a bad start.   Its gee-whiz style and creaking plot, which finds three boys and the atomic-physicist-uncle of one of them building their own rocketship to go to the moon, where they wipe out some evil Nazis (!), could hardly have convinced or impressed anyone older than ten.[21] *Space Cadet* (1948) was a great improvement, adapting to the space age the old formula of surviving military school.   The real protagonist is the academy itself, from its ingeniously worked out physical and psychological tests, through the inevitable dormitory capers and noble-sounding rituals, to the maiden voyage of the three boys whose careers we follow through the book.   The voyage itself is overly spectacular, with heavy happenings every chapter, but the melodrama is undercut somewhat by the boys' limited rewards; their derring-do is treated by the Commandant as well within the line of duty.   The best parts of the book are individual scenes: the obligatory set-piece of the first look back at Earth from the orbiting academy, the ghostly echoes of the muster of four missing heroes, the family mis-communication during Matt Dodson's furlough, the extended family of Venerian natives, and *deja vu* of green cadets taken in hand by the once-green Matt.   A good boy's book, it is relatively conservative in its extrapolations and limited in its interest- and age-group, when contrasted with later novels with their wider considerations about the nature of society and the psychological characteristics that make for success, or even bare survival.

Red Planet (1949), Heinlein's first portrayal of life on Mars, uses the old conventions of canals and life-supporting atmosphere.[22] Indigenous life forms described are few: plants that fold up all night to conserve precious moisture, deadly animals called "water-seekers," and an intelligent species with three distinct stages of development. Each of these affects the story, in which two boys precipitate a revolution and save the human colony. Though greed has tempted certain political appointees into halting the semi-annual colonists' migration (an unlikely self-destructive premise), they fail to reckon with the initiative of the gun-toting colonists, themselves, or with the Martians. Jim Marlowe and Frank Sutton are crucial not only to the revolution, which they set off by carrying tales from school, but also to good relations with the natives, whose mental powers are considerable. The villains and melodrama may be a bit tiresome, to adult readers at least, but the main emphasis is on the reader's learning to understand this strange world and its inhabitants. The scenes at school, the town meeting, even the staging of the revolt pale next to the scenes involving Mars and the Martians. The landscape is functionally visualized, and Willis, the "bouncer," a round, furry creature who can reproduce sounds exactly, steals most of the scenes he's in. Having rescued Willis twice from "water-seekers," Jim is a welcome guest of the Martians, because "bouncers" are first-stage Martians, and Willis is a highly-regarded one. His people introduce Jim to their "water-sharing" ritual, to their technological and mental powers, and to their "Old Ones," third-stage Martians who may be what we would call ghosts. The story's fairy-tale charm—godlike aliens, humble heroes, cooperation between species—is fastened securely to an extrapolative base, but it is also counterbalanced by the barely avoided possibilities for violence on the frontier and between humans and Martians.

Farmer in the Sky (Boy's Life, August-November 1950), reduces the colonial problem to its man-against-nature essentials, once the hero and his family arrive at the Jovian moon, Ganymede. Earth's overcrowding and scarcity economy provide motivation for escape, but the pioneers also need initiative and determination, hard work and know-how, plus a little luck, in order to survive.

With little melodrama and no villains—just some caricatured contra-survival types—the emphasis is entirely on discovery, with a minimum of event. Half the book is spent in getting there, the other half on frontier life, punctuated by a natural disaster and a planetary survey that turns up evidence of prior civilization. The hero's involvement with the Boy Scouts may not wear well to an adult audience, but it explains some of his behavior and demeanor, and it does give an edge to his attitude toward the discipline and practical education needed for survival. He would have been more rounded, however, were we given more information about his deceased mother and about his prospects for a family of his own. These two emotional involvements are suggested, but only as sentimental clichés, too sketchy to be convincing.

War is the background for *Between Planets* (*Blue Book,* September-October 1951), a war between Earth and her colonies, and Don Harvey is caught in the middle. Born in space, he's at school in New Mexico, when his parents on Mars send for him just as hostilities are about to break out. Never sure where his loyalties should lie, he makes intuitive choices against repression, which lead him inexorably to take sides against Earth. Much space is devoted to the revolution—Don's part in it centers on his possession of a message-bearing ring, though he also serves in the colonial army—but the depiction of an alien world is dominant. Venus is again hot, overcast, wet, with colonial ethics and economic development worthy of the American West.[23] Its native life forms include cuddly "moveovers," whose nomadic habits save Don's life, and intelligent dragons. One of the latter, a physicist named "Sir Isaac Newton," is part of the interplanetary organization of scientists, including Don's parents, who end the war bloodlessly, with faster-than-light travel and force fields developed from the secrets of the "First Solar Empire," in the melodramatic nonsense which may well ruin the book for a mature or perceptive reader.

The nonsense is more inspired in *The Rolling Stones* (*Boy's Life,* September-December 1952), a guided tour of the spaceways in the company of the outrageously multi-talented Stone family. This time the emphasis is more on character than on settings, though the latter are done well, with touches of satire: used spaceship lots, Mars and its moons, the Asteroid Belt, and the family spaceship. None of the characters is well-rounded, though the whole family is, and the fun lies in trying to figure out what they will pull off next, their adventures being eminently sensible in contrast to those of the space opera serial they write for Terran stereovision, "The Scourge of the Spaceways." The Stones' own romance of the road balances excitement with the comedy of situations, most notably the commercial ventures of the twin boys: importing bicycles to Mars, coping with the breeding habits of the Martian "flat cat" in the closed quarters of the spaceship, and dealing with the laws of man as well as those of nature.

Starman Jones (1953) has a more dystopian air to it; although Max Jones rises from rags to riches, his climb is a fluke, aided by luck, remarkable mathematical abilities, and a powerful helping hand of the altruistic Sam Montgomery. Max's ability is never in doubt, and presumably would have been rewarded as a matter of course in a more meritocratic society. However, the collation of circumstances needed to let him percolate upwards at a phenomenal rate is not just a Horatio Alger story; it is also an indictment of Earth's stagnant society, in which hereditary guild membership is the key to survival. The action and backgrounds, social as well as technological, are credible; Sam's dream of escaping to a frontier planet is never realized, and each planet we actually see is so organized, by humans or aliens, as to be stifling. The fairy-tale characterization, however—hero, helpers, girl friend, human villain, enemy aliens—is no more than appropriate to the romance plot.

Another comedy, *The Star Beast* (*F&SF,* May-July 1954), centers on cultural misunderstandings between alien species. The minor plot, with which the book opens, finds John Thomas Stuart XI maneuvering clumsily, helped greatly by his too-wise girl friend, to maintain his master-pet relationship with the eight-legged Lummox, whose ungainly appearance and behavior have alienated the townspeople. The major plot, enveloping this one, concerns interspecies diplomacy, between the belligerent Hroshi, come to Earth to reclaim their "queen" (Lummox) carried off long before, and three Earth representatives: Henry Gladstone Kiku, Permanent Undersecretary for Spatial Affairs; Sergei Greenberg, his aide; and Secretary McClure, their nominal superior. Kiku, the indispensable bureaucrat, is a fascinating character, who juggles the Hroshi, the Secretary, the "Friends of Lummox," the "Keep Earth Human League," and other powers in a successful attempt to expand

Earth's interstellar relations. Even his idiosyncracies are functional in the story, his overcoming of his phobia against Dr. Ftaeml, the Hroshi's Medusa-like interpreter, for example, being a part of the motif of cultural misunderstanding and the lowering of barriers. Some of the satire is laid on very heavily: John Thomas' mother and the other townspeople are meanly caricatured, the heroes—Kiku and Greenberg—are pointedly not Anglo-Saxons, and Lummox turns out to be a she, not a he, and to regard John Thomas as *her* pet. The setting in time is a bit fuzzy, though perhaps Heinlein is deliberately mixing an interstellar travel and a Solar Federation with a hick town and twentieth century mores and furnishings, in what is essentially a romp.

After such charming nonsense, *Tunnel in the Sky* (1955), is a bit of a shock. Named after the mode of transportation in use—space/time anomalies called "gates," or "tunnels," which connect distant points as if they were adjacent—this book takes place after the golden age of spaceships, but still its major action is on another planet. Earth is crowded, static, perhaps a bit decadent, with excitement and living space available only on frontier worlds, some of which are being settled, some of which are used as testing grounds for classes in survival. One such course gives rise to this story, essentially a propaganda piece on the necessity of preparedness, the ferocity of mankind, and the durability of civilized behavior. Whereas William Golding's *Lord of the Flies* (1954) had depicted young and adolescent boys turning savage when stranded on an isolated island, Heinlein's young men and women (ages 15-25) establish a frontier foothold during the two years they are isolated by a gate's malfunction. The world of which they stake out a portion is idyllic, except for yearly lemming-like migrations of the animals, whose ferocity at that time is the only serious outside threat to the community. The real problems are communal, husbanding resources, getting along together, governing themselves; they succeed pretty well, seen from inside, even if the media, after their rescue, does label them as savages. These problems give Heinlein an excuse to analyze man as a political animal, as well as thinking individual, and to question the traditional connection assumed between age, education, and maturity. In such a context, romance and even babies are inevitable, but they are handled at a distance; the protagonist and viewpoint character, a leader by default, is more innocent even than John Lyle (of " 'If This Goes On . . .' "), and perhaps too simple to serve appropriately as the reader's stand-in. But the book as a whole stands up quite well as the concentrated distillate of Heinlein's major theme.

Time for the Stars (1956) is another sobering tale, though handled with a lighter tone. Population pressure again is the cause of man's search for other habitable planets. In torchships, which approach the speed of light, communication back to Earth is impossible, except by the "instantaneous" means of telepathy. Pat (for Patrick Henry) and Tom (for Thomas Paine) Bartlett are among the twins and other close relatives found to be telepathic and hired to serve as communication links; Pat, the one who goes, is writing this book as a journal requested by the ship's psychologist so that Pat may understand his roots, the changes he is undergoing as his time and Tom's diverge, and the way to make a balanced adjustment. He also tells the story of his adventures on board the ship, but the guided tour seems to break down once Pat has found himself. The last third of the book is almost perfunctory, with its planet-hopping incidents (one of which takes only a paragraph, one of which decimates the ship's company) and its series of surprise endings. The ship is recalled, since a faster-than-light drive has been developed in their absence; their return to Earth creates no sensation, since the novelty has already worn off; and Pat gets married to the fourth telepathic link in his family, his brother's great-granddaughter. The "happy ending," however, does not blunt the effect of more somber themes—allied to Pat's earlier brooding, which precipitated the journal—such as the essential severing of relations caused by the differing rates of time lived by the brothers and the great risk involved in the expeditions in the first place. Other ships were totally lost, Pat's lost many of its crew (including Pat's uncle), and the telepaths, especially those on Earth, were put through heavy strain. The suspicion that this was all unnecessary, given the technological advances of the next few generations, is only partly mitigated by the assurance that research with the telepaths was what led to the discovery of space/time discontinuity which led to the invention of the faster-than-light drive. As in *Between Planets* and *Farmer in the Sky,* significant losses have to be lived with; their matter-of-fact acceptance requires the long view of expansion as the destiny of man.

Other sacrifices to this ideal are explored in *Citizen of the Galaxy* (*Astounding*, September-December 1957), a study of slavery far advanced beyond "Logic of Empire." The survival of the slave boy, Thorby, to be restored to the vast fortunes on Earth of Thor B. Rudbek, is the stuff of fairy tales, but the experiences he lives through are rather somber, encompassing several degrees of enslavement. Physical slavery is practiced in the Nine Worlds Empire, a distant corner of the Galaxy, where Thorby is bought by the crippled begger, Baslim, who raises him as a son, educating him in memorization, mathematics, survival, and espionage. After Baslim's death, his request is enough to get Thorby adopted by a ship of Free Traders, whose "freedom" of movement and trade is ensured by a rigid social hierarchy, and hedged by rules and folkways equivalent to mental slavery. Thorby's acceptance and his rise in status in the ship's family are illuminated by discussions with a "live-in" anthropologist, punningly named Margaret Mader. After transfer to a vessel of the Hegemonic Guard, Thorby learns his identity and that of Baslim; a Colonel in the "X" Corps, he once had freed an enslaved Trader ship, and had gone into a kind of voluntary servitude in order to help wipe out the entire slave trade. Finally on Earth, Thorby finds himself less free than ever, hampered first by unscrupulous guardians, then by his own wealth and the need to look after it, and finally by his own commitment to help realize Baslim's goal. Each social background is filled in well, with Earth's being most obviously caricatured, her citizens being enslaved by their own decadence and self-interest. Thorby's education, however, is uncertain; he seems to begin each episode with a blank slate, and his romantic naiveté is extremely hard to believe, given his experiences with Baslim and the "underworld" of the planet, Sargon.

Returning to comedy, Heinlein wrote *Have Space Suit—Will Travel* (*F&SF*, August-October 1958), if not a parody, at least a *tour de force*, exposing a number of familiar themes. Trying to win a trip to the moon in the near future, Kip Russell wins second prize in a slogan contest, a used spacesuit, which he refurbishes for the fun of it. Trying it out, he is kidnapped by a flying suacer, and the action becomes progressively more melodramatic and outrageous as the distance from Earth grows progressively greater— first the Moon, then Pluto, then a planet of the star Vega, then a world in the Lesser Magellanic Cloud, a "nearby" sister Galaxy of our Milky Way. A well-structured chase sequence, with aliens for both cops and robbers, this tall tale features a girl genius as Kip's fellow-victim, a desperate trek across the lunar surface, imprisonment with the threat of being eaten, blowing up the enemy's quarters and braving incredible cold to set an emergency signal on Pluto, and going on trial on behalf of mankind (along with a Neanderthal and a Roman Legionary) before the "security council" of the Three Galaxies "federation." In the best tall tale tradition, everything takes place in only a few days, and the folks back home hardly notice the kids have been gone. Kip returns to his soda jerk job before starting college, but, as a logical conclusion to the book's satirical jabs at modern education, scientists who have debriefed him at Princeton arrange, as an afterthought, for him to be admitted to M.I.T. A mind-stretching joy-ride, this novel seems to demand of its readers not only a certain amount of sophistication, but also a willingness to go along with the gag.

A fitting climax in some ways to Heinlein's production of "juveniles" is *Starship Trooper* (*F&SF*, October-November 1959), intended for but refused by Scribners, perhaps because of its attitude toward war, a traditional pose given a new twist or two to make it more controversial. As he defines patriotism in his April 5, 1973, lecture at the naval academy—"It means that you place the welfare of your nation ahead of your own even if it costs you your life."[24]—so in this novel does he define, and illustrate, "the moral difference . . . between the soldier and the civilian" (p. 24). This is the story of the training of a Mobile Infantryman for rocket-delivered action duty against an implacable alien enemy, on behalf of an Earth which "honors" its military, and other veterans of Federal Service, with exclusive rights to citizenship (i.e., holding and voting for political office), but has little use for them otherwise except in time of crisis. The training, in the foreground, is rigorous and unflinching in the old Marine tradition: the narrator witnesses floggings and capital punishment and undergoes a flogging himself in the name of discipline. Background memories fade in and out of his high school class in History and Moral Philosophy, citizen-taught, which everyone had to take but no one had to pass. As intellectual justification for the system he will defend, its arguments are self-serving on behalf of the status quo, but his acceptance and parroting of its principles are consistent with his character and understanding.

Structurally, this is Heinlein's most ambitious work, beginning in the middle, replete with flashbacks, rituals, sentimental coincidences, slick as a military training film, as Panshin rightly points out. Like a training film, too, the book is heavy with propaganda, supporting emotionally its basic premise: survival may ultimately depend on war, and discipline is the indispensable requirement of military training. War is dirty and dangerous, but also necessary, exciting, even glorious, in defense of mankind, especially since the enemy is literally dehumanized. "The Bugs" are implacable, intelligent aliens—the traditional "Bug-Eyed Monsters"—biologically hive-like in efficiency and determination. Even if they were not, a case could be made that "war is the health of the state," with the military ethic as the most blunt way of putting the case for expansionism. In all the frontier situations, wherever Heinlein pits man against nature, a kind of war is at least implicit, and a disciplined education is the survivor's *sine qua non*. Those who feel betrayed by Heinlein's apologia for the military hero may not have been paying attention when the military were heroically cast in earlier books, or they may be caught in the philosophical position Heinlein derides in several works, recognizing that water runs downhill, but never expecting it to hit bottom. That either the society or the military would ever run as smoothly as is postulated here I doubt; 1975 American society does not provide a position of strength to offer as a better alternative. And for all that I am not in sympathy with the military, I am astonished at how well he makes the case, and can almost convince me, inside the book: the philosophy is internally consistent, the narrator a perfect example of selfless goal-involvement, and the action scenes are among the best Heinlein has ever done.

After all these blaring horns and thundering drums, the last of his "juveniles" is rather a disappointment. *Podkayne of Mars* (*If*, November 1962-March 1963) gives me the impression that Heinlein no longer cared, that the piece was left over from a few years before and finished off for a quick sale.[25] It does, however, present his most authentic use of the journal form, the journal this time being kept by a teen-age girl; her story of taking a tour from her home on Mars to the "inner planets" is interrupted by political melodrama on Venus, and she never does get to Earth. Shipboard life and technology are well done, of course, and Venus is beautifully decadent, reminiscent of Earth in *Between Planets*, but governed, if that's the word, as "corporate fascism," which Poddy's uncle (the story's *raisonneur*) thinks is either "the grimmest tyranny the human race has ever known . . . [sic] or the most perfect democracy in history" (p. 106). The melodrama, however, is never convincing, it seems almost a self-parody, and the choppiness of the narrative—the journal is contemporary with the events—is not aided by the shortcut device of adding three slices of commentary by Carlk, Podkayne's incredibly brilliant and amoral kid brother.

As the later examples particularly illustrate, novels labelled "juvenile" are not necessarily childish. They may be quite serious in their extrapolation and exploration of technological and social problems and, indeed, five of Heinlein's fourteen "juveniles" were published first in "adult" science fiction magazines. The innocence, energy, and willingness to please of the youthful protagonists is often endearing, if sometimes quaint, but allows for only limited distinctions between the heroes of different novels. Other debilitating problems include the apparent formulaic need for something eventful to happen in every chapter and the perennial Heinlein problem with endings. He claims he ruthlessly edits his first draft endings, so as not to spell everything out for the reader, but the effect, frequently, is of the author's having run out of gas in bringing the novel to a conclusion. But the general effect of focusing on a single character in a lengthy narrative is to involve the reader in the development of that character, and in the effect on him of adapting to the changing world around him. Since Heinlein's heroes are survivor-types, their personal stories have happy endings, however somber the background or the theme of the novel may be. But if Heinlein could have taken the same care in developing those characters that he did on their backgrounds, I could agree more easily with Panshin's assessment of the "juveniles" as Heinlein's best. Seen as a whole, the series provides a kind of transparent overlay of other adventures taking place against the same general background as that sketched out for the Future History. Seen as a sequence, the series shows the same growing seriousness of tone, the same growing seriousness of characters' social and personal insecurity, that is reflected in Heinlein's other works.

FRONTIERS OF THE MIND: the explicit fantasies

Since the earliest days of Heinlein's writing career, his published works have included stories that were unabashed fantasies, which some readers even prefer to his more probable pieces. Why that should be is not immediately apparent, since most of his fantasies show much less care about composition and craftsmanship than do his science fictions. But in so far as science fiction is a rationalizing process, its emotional burden rests largely in the fantasies that underlie the rationalizations. Heinlein's prose is rarely emotional, but his themes usually are. Commercial reasons surely are involved, as he has striven to reach a larger reading public, but I presume there are also personal reasons why he prefers certain emotional themes and motifs to others, and why he has risked alienating his traditional public in recent years by stripping the rationalizations, especially the science fiction rationalizations, down to barest minimums. Before examining these later, more serious works, it should be instructive to review his earlier, often more frivolous ones.

" 'And He Built a Crooked House' " (*Astounding*, February 1941) is sheer horseplay, a *tour de force* about an innovative house shifted by an earthquake into the form of a tesseract, resulting in people's finding all their directions wrong in going from room to room. Its analogy to a nightmare of being lost in labyrinthine rooms should be apparent. The fear of superior beings playing with man is dramatized in "Goldfish Bowl" (*Astounding*, March 1942). Two would-be explorers of newly-risen stationary waterspouts in the Pacific wind up in an unearthly prison of sorts, under observation analogous to that suggested by the title and hammered home by the parallel of pet goldfish left behind by one of the men. This well-wrought story, connecting a variety of uncanny phenomena, has an unnerving Kafkaesque conclusion: the body of one of the scientists reappears, his skin self-mutilated with the message, "Creation took eight days." Another threatening puzzle is only sketched in "The Year of the Jackpot" (*Galaxy*, March 1952): a large number of social and natural cycles are peak-ing all at the same time. The protagonist is a statistician who acquires a new girl friend, first because she's a statistic, an unconscious participant in a new "fad" of stripping in public. As the figures indicate increasing reasons for concern, they leave Los Angeles in a hurry, just before the bombs start to fall, only to discover once they are in their rural retreat that the sunspot cycle spells disaster for all human life.

In at least six early stories, the defeat of absolute evil by means of superior technological or mental powers is central, in what does not always escape comic-strip quality. "Magic, Inc." (*Unknown*, September 1940) explicitly brings in devils and witches; in a parallel universe where magic works, a minor devil takes over a crime syndicate, and is defeated only by a female white witch who invades Hell and makes Satan call off his underling. In "Elsewhen" (*Astounding*, September 1941), five students and a professor of metaphysics "experiment" with travelling to parallel subjective universes. One becomes an angel, two take part in a revolution against enslavement, while the other two, and eventually the professor, take up sybaritic residence in a Roman-like hedonist empire. Stereotyped cops and robbers, and the professor's escape from arrest, through mental powers, supply most of the action. "Lost Legacy" (*Super Science Stories*, November 1941) finds a psychologist, a brain surgeon, and a girl student disgraced for testing, and proving, the efficacy of mental powers, then running off to California's mysterious Mount Shasta, where they come upon a band of mystics who give them advanced training. After an idyllic period, the three of them try to infiltrate the whole nation by means of a Boy Scout Jamboree, then are forced and helped to overcome the evil controllers of the world. A detective couple, like Mr. and Mrs. North, in "The Unpleasant Profession of Johnathan Hoag" (*Unknown Worlds*, October 1942), get involved in another melodramatic tussle for souls, this time with an organization called "sons of the bird" who operate through the looking glasses of the world. Confusing action culminates in a lengthy explanation that these men were an early sketch by the artist of this world, which he failed to erase when he revised his work. Mr. Hoag is an "art critic" who decides to eliminate them and spare us, thanks to his enjoyment of the tastes of this world, especially the tragicomedy of human love.

More science fictional in nature, *Sixth Column* (*Astounding*, January-March 1941) is still recognizably a fantasy because of the basic premise of John Campbell, which Heinlein developed for quick sale, that six American military scientists, hidden in a mountain installation, can overcome a successful "Pan-Asian" occupation by means of "super-technology" and a religious front organization that the invaders are too stupid to see through. Written before Pearl Harbor, this has obvious propaganda value, labelling the enemy as indistinguishable Asians and touting the superiority of American technology, but it has little to offer a mature reader. Also ostensibly science fiction, "Gulf" (*Astounding*, November-December 1949) is an ill-constructed botch composed of roughly equal parts of nonsensical melodrama, educational philosophy (including much talk about semantics, speeded-up language, and freedom), and illogical wrap-up. The superman concept has a certain fascination about it, perhaps especially because it does not rest upon "super powers" but seems reachable by means of education, but the story as a whole is poorly told, as might be expected of a tale commissioned rather than volunteered. Each of these six tales appeals to basic fears, desires, and prejudices of many readers and may have been turned out simply as a potboiler. They do not seem to have involved the author enough for him to finish the job of writing, but the ideas—super powers, black-and-white conflicts—come back more insistently in later years, in works of a more serious nature.

Three of Heinlein's fantasies, however, are reprinted with some regularity, presumably because of their theme, but also be-because their presentation is expert enough to disarm even a critical reader. "They" (*Unknown*, April 1941) appears to be a classic study of paranoia, until a trick ending shows that the entire world really was constructed to confuse the narrator and force him to believe other people like himself actually exist. More playful, "By His Bootstraps" (*Astounding*, October 1941) recounts how a young man, stymied over his thesis on mathematics and metaphysics and the impossibility of time travel, is drawn into a future time by his own later self, thus triggering the actions which lead inevitably to the act that opens the sequence. Future and past interact physically, not just subjectively, and the hero's personal sense of determinism seems to control the lives of others.

The whole adventure, which results in his becoming a presumably benevolent dictator over long-enslaved people far in the future, can be regarded as another solipsistic fantasy, if not of the hero, at least of the author.

Combining solipsism and time travel, "All You Zombies" (*F&SF*, March 1959) also adds an uncomfortable degree of self-awareness and a hint of real personal terror. Fast-paced, the story is told in perhaps too few words, since the Temporal Bureau's context and functions are a bit vague, but the knots in the tangle appear to be tied tightly, and the emotional impact is strong. Although Heinlein sketches in a few supernumary characters—an assistant bartender, a Sergeant in the Temporal Bureau, and unidentified hospital and orphanage personnel—all the major characters are the same person, who is his/her own father and mother, as well as the Temporal Bureau employee who makes sure that the paradox is enacted successfully. Construction is particularly important in such a story, and Heinlein's handling is deft, given the necessity for the characters to use dialogue to carry out the exposition. Comprising two-thirds of the wordage, the first section (of eight, each carefully headed by a precise time, date, and place notation) introduces the bartender-narrator and the true confessions writer who calls himself "the Unmarried Mother," lamenting his sex change. Hints are dropped that this is more than a simple time-travel tale: the bar is called "Pop's Place"; the bartender wears a ring displaying the "Worm Ouroboros," with its tail in its mouth; and the juke box is overheard playing a once popular song, "I'm My Own Granpaw." Six fast passages follow, showing how the Temporal agent arranged things; then the narrator lets the mask drop:

I felt a headache coming on, but a headache powder is one thing I do not take. I did once—and you all went away.
So I crawled into bed and whistled out the light.
You aren't really there at all. There isn't anybody but me—Jane—here alone in the dark.
I miss you dreadfully! (p. 15)

I don't know that these stories offer the indispensable key to interpreting Heinlein, as Panshin maintains, but they do strike at common human fears; they relate to the significance of freedom and slavery for him and to the scarcity of solid characterizations and the strength of fantasy in his writing.[26] Heinlein is far from unique in exhibiting these qualities, of course; single-character novels are endemic in the twentieth century, solid characterization is rare in anyone's science fiction, and science fiction in general is preoccupied with fantasies of power and control, though often technology-centered. In Heinlein's late work, technology is only minimally developed; the fantasies predominate, with at least a tinge of solipsism in almost every work, as if the writer were overly self-conscious about being the creator of all that goes on in his work. " 'All You Zombies' " is an extreme example, prototypical perhaps for the identity problems that have occupied Heinlein, as subject matter at least, since his first post-war adult novel.

The Puppet Masters (Galaxy, September-November 1951) is a masterpiece of a horror tale. If freedom is the thing dearest to a Heinlein hero, imagine his recoil against alien beings ("slugs") who fasten themselves parasitically to the nervous system and take over absolute control. Heinlein describes this for us twice in first person and, for good measure, also shows them once taking over the hero's girl friend. The obvious emotional appeal of the vampire motif should not blind us, however, to the superb story-telling. From the landing of the flying saucers to the humans' mopping-up exercises, the pace never slows as the pseudonymous narrator gives us inside looks at both sides of the war. In the highest echelon of a secret governmental security agency, he is aware of the planning and carrying out of nationwide operations, and also is involved personally in specific aspects of most of them. The date of 2007 is arbitrary, since the technology, politics, and mass media involved in the story had a near-future credibility at the time of the writing, while the local color, shock value vignettes, and characterizations are quite convincing enough for a thriller.

The hero's closeness to his father, the head of the agency, and his rigid (puritanical? lovestruck? satirical?) insistence on a binding marriage to his willing girl friend could have been explored more fully, especially the latter in a society where temporary contracts are the rule and modesty is no serious barrier to the stripping down required to reveal the slugs. In both cases, however, a conventional 1950's relationship apparently was assumed in order to increase the shock value of the slugs' temporary control over the hero's closest associates. The emotional values of the theme, in fact, are exploited everywhere, from the hero's own psychological changing of sides under slug control, to the girl friend's repressed memories of a slug invasion of Venus, to the government's need to take extremely autocratic control measures in order to fight the slugs. The important distinction between the different kinds of control, of course, is that such self-defense measures are essentially voluntary on the part of the human society, if not of every individual, and that they are temporary and reversible. Indeed, Heinlein's virulent opposition to totalitarianism throughout his career seems to me to be based less on political ideology than on this quasi-mystical opposition between "free men" and the "hive" mentality, nowhere more clearly and emotionally illustrated than in this novel.

Loss of identity is not a nightmare, but a dream, in Heinlein's next adult novel, *Double Star* (*Astounding*, February-April 1956), possibly his best crafted example of the long narrative. The other side of the military coin, politics, is the subject of examination, as the actor Lorenzo Smythe ("the Great Lorenzo") is hired, after a gangster-like kidnapping, to impersonate, then required to become John Joseph Bonforte, leader of the Expansionist Coalition in the world parliament, in a success story worthy of the dreams of any juvenile hero. Heinlein does not minimize the problems of getting away with such an impersonation; Smythe must convince participants in a Martian brotherhood ritual (at the risk of his life), Bonforte's old friend the Emperor (who does see through Lorenzo, but accepts him), the press (in another close call), and the relatively easy-to-fool public. To pull off this feat requires a consummate performer, and Lorenzo, in a highly distinctive first-person narrative, shows us his capabilities. Fully aware of his own tools, experience, and inadequacies, as well as the requirements of the job, he studies carefully the man and his public image until, with the aid of Bonforte's personal staff, he reaches the point where he knows better than they what Bonforte would say and do. Standing for tolerance, free trade, expansionism, and general goodness, Smythe-Bonforte also stands in as a representative of any creative person, artist, writer, or politician, doing what he can and must.

Identity problems are also central to *The Door into Summer* (*F&SF*, October-December 1956), which might be labeled a story ormat not—

of identity crisis. Three conventional gimmicks identify this novel as science fiction: time travel, cryogenic freezing, and the simple, functionally shaped "service" robots which Daniel Boone Davis designs for a living. But they help to construct an adult fairy tale, in which the hero, oppressed by the ugliness and rapacity of the contemporary world, manages to beat the system, almost through no fault of his own. Naively concerned for little else than his beloved designs, he finds himself hustled into cold sleep by his scheming ex-partners, to wake up thirty years later, broke and out of touch with the times. Yet he is able to capitalize on his reputation as a designer, which goes far beyond what memory tells him it should.

In a complex plot—typical of time travel tales—Dan has his suspicions aroused by discovering his own initials on unfamiliar designs. They deepen when, in looking for Ricky, the little girl who was once his only real friend, he finds she has just checked out of a cold sleep "sanctuary," not alone. Knowing he must have succeeded already, he connives to be sent back in time by a secret device which is normally erratic in terms of temporal direction. Once again in his "own" time, he does the necessary designing and careful financial planning this time, and sees to it that he and Ricky—closer in age this time—will wake from cold sleep at about the same time thirty years in the future again. In other words, not only does Dan get a second chance, but he uses it carefully, keeping his youth and getting the girl, winning both riches and fame in a world more congenial than the one he left.

Every man's dream, this story is underwritten by Heinlein's usual sense of detail and local color (California and Colorado), by an unusual care for plotting, and by an excellent feel for design. Any story of time travel seems to me, technically speaking, a fantasy, but the fairy tale quality of this one is kept before us by the presence of Dan's cat, Petronius Arbiter (Pete). A literary descendant, I suppose, of Puss-n-Boots, he is Dan's closest companion, even "speaking" when spoken to, who is lost in Dan's first sleep, but regained in the second to share in the triumph. Even the book's title derives from Pete's habit, when he and Dan once lived in a Connecticut farmhouse, of trying door after door in a search for one which did not lead into the winter snow and cold outside.[27] And this wintry world, symbolic of our present and near future, chills the tone of the whole novel; for all that it has a happy ending, it is clearly linked to later novels of "alienation."

The year 1961 brought the book for which Heinlein is now most widely known, the one which established his reputation as a "guru" and solidified his alienation from many science fiction critics, though not from the fans who voted Heinlein his third of four "Hugo" awards for *Stranger in a Strange Land*. One surprising thing is how well this novel has worn, despite publicity over its being used as a guidebook by the Manson family, and despite the obvious heaviness of its content and delivery.[28] Part satire, part horseplay, part religio-sexual parable, this novel has been taken up, and put down, for various extrinsic reasons, to some extent because it is hard to be certain which way the satire is supposed to cut. A dark pessimism underlies the often frivolous tone, and the putdown of contemporary mores is done in the name of a religion itself impossible to take with a perfectly straight face, however appealing it may be to some would-be converts. A confusing book, *Stranger* combines a number of elements from earlier Heinlein works with a new attitude toward human sexuality, a heavy-handed gaiety as irritating in some ways as the earlier prudery was in others.

The technological content is minimal, reduced to a few comforts and conveniences not unforeseeable as early as 1941, and largely restricted to the first half of the book. Indeed, stylistic differences also support the contention of Moskowitz that the first half was written years before the last.[29] The one essential "science fiction" is a long-standing convention of Heinlein's, the superior mental powers of the inhabitants of Mars, powers such as he previously had attributed to humans only in inconsequential fantasies. There they were also allied to infallible judgment and used to destroy evil-doers, but were not connected to the sexual purposes involved here. Though nudity was alluded to, frequently, in earlier works, sexuality was restricted to innocent kisses and all but kissless romances, and even marriages, which were all that science fiction publishing conventions would allow. Sex is a major component in all of the later novels, although its treatment is still unreal, if characters' speech and behavior should be adequately motivated, rather than mere conveniences for the author's didactic purposes. In *Stranger,* the problem is alleviated, but not eliminated, by the integration of sex into the total symbolic fable. This is of course another *Bildungsroman,* or novel of education, this time one in which the education is that of an innocent superman, with a growing awareness of what it means to be human, as well as to be Martian. His mixture of Martian upbringing with human education—the latter gained primarily from an aged eccentric, Jubal Harshaw; a show biz religious cult, the Fosterites; and a tour with a carnival—leads, not illogically, to Valentine Michael Smith's founding his own cult of mysticism, sex, and total understanding (or "grokking"), and becoming its first martyr. As innocent as Voltaire's Candide, as amoral and indestructible as Mark Twain's "mysterious stranger," Smith attempts to superimpose Martian customs on human biology and society. Gradually, however, he comes to recognize and even revere human ways, and to recognize the need for his own "discorporation" as both a confession of failure and a rallying symbol. That this is parallel to Christ's death is no accident, but it seems not merely a blasphemy, rather a parody. The interlocking symbols of water, sex, linguistic patterns, psi powers, godhood and cannibalism, snakes and tattoos tap depths of feeling, to be sure. But the carnival showmanship, the silliness of some character reactions, and the ludicruous superimposition of wise-cracking angels in variable heavens direct the reader's attention back to a recognizable world so unregenerate that it can be set right only by fantasies, only in the imagination. The mysticism and joy are presented as being very real, for all the wordy philosophizing and silly avoidance ploys. But the cynicism and satire are also intense, and an unequivocal reading is only possible to someone intent on finding it, from a believing Charlie Manson to a scoffing Robert Plank. Heinlein's most moving book, partly because of the tension between realities and wish-fulfillment, it is also as seriously flawed as any of his works, and no more a masterpiece than it is a disaster.[30]

His next adult novel, *Glory Road* (*F&SF,* July-September 1963), again strikes out on the archetypal trail made familiar in critical contexts by Frazer, Jung, and Joseph Campbell. Dedicated to *Amra,* a fan magazine dedicated to sword-and-sorcery fantasies, this novel is superficially a satire of that genre. More precisely, I think, it satirizes the traditional romantic yearning for escape, heroism, and deference to authority. Adventurism, in the Horatio

Alger mode, underlay most of the juveniles; this time, Heinlein brings it into the open and turns it against itself. That the adventure episodes are done well may have misled some readers into thinking that they were primary, that their essential meaninglessness is accidental, and that the desultory conversations between the hero and his girl are secondary. But this book has another venerable ancestor, the "road" novel, which generally plays off romance against realism. The hero is hired by means of a classified ad, planted especially for him. He is sexually backward, and satirically so, as representing all Earthmen. His quest is for "the Egg of the Phoenix," an object meaningless to him until after he has won it; it contains the wisdom of the ages, and other characteristics contained in the memory patterns of previous "Emperors." His "tools" are supplied by a magic box, four-dimensional apparently, which he promptly loses in a swamp, and inexplicably gets replaced. His "Queen," or "Empress," whom he wins by doing her bidding, turns out to be much older and more powerful than he is. His very success results in his becoming a gigolo and a useless "retired hero." All of these factors seem to me parodic commentaries on the traditional hero-myth, which is contrasted to the "rational" framework of the conversations and the "reality" of the Galactic Empire, with its *laissez-faire* government and its sexual freedom.

Farnham's Freehold (*If,* July-October 1964) is a cold war parable, but not in any simplistic sense. Hugh Farnham is a hard-line cold warrior, a fancier of cats and "freedom," an unconscious stereotype of white male superiority, who has had the foresight to build and stock a bomb shelter that saves his life and that of his family. When the bombs drop on nearby defense installations in Colorado, the third blast knocks them some 2000 years into the future. Set against an idyllic landscape, their pioneer-like survival and growing intra-familial rancor are perhaps the best part of the book, despite some regrettable lapses in the cause of sensationalism.[31] The idyll comes to an end, however, when the region's rulers show up; being black, they accept the Farnhams' house-boy Joe, and enslave the whites. Survival-conscious, Hugh suffers indignities rather than risk the castration normal for slaves not being used for stud purposes and becomes chief historian and bridge partner for the reigning Lord Protector. Meanwhile he passes messages to Barbara, his daughter's friend whom he just happens to have impregnated on one try, the night of the bombing, so that they and their twin sons can try to escape. The escape fails, the chief domestic is killed, but nevertheless the four of them are sent back to our time, where subtle differences make possible their surviving the bombing this time, to preserve the limited freedom of the pioneer outpost amid disaster's remnants.

The satire, again, is equivocal. Ostensibly directed at first at those Americans who think they can trust the Communists (and their own government?) not to resort to nuclear war, it carries this line of thinking to what most (white) Americans might think the worst possible social result of such a war. But the Farnham household is satirized, too, in what seems to be a scathing attack on Americans' spoiled way of living, getting whatever they want without struggle, unable to cope with different conditions. Hugh's wife is an alcoholic, his son a mama's boy, his daughter an unwed mother who dies in childbirth, and Hugh, himself, for all his technical competence at survival, (i.e., he does survive, whole, the entire adventure), is little more than competent; he is neither a master technician nor a model of civilized adult behavior, whether observed before or after the time shift. He does learn the results of atomic war, he gains perspective on his own culture and his own institutionalized racism, and he senses the futility of overt rebellion for pride's sake and of covert rebellion for freedom's sake. The time travel device, for which Hugh and Barbara are experimental guinea pigs, does not meet the logic of the plot so much as it gives the reader a vicarious second chance, a chance to see that chauvinism and selfishness may be legitimate only in very particular, circumscribed contexts. Yet the shock treatment and sensationalism Heinlein employs—black rule, enslavement, cannibalism, incestuous desires, voluntary castration, bloody deaths on the part of whites— call a tremendous amount of attention to themselves for their shock value alone. And the flawed construction and extreme talkiness of the book, as of most of Heinlein's novels since and including *Stranger*, are also serious drawbacks, blurring whatever other effects he may have had in mind.

To many readers, *The Moon is a Harsh Mistress* (*If*, December 1965-April 1966), seemed a return to the old Heinlein. The setting was the familiar underground lunar colony, the central topic was revolution against repressive Earth imperialism, an inevitable step in the Future History sequence, but played for propagandistic pruposes as a discomforting parallel with the American Revolution exactly three hundred years before. The narrator, Manuel or "Manny" (sometimes called "Man"), is a fairly simple-minded technician who sees everything operationally, but with more than a dash of sentimentality. A one-armed computer repairman, he is a reluctant revolutionary who becomes a putative leader, thanks to his contact with the central computer, but conveniently misses key battles. Often slow to catch on, but usually making a good case for himself, Manny is not a fully reliable narrator, as is perhaps emphasized by the distancing effect of the peculiar slang through which he addresses the reader.[32] The real hero, of course, as Budrys pointed out, is a sentient computer named "Mike" (cf. Michael Valentine Smith in *Stranger in a Strange Land*), who oversees the entire operation of the lunar colony, including life support systems and media channels.[33] Mike regards his/her/its participation in the revolution as a kind of joke on his nominal bosses, who don't pay any personal attention to its quirky personality. Undertaking a study of humor, Mike is not an entirely trustworthy ally; as the revolution proceeds on course, it keeps reporting that the odds against success are increasing, thus giving rise to the only serious doubts reported in anyone's mind. Mike's loss of sentience after Earth's bombardment of nearby territory is convenient, if the revolutionaries are to consolidate their gains without worrying about the computer's playing games against the new government.

Although the revolution supplies most of the action in this book, it seems perfunctory; certainly it is long overdue in terms of Heinlein's Future History scheme. Yet the lunar lifestyle, the background which should make the revolution meaningful, isn't all that solid either, for all the experience Heinlein has had in describing it piecemeal in the past. Inconsistencies abound, but some of the main points asserted are the following: its citizens have a heritage of political exile and of scarcity of women, they have a high regard for custom but not for laws, they have an exaggerated sense of chivalry and of free enterprise, they are racially and sexually tolerant of others, they are highly conscious of the thin threads by which their individual and communal survival depend, and they are capable of exerting a united effort only under the stress of an extended propaganda program which emphasizes their oppression by a greedy Earth. Ecologically, this oppression may be very real, threatening to exhaust their resources within seven years, although Heinlein never supports this assertion. Economically, however, they manage to support, on the basis of exports to Earth (primarily of grain), a rather high standard of living and a remarkably "free" society, which is pointedly not a democratic one, either before or after the war. The whole picture, inconsistencies and all, is that of a rather insubstantial dream, incorporating both traditional and unconventional wish-fulfillments.

Heinlein does try something new, for him, in his next novel, *I Will Fear No Evil* (*Galaxy*, July-December 1970), but the result is aesthetically little short of disastrous, however successful it may be commercially.[34]   Sex is the primary topic, led into by the theoretical premise of transplanting the brain of a dying rich old white man into a new body, that of his nubile young black secretary, killed but left perfectly intact. Some satirical points are made about legal shananigans establishing identity, about city areas being unpoliceable, about bureaucrats and credit sales and the prison of being rich, but most of the book consists of interminable talk about Joan (for Johann) Eunice (for the secretary) Smith's learning the role of a sensuous woman, in hetero-, homo-, and bisexual combinations. The upshot of it all is that Joan, in the best solipsistic fashion, gets herself pregnant by the banked sperm of Johann, and marries his old lawyer, Jake. The dual consciousness, whose internal dialogues comprise the largest portion of the book, becomes triple when Jake dies.[35] Emigrating to the moon, Joan dies in childbirth, and the three depart from consciousness cheerfully, whether to death or the mind of the newborn child is left indeterminate. Heinlein's career-long dream of escape and off-earth emigration is extended here to the escape from the limits of a single consciousness and of the mortality of the human body. But, for all that the argument may have serious intent, the clichéd characterizations, the simplistic sexual fantasies, and the incredibly arch style make the book all but unreadable; caught between fantasies, it is poorly anchored for science fiction, and too serious and talky to be pornography.

His latest book to date, *Time Enough for Love* (1973), is not an aesthetically successful work either, but it is a revealing document, summing up many of the themes and ideas of Heinlein's *oeuvre,* through its cursory examination of some of the later lives of Lazarus Long, hero and mouthpiece of *Methuselah's Children.*[36] Longer by far than any other Heinlein novel, it is offered as archive records collected over 2000 years from now, comprising stories told by Lazarus out of his past and his selected aphorisms, interspersed with a continuing narrative (with varying viewpoints) of the time in which these records were collected.

Life in the novel's "present," beginning on a world he once founded as a "corporate tyranny" headquartering the Howard Foundation, has some utopian features corresponding to those of early and late Heinlein novels. Long life and its perspective presumably make eminently sensible such wish-fulfillments as sexual promiscuity, "logical" distinctions between masculine and feminine roles, and a libertarian government which respects the wishes of the individual (including suicide), in addition to the usual technologically-based comforts and conveniences. But this society is becoming too stale and "civilized," more orderly, and the chief administrator, unsure of his course of action, overrules Lazarus' wish to let himself die, in order to record some of his "wisdom" and to share life with him. In the process of settling another new world, the group which surrounds Lazarus takes on some interesting scientific and technological puzzles. They successfully transfer a computer's mind into a "blank" human body, make twin girls out of clones derived from Lazarus, himself, and develop a method of time travel which really interests him as something new; and everyone loves, and eventually makes love to, everyone else, regardless of sex or biological relationship (by this time, Lazarus feels he's related, as an ancestor, to almost everyone in the Howard families).

Recalling his past lives, Lazarus tells rambling stories, some of which are major building blocks of the novel. As meanderings of this old man, of course, they carry an interest not wholly justified by their structure or the manner of their telling. The first tells of a World War Two Navy officer who avoided physical labor and danger by using his head; drawn in part from Heinlein's own life experiences, it portrays our century's illogic in ludicrous but loving perspective, showing us Lazarus' view (and apparently Heinlein's) that the life most worth living is that which involves the least effort. The second relates Lazarus' buying and re-educating of a slave couple; brother and sister, but genetically compatible, they marry, settle down, and succeed in the restaurant business, owing it all to him as surrogate father. The third tells of the one real love of Lazarus' life, love for an "emphemeral" (a girl of our normal life span) on a frontier planet, describing with loving detail the daily joys and hardships of pioneer life (and who but Heinlein would have the audacity to present as science fiction, which in context it is, a straightforward tale of settling the new land with little more than horses and hand utensils?). A fourth story emerges from his trip in time, whereby Lazarus finds that he can go home again, to meet his own mother in her youth, and even to make love with her (his own childhood self already existing), before being killed in the trenches of World War One. Of course, he is not really killed, or rather the twins, by means of a time travel ship, rescue him just before it's too late, assuring him in the book's last words that it was "Just a dream, Beloved. You cannot die."

Given the premise of longevity, going on immortality, it does not seem illogical that for Lazarus Long, having experienced everything, the most important thing in the universe would be love (including, but not limited to sex), that his experiences concerning love would be multifarious, and that his opinions about it would be idiosyncratic. And it is moving to me to see Heinlein, in what may be the twilight of his career, connecting love and family, struggle and immortality in what is often a direct and personal-seeming narrative, the whole of which suggests that simple pleasures are the best, although we may only be able to gain them fully in our imaginations. But the tales of Lazarus are extremely long-winded and the arch dialogue and giddy behavior of the people in Lazarus' "love-circle" of the fictional present are unconvincing, betraying once more what appears to me to be Heinlein's apparent nervousness in writing about sexual matters.[37] And though I can see the need for structural innovations in chronicling (even in representative snippets) a life that spans 2000 years, the shifting points of view, the intrusive narrative voices, the elaborate analogy to a musical composition all seem rather forced.[38]

Heinlein has always had some difficulty dramatizing his fantasies, those that he could not tie down to hard facts by close-order approximation and extrapolation. The early e.s.p. or psychic power stories, for instance, deteriorate into simple melodrama, and the later flights of sexual fantasy, encumbered with talk and disconnected from ordinary character motivation, never get off the ground. On the other hand, *Double Star, The Door into Summer,* and the solipsistic "They" and " 'All You Zombies' " are far more successful, because they are anchored to analogies with observable human behavior. A sense of psychological reality, though obscured with symbolism, also keeps *Stranger in a Strange Land* and *Glory Road* from drifting off completely into Never-Never Land. But psychological realities, his own at least, are things that Heinlein often seems to have tried to hide behind such stereotyped emotive labels as "freedom," "power," and "cannibalism." It is not, in fact, until *Time Enough for Love,* for all its faults, that he finally seems to confront that vast territory within the mind, of which such stereotypes are only the most distant frontier outposts.

CONCLUSION

In analyzing the works of any writer, the critic runs into problems in disentangling his subject's personal contributions from the corporate fantasies of his reading public. In the case of someone like Heinlein, who is unabashedly a writer of commercial fiction, with its often rigid rules and arbitrary editorial strait-jackets, this problem is still more complicated. Certainly Heinlein shares with his whole society, including the makers of scinece fiction, a positive attitude toward the frontier, toward adolescent potential, and toward the proper use of gadgetry. The frontier, with its challenge of the unknown, inviting expansion of man's territory and his knowledge, and often threatening his survival, is a staple of Western literature and philosophy. So is youth, with its romantic dreams, and the volition and potential to learn in order to achieve them. And the ambivalence of man toward science and technology, his fascination with gadgets coupled with his justifiable fear of their progressive disruption of his way of life, is a key theme continuing through at least the last two centuries in Western civilization. The settings against which these themes are sounded, and to a large extent the manner in which they are presented, Heinlein shares with many other writers of science fiction. Space and the future, instant wisdom and quick technological fixes recur functionally in almost all of his writings, providing the typical science fictional perspective on the present which, it is pretended, allows us to see it whole. Given a single human species, planet, and period in time, differences in race, religion, even sex, and lifestyle, become relatively unimportant.[39] And any single-minded assertion of supremacy, of sex or nation, race or religion, and almost any intolerant attitude (except perhaps one's own) becomes fair game for satire. But Heinlein's own adaptation of these views is also individual, as may be visible in a short historical cross-section.

When Heinlein began writing science fiction, escapism was assuredly the name of the game. Readers of science fiction, scarred by the Depression, wanted to believe in habitable planets, conquests and utopias, miraculous cures and technological fixes, god-like or demoniacal aliens; and they were willing to meet the writer more than half-way.[40] Heinlein was a leader in the adaptation of these fantasies to a fictional world which also allowed for the realities of dining room and board room; for the phenomenal effects, direct and indirect, positive and negative, of technological fixes; and for the ornery resistance and resilience of human behavior. As the United States came out of the Depression and into World War Two, back into its self-appointed role as savior of the Western democracies, Heinlein helped to develop in the pulp magazines "social science fiction," with its more responsible attitude toward the future modern man and his technology were bringing into being, including the unlikely survival of democracy, except as a label. The prediction-consciousness of Campbell's *Astounding* was echoed in the grand design of Heinlein's Future History which, in its relatively detailed projection of progressive expansion, despite setbacks in the near future, probably summed up the predominant feeling of the science fiction community.[41]

After the war came initial exuberance, then the Korean War and McCarthyism, and a kind of sinking, by most people, into complacent acceptance of the status quo of cold war jitters accompanied by unprecedented and ostensibly unlimited growth. Science fiction's critique of this mix of secrecy and stagnation has probably been overrated; certainly Heinlein's view was an oblique one, suggesting by examples of change that apparently stable situations were not permanent. Like other science fiction writers, he continued to be involved in a kind of special pleading (with which I am in almost complete sympathy) for space travel and expansion off Earth, for technological education and a one-world viewpoint, things emphasized in science fiction of the 1940's and 1950's. With the abortive East European revolutions, with increased security-consciousness at home, with the failure of even the first Sputnik to arouse the American competitive spirit to serious educational reform, the dreams of science fiction seemed to fade. The bite of satire, turned against the present, went deeper, but science fiction writers also turned inwards, paying more attention to psychological states and to the means by which such states must be expressed—words, language, style. Showing the effects of this same pressure, if in no other way than that he was selling to the same markets, Heinlein's writing became more somber, more sharply satirical, more interested in the individual and his fantasies. Amid these tensions, too, his writing improved, reaching its peak in the mid-1950's, though he was no longer the pace-setter he had been a decade before.

Introduced by a dream of Camelot and the launching of a crash space program, the 1960's soon bogged down in assassinations, another land war in Asia, mass protests in the streets, worries about overpopulation and ecological imbalance, and the relative boredom of the actual landings on the Moon. Science fiction, corporately, showed the strain, with a continued emphasis on war and conquest, with increasing shrillness concerning overpopulation and ecotastrophe, and with a further shift toward style and "speculative fantasy."[42] Heinlein's interest in the cold war consciousness as subject matter apparently peaked around the turn of the decade, for his later novels turn away from the social contemporaneity of the *Farnham's Freehold* frame-story toward the fantasies of sex and hedonism already adumbrated by *Stranger in a Strange Land.* An older man now, called by many the "Dean" of science fiction writers (though Leinster, Simak, and Williamson all predate him), Heinlein did not have the incisive style or craftsmanship of younger writers, or their seriousness about brooding, negative themes. His dreams of progress postponed (not that he ever believed in any linear kind of social progress), he fantasized about his dreamworlds and, not unwilling to assume the role of elder statesman, seemed preoccupied with immortality.

In all these phases, Heinlein was an important moving force, speaking at times directly, but mainly through the strength of his example. From the first, there was his sense of realism, of ordinary actions in daily life, or the detailed texture of a limited range of experience, of the continuity between future and current behavior. Then there was his caring about the larger canvas, the Future History so many readers, and other writers, took to heart, only to have a younger generation rebel against it. Having fitted these to the adventure-story formulas that sustained the science fiction magazines, Heinlein then adapted them to the formulas of the mass magazine and juvenile novel markets, selling all the time to the sf magazines as well. Finally, as other writers, more competent with words, more careful with design, surpassed him, and gradually did away with the need to follow formulas so faithfully, Heinlein tried to keep up. The results were highly individual, but far from unqualified successes, since Heinlein, shifting more and more from pulp adventure toward philosophical dialogue, did not have the necessary resources of style to fall back on.

Although his latest work shows belated influences of the great "modernist" writers of the earlier part of the century, Heinlein's attitude toward style and manner which was not, like his, lucid, transparent, ostensibly objective, generally has been, if not antagonistic, at least indifferent; in that, too, he reflects the attitude of most sf writers of his generation. In lectures, talks, and articles he emphasized the content, more or less dismissed technique as formula, and deprecated those writers for whom words were more important, mirroring psychological states which often did not have the, for him, requisite, positive outlook.[43] His very mastery of formulas was, in a sense, his downfall, for it obviated the need to create distinctive characters, to explore more than a very narrow emotional range, even to complete the plots and constructs he had begun. Having been successful, too, under formulaic limitations, at suggesting a philosophy rather than spelling it out, he was either unwilling or unable to support his positions more fully in his talky later novels, where no taboos or limits on length were operative. And the authoritative insider manner, replete with wisecracks and homey sayings, which he affected in the early 1940's, has become dated, while the garrulousness of the 1950's and 1970's has not been an adequate replacement.

Generally a competent craftsman, if nothing else, Heinlein stood out among his contemporaries before the War, and again as a writer of "juvenile" novels, and his level of consistency over all is probably unmatched except by H. G. Wells. But his best works do not rise above that level as much as his worst fall below it. " 'We Also Walk Dogs,' " "Blowups Happen," and " 'The Roads Must Roll' " are more than competent, as are such postwar stories as "The Green Hills of Earth" and "The Menace from Earth"; but all five are dated, in substance or style or both. More universal perhaps because set in the more distant future, *Methuselah's Children* and *Beyond this Horizon* show serious cracks and flaws after thirty years, while the attitudes frozen into "The Man Who Sold the Moon" and *The Puppet Masters* have come to seem somewhat quaint. The "juveniles" stand up as an overall achievement, but none of them really stands out, though my personal preference is for *Citizen of the Galaxy* and *Starship Troopers,* despite my reservations about their philosophical-political underpinnings (i.e., the inevitability and acceptability of slavery and war), over such rollicking jaunts as *The Rolling Stones* and *Have Space Suit—Will Travel.* But Heinlein's best—such stories as " 'It's Great to be Back,' " "They," and " 'All You Zombies' "; such novels as *Double Star* and *The Door into Summer*—do not seem to me to match the best single novels of a dozen or more other wirters, even limiting the list to those whose fame lies mainly in the science fiction field.[44] And his worst, such as "Elsewhen," "Gulf," "Searchlight," *Rocket Ship Galileo,* and *I Will Fear No Evil* are as bad as anything ever used to show science fiction up as inept and infantile.

Today, Heinlein is known to many, thanks to paperback advertising techniques at least, as the "Dean" of science fiction writers, not so much because of his length of service as because of his relationship to the corporate body of science fiction. He is "historically" important as a pioneer in realistic and extrapolative science fiction, and as a representative writer whose craftsmanship and technical knowledge-ability were generally quite high. But he may also be a victim, in a sense, of another basic lesson of the frontier: the earliest settlers, laying the groundwork, making possible further developments and greater accomplishments, may be indispensable, but frequently they are remembered, if at all, only for being there first.[45]

Beverly Friend

THE STURGEON CONNECTION

Before Theodore Sturgeon's
Unicorns always picked virgins!

Awriter who would have his unicorn walk directly up to the girl who . . . (as Theodore Sturgeon did in "The Silken-Swift" back in 1953)[1] just isn't safe. If he would so impugn unicorns, what might he do with mother-love, filial devotion, romantic courtship? More importantly, perhaps, what would he have to say about incest, vampirism, homosexuality?

Before spurning that unicorn, however, as being a maverick of its breed, one just might note that the virgin in the story is self-centered, cruel, and totally undeserving, whereas the "other lady" is filled with love, understanding, and kindness (leading, of course, to her present situation). There is, thus, some justification for the unicorn's choice—for the shattering of the classic mold as, in most of his stories, Sturgeon shatters most contemporary (although still universal) taboos and mores. He is a rule-breaker beyond compare.

That role was not immediately apparent. His first stories were published by John Campbell in that seemingly magic year, 1939, when Asimov and Heinlein also first published in *Astound-*

ing. His earliest science fiction was competent enough, but he did not gain attention until the appearance of "It" (*Unknown,* August 1940), generally regarded as one of the finest monster fantasies of modern literature. He followed this with "Poker Face" (*Astounding,* March 1941), in which he suggested that alien humanoids already live among men, but it was "Microcosmic God" (*Astounding,* April 1941), which gained a place in the Science Fiction Hall of Fame.

From it one might have inferred something of the development of Sturgeon thematically. It is a variation on the Frankenstein story, for the scientific genius, James Kidder, its protagonist, creates life—creates a race of microorganisms "which would develop and evolve so fast that it would surpass the civilization of man; and from them he would learn."[2] He becomes the god of these Neoterics, as he calls them, and although he may be a harsh god in the sense that he makes them adapt quickly to the changes he brings about in their environments, he does share their accomplishments with mankind. The real conflict of the story arises between Kidder, who works for the good of mankind, and Conant, the ruthless bank president whose "organization yielded him more money and power than any other concern in history, and yet he was not satisfied" (p. 95). When Conant tries to gain complete control by bombing the island where Kidder has conducted his experiments, the scientist tells the Neoterics to build an impregnable shield. They do, thereby breaking off communication with Kidder for the first time; this permits Sturgeon to strike a note of horror, for the narrator fears the day those creatures will let down the shield and emerge again into the world of man.

Then came World War Two and with it a move to the Caribbean. There, among other jobs, he learned to operate the new bulldozers which fascinated him. The experience produced another memorable story, "Killdozer" (*Astounding,* November 1944). It, too, turned on the monster theme, for the machine developed some twisted intelligence (perhaps reflecting men at war, carving airfields from the islands of the Pacific) and turned upon the men who used it, seeking to destroy them. In a recent remark Sturgeon has implied that it was the only narrative he had written between 1940 and 1946. Of this six-year gap in his bibliography, he wrote:

What wonders I might have produced had I not clutched up, I wailed. And [his "perceptive friend"] said no, be of good cheer. He then turned upon the whole body of my work a kind of searchlight I had not been able to use, and pointed out to me that the early stuff was all very well, but the stories were essentially entertainments; with few exceptions they lacked that Something to Say quality which marked the later output. In other words, the retreat, the period of silence, was in no way a cessation, a stopping. It was a silent working out of ideas, of conviction, of profound selection. . . .[3]

One of his first efforts after the war, "Mewhu's Jet" (*Astounding,* November 1946), provided the familiar initial encounter between humans and an alien who comes to Earth with a wry twist proving Sturgeon's keen humor. The alien is a lost child who will never be able to explain the adult, scientific wonders of his civilization to mankind. Other than that, however, Sturgeon emerged from World War Two as "clutched up" as any member of the scientific or science fiction communities. In "Memorial" (*Astounding,* April 1946), the visionary (or mad) scientist, Grenfell, seeks to create an atomic horror, The Pit, as a lasting memorial which will make man realize that he must never use atomic power in war. Largely structured as a dialogue between Grenfell and the journalist Roway, the story voices the fear of the period. Sturgeon reveals his stance by allowing Roway and the government agents whom he has brought with him to force Grenfell to use his development as a weapon—not Grenfell's idealism—to cause the nuclear explosion. It initiates not one but two atomic wars; there were no more after that . . . only "half-stooping, naked things whose twisted heredity could have been traced to mankind." In 5000 A.D. with The Pit still radiating, "the earth could never forget the horror that could be loosed by war. That was Grenfell's dream" (p. 286). In contrast to such horror, in "Thunder and Roses" (*Astounding,* November 1947), after the United States has been devestated by atomic attack, the beautiful Starr Anthrim, a singer mortally poisoned by radiation in the first attack, wanders from military base to military base searching for the last command post that will activate a retaliatory attack. She has but one message:

'They have killed us, and they have ruined themselves. As for us—we are not blameless, either. Neither are we helpless to do anything—yet. But what we must do is hard. We must die—without striking back.'[4]

She dies, but she wins the heart of an army sergeant who kills his buddy in order to prevent the attack and then destroys the lever: " 'You'll have your chance,' he said into the far future" (p. 49).

However incompletely developed, Sturgeon had discovered his central theme. Perhaps he stated it most fully, most completely, in "To Here and the Easel" (1954), published a year after the book edition of *More Than Human*, the novel which more than anything else established him at the forefront of science fiction writers and gained him the International Fantasy Award.

Richly complex in technique and symbolism, "To Here and the Easel" tells how a painter dissatisfied with his earlier work regains the inspiration to paint. At one point he asserts:

For when you were stripped and alone, somewhere in yourself you found a way to travel, through wild countries, through poverty and sickness and hardship, certain that they would refine you for your destiny. You see, dear dopple, the twentieth-century man has no destiny; at least, he has no magicians to read it off for him, so he can never be quite sure. But take his amulets away, his spells and cantrips graven with the faces of dead presidents —and he'll look over no mountains toward an unshakable faith. He'll stare at nothing but his own terror.[5]

And he concludes:

Does anyone ask a painter—even the painter himself—*why* he paints? Now me, I painted . . . used to . . . whatever I saw that was beautiful. It had to be beautiful to me, through and through, before I would paint it. And I used to be a pretty simple fellow, and found many completely beautiful things to paint.

But the older you get the fewer completely beautiful things you see. Every flower has a brown spot somewhere, and a hippogriff has evil laughter. So at some point in his development an artist has to paint, not what he sees (which is what I've always done) but the beauty in what he sees. Most painters, I think, cross this line early; I'm crossing it late.

. . . .

The only key to the complexity of living is to understand that this world contains two-and-a-half billion worlds, each built in a person's eyes and all different, and all susceptible to beauty and hungry for it. (pp. 54-55)

The year before he had published *More Than Human*. That three-part novel had its core in the novelette "Baby Is Three" (*Galaxy,* November 1952), the only section to appear in magazine form.[6] Structured as a psychoanalytical session involving Dr. Stern and the boy Gerard, it allows the reader to reconstruct the boy's experience as he becomes part of a complex organism: himself; the girl Janie, who has the powers of telepathy and telekinesis; Bonnie and Beanie, the black twins who have the power of teleportation; and the baby who, Gerard says, coordinates them all. At the climax of the story, however, the reader learns that that power belongs to Gerard himself. As he explains it:

'I'll tell you. I'm the central ganglion of a complex organism which is composed of Baby, a computer; Bonnie and Beanie, teleports; Jane, telekineticist; and myself, telepath and central control. There isn't a single thing about any of us that hasn't been documented; the teleportation of the Yogi, the telekinetics of some gamblers, the idio-savant mathematicians, and most of all, the so-called poltergeist, the moving about of household goods through the instrumentation of a young girl. Only in this case every one of my parts delivers at peak performance.'[7]

The result is a superorganism, *Homo Gestalt,* which not only has greater power than mankind, but perhaps more importantly overcomes the fragmented isolation of individual man. What is perhaps most important is the suggestion that the individual units maintain their own identities while working together. As a unit they are able to "blesh" (p. 340)—to blend and mesh together into something more than human.

Writer Robert Bloch has cited the novel as a book which "stands virtually alone in its consideration of empathy, the basic problem of MAN AGAINST HIMSELF, and even more important, MAN *FOR* HIMSELF and MAN *FOR* MANKIND." He further states that *More Than Human* preaches "evolution rather than revolution, evaluation rather than revelation, individual right rather than individual might."[8] And these words can apply to the entire canon of Sturgeon's fiction. As William Nolan wrote, "He is a searcher, seeking love, communication, emotion which he can put to paper, trapped in the skin of a story."[9]

In a passage echoing the "Foreword" to *Sturgeon Is Alive and Well . . .* he himself recalled that at one of the first Milford Conferences, Damon Knight and James Blish had suggested that "a writer has a thing he says and he tends to say it over and over again—not by any means repetitiously, but thematically or in his

selection of image and relevant metaphor."[10] To "blesh"; to connect: that is what Sturgeon says over and over again. Connect the
parts of the body, the phases of personality, one human to
another, each to a group; form something larger than self, something beyond individuals, something greater and more enduring.

The means to such ends, for Sturgeon, is love. The fate of
the old woman in "How to Kill Aunty" emphasizes that point
nicely. In a hate-filled tale of nephew and aunt attempting to murder one another, Sturgeon says of her after she has succeeded,
thereby leaving herself entirely alone:

. . . All her life she had been too busy to be loved, too busy to be liked. She
had been too busy to have a childhood and she had been too busy to be old.
  Not any more. The Hubert [nephew] business was the last thing she had
to be busy about; for years it had been everything and the only thing, and
now she'd finished it, and though she lingered on for a long while, it was the
finish for her.[11]

Since his theme is love, his subject matter has often been
sexuality, and it is here that he deliberately employs the taboos
and mores of traditional society to emphasize his themes. In the
same year as the publication of *More Than Human,* he shocked the
science fiction audience with the story, "The World Well Lost"
(*Universe Science Fiction,* June 1953).[12] Two aliens land upon
Earth, their ship disintegrating so that they are marooned. They
had stepped from their ship "hand in hand. Their eyes were full
of wonder, each at the other, and together at the world. They
seemed frozen in a full-to-bursting moment of discovery."[13] Immediately they become known as "loverbirds" and create a nine-
day wonder on a world immersed in its sensuality. "Like a sudden
bloom across the face of the world came the peculiar magic of the
loverbirds. . . . But watch the loverbirds, only a moment, and
see what happens. It's the feeling you had when you were twelve,
and summer-drenched, and you kissed a girl for the very first time
and knew a breathlessness you were sure could never happen
again" (p. 81).

Computers identify them as citizens of Dirbanu, a planet
which has refused any relationship, even commercial, with the
Earth, its ambassador having shown a "most uncommon disdain
of Earth and all its works, curled his lip and went wordlessly

home" (p. 83). A message from Dirbanu advises Earth not to give the loverbirds sanctuary since they were fugitives. "So from the depths of its enchantment, Terra was able to calculate a course of action. Here at last was an opportunity to consort with Dirbanu on a friendly basis—great Dirbanu which, since it had force fields which Earth could not duplicate, must of necessity have many other things which Earth could use . . ." (p. 84). Thus the loverbirds are arrested, and a ship with a carefully screened crew of two is prepared to return them to their planet.

The two men are described as "a colorful little rooster of a man and a great dun bull of a man." They will not ship out with any other individual. The former, Rootes, chatters of his "conquests in port" in a manner that "carries the tones of thirst rather than of satiety" and asks if his companion has any pornography, relying finally upon a volume of Michelangelo. The latter, Grunty, is, of course, the latent homosexual in love with the "unaware-other." He condemns the society of Earth as roundly as any of Sturgeon's protagonists:

A filty place, Terra. *There is nothing,* he thought, *like the conservatism of license.* Given a culture of sybarites, with an endless choice of mechanical titillations, and you have a people of unbreakable and hidebound formality, a people with few but massive taboos, a shockable, narrow, prissy people obeying the rules—even the rules of their calculated depravities—and protecting their treasured, specialized pruderies. In such a group there are words one may not use for fear of their fanged laughter, colors one may not wear, gestures and intonations one must forego, on pain of being torn to pieces. The rules are complex and absolute, and in such a place one's heart may not sing lest, through its warm free joyousness, it betrays one. (p. 93)

He realizes that the loverbirds are telepathic and is afraid they have learned his secret. He plans to kill them, but as he raises his gun, they begin to show him a series of pictures: first of mankind, both male and female, beautiful whether clothed or nude. Then Dirbanuans—whose females are grotesquely different from the graceful loverbirds. Grunty releases them in a space raft; Rootes declares that he would have killed them had he realized they were "God damned *fairies*"; and the story ends as Grunty acknowledges his own homosexual love for Rootes. So shocked was the science fiction community that its members apparently failed to realize, first, that Sturgeon used the device to attack the immorality of a sensuous Earth, and, secondly, that because men and women had been so alike, the ambassador from Dirbanu had thought homosexuality was rampant upon Earth and, therefore, Dirbanu refused to have anything to do with so decadent a world.

Homosexuality is again the focal point in a longer, more elaborate work, *Venus Plus X* (1960), which saw no magazine publication in America but was serialized in the British *New Worlds* (January-April 1961). It presents the world of Ledom, dual-sexed creatures who are not, as the protagonist Charlie Johns, imagines, logical mutations of humans in some golden future, but "self-made, surgically adapted creatures inhabiting a Shangri-La adjacent to and congruent with our own world."[14] Sympathetic until his discovery, Charlie Johns cannot tolerate the revelation:

'. . . What changed you?'
'Only the truth.'
'What truth?'
'That there is no mutation.'
'Our doing it to ourselves makes that much difference? Why is what we have done worse to you than a genetic accident?'
'. . . Why is what you do evil? Men marrying men. Incest, perversion, there isn't anything rotten you don't do.'

. . . . .

'Yet a mutation would have made us innocent?'
'A mutation would have been natural. Can you say that about yourself?'
'Yes! Can you? Can homo sap? Are there degrees of "nature"? What is it about a gene-changing random cosmic particle that is more natural than the force of the human mind?'
'The cosmic ray obeys the laws of nature. You're abrogating them.'
'. . . Tell me, Charlie Johns: what would homo sap do if we shared the world with them and they knew our secrets?'
'We'd exterminate you down to the last queer kid . . .'[15]

Perhaps the most effective attack upon the hypocrisy of man's society occurs in Sturgeon's "If All Men Were Brothers, Would You Let One Marry Your Sister," written especially for Harlan Ellison's *Dangerous Visions* (1967). At the opening of the story, its portagonist, Charli Bux, bursts into the office of the Archive Master because he has been refused a hearing at any other level of the bureaucracy. He has been to the planet Vexvelt, discovering there a glorious Eden complete with, for example, a cancer cure, but on Terratu he cannot get anyone to admit that planet's existence. Structurally, the story alternates between the dialogue of Charli and the Archive Master and flashbacks to Charli's experiences relating to Vexvelt. Early in the narrative the reader learns that he reached Vexvelt only through a contact he had made on the planet Lethe. He asks if the Master knows what goes on on Lethe, and is told, "Everyone knows about Lethe. . . . That kind of thing has its function. Humanity will always— . . . One neither approves or disapproves. . . . One knows about it, recognizes that for some segments of the species such an outlet is necessary, realizes that Lethe makes no pretensions at being anything but what it is, and then—one accepts, one goes on to other things." Charli reminds the Master that "On Lethe . . . you can do anything you want to or with any kind of human being, or any number or combination of them, as long as you pay for it."[16] Rather than accept the manner of life on Vexvelt, however, the Master cries out: "Abomination. . . . I—would—rather—die—eaten alive—with cancer—and raving mad than live with such sanity . . ." (p. 353).

Such sanity permits incest. When Charli first meets the people from Vexvelt on Lethe—where a mob was trying to burn their ship—the lovely Tamba has Vorhidin ask if Charli would like to sleep with her. He does, and because freely given, the relationship is meaningful, but he is confused when on Vexvelt she says that she must spend that night with someone whom he suspects is her brother. He cools toward her, but her place is taken by the lovely Tyng. That relationship leads Sturgeon to voice one of his most basic themes:

The pre-Nova ancient Plato tells of the earliest human, a quadruped with two sexes. And one terrible night in a storm engendered by the forces of evil, all humans were torn in two; and ever since, each has sought the other half of itself. Any two of the opposite sex can make something, but it is usually incomplete in some way. But when one part finds its true other half, no power on earth can keep them apart, nor drive them apart once they join. This happened that night, beginning at some moment so deep in sleep that neither [Tyng nor Charli] could ever remember it. What happened to each was all the way into new places where nothing had ever been before, and it was forever. The essence of such a thing is acceptance . . . (p. 357)

Lest he be judged, Charli Bux ceases to judge and begins to observe closely the society about him:

Life around him certainly concealed very little. The children slept where they chose. Their sexual play was certainly no more enthusiastic or more frequent than any other kind of play—and no more concealed. There was very much less talk about sex than he had ever encountered in any group of any age. He kept on working hard, but no longer to conceal facts from himself. He saw a good many things he had not permitted himself to see before, and found to his surprise that they were not, after all, the end of the world. (p. 357)

Once again, then, Sturgeon uses the idea of sexual freedom as a means to criticize his own contemporary society. But Charli Bux is put to a final test, for he finds his beloved Tyng in bed with her father, his friend, Vorhidin. He beats the unresisting Vorhidin until he is exhausted, and then Vorhidin gently carries him into the house. Then begins a long dialogue—lecture would perhaps be the better word—in which Vorhidin defends the concept of incest, declaring that the human species is the only one which holds it taboo. This allows an attack upon the concepts of guilt and sin, among others, and argues that two ecologists, Vexworth and Phelvelt, founded the society of Vexvelt, "the only culture ever devised on ecological lines. Our sexual patterns derive from the ecological base and are really only a very small part of our structure" (p. 364). Moreover, despite the almost obsessive popularity of sex as a topic on most worlds, only incest is uniformly "a horrifying thought" *morally,* although *biologically* speaking, Vorhidin finds nothing wrong with it; arguing by analogy to the breeding of fine strains of cattle, he insists that incest on Vexvelt brings about "stabilization, purification, greater survival value . . ." (p. 362). Charli is convinced; he returns to Terratu to face the Archive Master and prove to Vorhidin that the other worlds will accept the conduct of Vexvelt because "one greater force, greed" (p. 365) will compel them to seek the products which Vexvelt has to offer them commercially. When he learns he is wrong, he returns to the Edenic planet.

One could go on, compiling the many stories in which Sturgeon explores the nature of love—and sexuality—using it always as a weapon to criticize contemporary society. But the result would be essentially the same. Sam Lundwall summed it up well when he wrote:

Sturgeon has for some years been taking love apart in his stories, to see what makes it tick . . . and this has resulted in a number of short stories and novels in which the plot is nothing more than a background, a way of making the characters express themselves. Many of his best stories are not science fiction even in the broadest sense of the word. I have an uneasy feeling that this is what makes Sturgeon great; that he doesn't care about gimmicks and environment at all, just the characters themselves. He is the absolute antithesis of Robert A. Heinlein, to whom environment is all and the characters just part of the overall picture.[17]

Love: a meaningful, unifying relationship. For Sturgeon this is not a mere togetherness, as he proved so ably in the story "Mr. Costello, Hero" (*Galaxy,* December 1953), written at the same time as *More Than Human.* In it Sturgeon posits a dystopia in which no one is allowed to venture anywhere without a partner. The philosophy behind this is expressed thusly:

They say no human being ever did *anything.* They say it takes a hundred pairs of hands to build a house, ten thousand pairs to build a ship. They say a single pair is not only useless—it's *evil.* All humanity is a thing made up of many parts. No part is good by itself. Any part that wants to go off by itself hurts the whole main thing—the thing that has become so great. So we're seeing to it that no part ever gets separated. What good would your hand be if a finger suddenly decided to go off by itself?[18]

On this basis no one is permitted to be alone. But the unity is negative because it is imposed from without. The "hero," Mr. Costello, ultimately ends up restricted to supervising an ant hill, the type of regimentation which he had wished to force upon humanity.

Where, however, unity comes from within and the connection is made by telepathy and "telempathy," Sturgeon finds his positive values. He makes his strongest cases in the novels *More Than Human* and *The Cosmic Rape* (1958). Whereas *More Than Human* concentrated upon forging a single entity (*Homo Gestalt*) from disparate parts, *The Cosmic Rape* seeks to unite the whole human race and, ultimately, to blend humanity with another intergalactic entity, the Medusa. On this blending of humanity (the "bleshing" of *More Than Human*), Sturgeon wrote:

First, there was the intercommunication—a thing so huge, so different, that few minds could previously have imagined it. No analogy could suffice; no concepts of infinite telephone exchanges, or multi-side-band receivers, could hint at the quality of the gigantic cognizance. . . . It had . . . texture. Your memory, and his and his, and hers over the horizon's shoulder—all your memories are mine. More: your skills remain your own (is great music made less for being shared?) but your sensitivity to your special subject is mine now, and your pride in your excellence is mine now. More . . . Mankind, as never before, I am I as never before.

Nor does this "bleshing" destroy the individual; Sturgeon continues:

When Man has demands on me, I am totally dedicated to Man's purpose. Otherwise, within the wide, wide limits of mankind's best interests, I am as never before a free agent; I am I to a greater degree, and with less obstruction from within and without, than ever before possible.

To explain how this is possible, Sturgeon cries out:

For gone, gone altogether are . . . the They-don't-want-me devil, the Suppose -they-find-out devil, the twin imps of They-are-lying-to-me and They-are-trying-to cheat me; gone, gone is I'm-afraid-to-try, and They-won't-let-me, and I-couldn't-be-loved-if-they-knew.[19]

All of these hyphenated statements are the cries of the isolated, fragmented outsiders to whom Sturgeon referred in "To Here and the Easel"—twentieth century man staring at nothing but his own terror. And Sturgeon brings all outsiders in, selecting for his tales idiots and mongoloid babies, the unappetizing derelicts of humanity, and those kept outside by the restrictive, uncaring taboos of society. In a way he dramatizes the fate of the outsider most effectively in the short story, "Prodigy" (*Astounding,* April 1949); long after atomic holocaust, in a desperate attempt to regain human normality, the Guardians of the Norm incinerate as undesirable the only child who is not a telepath.

Alfred Bester has called Sturgeon "an imaginative, sensitive poet who can write about human emotions with so much power that he's wasted on science fiction." Bester labels his science as "plausibly makeshift," but cites the fiction as unique, concluding that "his understanding and approach to human beings . . . makes him too touching to be endured."[20] Bester has hit a key point, for in his own definition of science fiction, Sturgeon has insisted that the story must be "built around human beings, with a human problem and a human solution, which would not have happened at all without its scientific content."[21]   In explaining why he wrote science fiction, he stated:

If society doesn't suit you, you can . . . build a better one and see if it works. You may also alter parts of your culture and create new operating environments for the rest. *Most important of all,* since science fiction can never deal properly with anything but people, it can orient people in and out of its pages, to new placements of the heart and the head in an increasingly science-influenced existence.[22]

Of course, to do so—to offer new placements of the heart and the head—the author must, of needs, draw from his own experience. In his own life, Sturgeon has known many loves and many losses: in his childhood the separation and ultimate divorce of his parents; in adolescence, the lack of communication with his stepfather and the onset of illness; in adult life, both occupational and marital struggles, including several early divorces. He is a highly personal writer drawing from his own sufferings for his craft. And it may well be this intensely personal basis of so much of the experience that he transforms into his fiction which makes Sturgeon different from other science fiction writers. It may explain why he places his emphasis upon emotion and character while, as Lundwall suggested, Heinlein places his upon environment and idea. More than such a detail specifically, it may well be this difference in emphasis which leads many critics to downgrade science fiction as a whole—especially if they do not know or associate the work of Theodore Sturgeon with the genre.

Through his exploration of love, then, Sturgeon's ultimate concern lies with the individual character, particularly that one who does not know or cannot achieve a fulfillment of love. One of the most notable studies is "Maturity" (*Astounding,* February 1947), in which a brilliant and irresponsible young genius (described as a "child") is filled with hormones and sterones "to help you reorganize your metabolism and your psychology."[23] It permits Sturgeon to debate the nature of maturity in terms of society and the individual; in this case, the protagonist, utterly isolated by his increasing maturity, wills that he die. In some ways, however, the most touching of the stories is "A Saucer of Loneliness" (*Galaxy,* February 1953). A young woman attempts suicide and tells her rescuer what caused her to do so. One day while the nameless, seventeen-year-old New York girl walked in the park, a small flying saucer hovered near, striking her forehead, communicating with her. The saucer falls as a creature dead. Both public and government insist that she reveal the message given her; she refuses to, insisting that "it was talking to *me*, and it's just nobody else's business."[24] She is accused of concealing some important scientific message and is interrogated endlessly, tried, and jailed for contempt of court because of her silence. Her moment of fame, like her imprisonment, passes, but she continues to realize the effects of the saucer. It make her aware of her own loneliness and of the empty, selfish quality of the people—the society— around her. She throws bottles containing the message into the sea; the F.B.I. seeks to obtain them all; but when she attempts suicide, she is saved by a nameless man who has recovered one of the bottles and read the message from the saucer:

> There is in certain living souls
> A quality of loneliness unspeakable,
> So great it must be shared
> As company is shared by lesser beings.
> Such a loneliness is mine; so know by this
> That in immensity
> There is one lonelier than you. (p. 166)

Their mutual need, and their need to be needed, unite the nameless man and girl, for "even to loneliness there is an end, for those who are lonely enough, long enough" (p. 167). In that at last they have overcome their isolation and found a meaningful love, they have achieved "The Sturgeon Connection."

TWO VIEWS:

Willis E. McNelly

I. RAY BRADBURY—PAST, PRESENT, AND FUTURE*

A. James Stupple

II. THE PAST, THE FUTURE, AND RAY BRADBURY

I.

Ray Bradbury, hailed as a stylist and a visionary by critics such as Gilbert Highet and authors such as Aldous Huxley and Christopher Isherwood, remained for years the darling, almost the house pet, of a literary establishment other wise unwilling to admit any quality in the technological and scientific projections known as science fiction. Within the field of science fiction itself, Bradbury's star zoomed like the *Leviathan '99* comet he later celebrated in a significant but ill-fated dramatic adaptation of the *Moby-Dick* myth. Fans pointed to Bradbury with ill-concealed pride, as if to prove that, at least with him, science fiction had come of age and deserved major critical attention.

Certainly America's best-known science fiction writer, Bradbury has been anthologized in over 300 different collections. His own individual works number in the dozens and have been translated into even more languages. After some ten million words—his own estimate—he feels almost physically ill unless he can spend

---

*Some portions of this article were previously published in considerably different form in the *CEA Critic* (March 1969). Copyright Ⓒ 1969 The College English Assoiation.

four hours a day at the typewriter. His aim is to work successfully in virtually every written medium before he changes his last typewriter ribbon. His plays have been successfully produced both in Los Angeles and off Broadway. He is currently researching the history of Halloween for a TV special, and he still collects his share of rejection slips for short stories, novellas, or movie scripts, with a larger share of acceptances.

His first volume of collected poems was issued in November 1973, although for years he refused to publish his poetry. He had too much respect for the form to do it badly, but after thirty years of trying to get the better of words, he permitted his serious poetry to be judged. He reads poetry incessantly, an hour or two a day, and returns to Yeats, Donne, Kipling, Poe, Frost, Milton, and Shakespeare. He is already an accomplished parodist in light verse, and his version of "Ahab at the Helm," to the meter of "Casey at the Bat," convulses college audiences who are not accustomed to seeing any elements of humor in Melville.

Beyond poetry or light verse, the short story, the novel, or the drama, the motion picture script is the one form that Bradbury feels may be the most significant. There is no doubt in his mind that the cinema has an ability to move men more profoundly and perhaps more ethically than any yet devised by man. The cinema script, he argues, while deceptively easy to write on first glance, is the most demanding literary form. Screen writers, Bradbury maintains, are too prone to let the technical skills of cinematography carry the weight of the artistic impact. As a result, the ideal of art—to impose an artistic vision upon an order of reality—suffers, and the resultant vision is darkened.

Bradbury's major themes transform the past, present, and future into a constantly shifting kaleidoscope whose brilliance shades into pastels or transforms language into coruscant vibrations through his verbal magic. Contemporary literature to reflect its age, he believes, must depict man existing in an increasingly technological era, and the ability to fantasize thus becomes the ability to survive. He himself is a living evocation of his own theory—a sport, a throwback to an earlier age when life was simpler. Resident of a city, Los Angeles, where the automobile is god and the freeway its prophet, Bradbury steadfastly refuses to drive a car. He has no simplistic anti-machine phobia; rather his reliance on taxicabs or buses springs from the hegira his family made from Waukegan, Illinois, to Los Angeles during the depths of the Depression when he was 14. The roads, he recalls, were strewn with the hulks of broken cars. Since that time his continual concern has been the life of man, not the death of machines. Man must be the master of the machine, not its slave or robot. Bradbury's art, in other words, like that of W. B. Yeats, whom he greatly admires, is deeply dependent upon life. Like Yeats in "The Circus Animals' Desertion," Bradbury must ". . . lie down where all the ladders start, / in the foul rag-and-bone shop of the heart."

If Bradbury's ladders lead to Mars, whose chronicler he has become, or to the apocalyptic future of *Fahrenheit 451,* the change is simply one of direction, not of intensity. He is a visionary who writes not of the impediments of science, but of its effects upon man. *Fahrenheit 451,* after all, is not a novel about the technology of the future, and is only secondarily concerned with censorship or book-burning. In actuality it is the story of Bradbury, disguised as Montag, and his lifelong love affair with books. If the love of a man and a woman is worth notarizing in conventional fiction, so also is the love of a man and an idea. A man may have a wife or a mistress or two in his lifetime, and the situation may become the valuable seedstuff of literature. However, that same man may in the same lifetime have an endless series of affairs with books, and the offspring can become great literature. For that reason, Bradbury feels that Truffaut was quite successful in translating the spirit of the novel, and the viewer who expects futuristic hardware or science fiction gimmickry will be disappointed in the motion picture. "Look at it through the eyes of the French impressionists," Bradbury suggests. "See the poetic romantic vision of Pissaro, Monet, Renoir, Seurat, or Manet that Truffaut evokes in the film, and then remember that this method was his metaphor to capture the metaphor in my novel."

"Metaphor" is an important word to Bradbury. He uses it generically to describe a method of comprehending one reality and then expressing that same reality so that the reader will see it with the intensity of the writer. His use of the term, in fact, strongly resembles T. S. Eliot's view of the objective correlative. Bradbury's metaphor in *Fahrenheit 451* is the burning of books;

in "The Illustrated Man," a moving tattoo; and pervading all of his work, the metaphor becomes a generalized nostalgia that can best be described as a nostalgia for the future.

Another overwhelming metaphor in his writing is one derived from Jules Verne and Herman Melville—the cylindrical shape of the submarine, the whale, or the space ship. It becomes a mandala, a graphic symbol of Bradbury's view of the universe, a space-phallus. Bradbury achieved his first "mainstream" fame with his adaptation of Melville's novel for the screen, after Verne had aroused his interest in science fiction. *Moby-Dick* may forever remain uncapturable in another medium, but Bradbury's screenplay was generally accepted as being the best thing about an otherwise ordinary motion picture. John Huston's vision was perhaps more confining than Ray Bradbury's.

Essentially a romantic, Bradbury belongs to the great frontier tradition. He is an exemplar of the Turner thesis, and the blunt opposition between a traditionbound Eastern establishment and Western vitality finds itself mirrored in his writing. The metaphors may change, but the conflict in Bradbury is ultimately between human vitality and the machine, between the expanding individual and the confining group, between the capacity for wonder and the stultification of conformity. These tensions are a continual source for him, whether the collection is named *The Golden Apples of the Sun, Dandelion Wine,* or *The Martian Chronicles.* Thus, to use his own terminology, nostalgia for either the past or future is a basic metaphor utilized to express these tensions. Science fiction is the vehicle.

Ironic detachment combined with emotional involvement— these are the recurring tones in Bradbury's work, and they find their expression in the metaphor of "wilderness." To Bradbury, America is a wilderness country and hers a wilderness people. There was first the wilderness of the sea, he maintains. Man conquered that when he discovered this country and is still conquering it today. Then came the wilderness of the land. He quotes, with obvious approval, Fitzgerald's evocation at the end of *The Great Gatsby*: ". . . the fresh, green breast of the new world . . . for a transitory enchanted moment man must have held his breath in the presence of this continent . . . face to face for the last time in history with something commensurate to his capacity for wonder."

For Bradbury the final, inexhaustible wilderness is the wilderness of space. In that wilderness, man will find himself, renew himself. There, in space, as atoms of God, mankind will live forever. Ultimately, then, the conquest of space becomes a religious quest. The religious theme in his writing is sounded directly only on occasion, in such stories as "The Fire Balloons," where two priests try to decide if some blue fire-balls on Mars have souls, or "The Man," where Christ leaves a far planet the day before an Earth rocket lands. Ultimately the religious theme is the end product of Bradbury's vision of man; the theme is implicit in man's nature.

Bradbury's own view of his writing shows a critical self-awareness. He describes himself essentially as a short story writer, not a novelist, whose stories seize him, shake him, and emerge after a two or three hour tussle. It is an emotional experience, not an intellectual one; the intellectualization comes later when he edits. To be sure, Bradbury does not lack the artistic vision for large conception or creation. The novel form is simply not his normal medium. Rather he aims to objectify or universalize the particular. He pivots upon an individual, a specific object, or particular act, and then shows it from a different perspective or a new viewpoint. The result can become a striking insight into the ordinary, sometimes an ironic comment on our limited vision.

An early short story, "The Highway," illustrates this awareness of irony. A Mexican peasant wonders at the frantic, hurtling stream of traffic flowing north. He is told by an American who stops for water that the end of the world has come with the outbreak of the atom war. Untouched in his demi-Eden, Hernando calls out to his burro as he plows the rain-fresh land below the green jungle, above the deep river. "What do they mean 'the world?' " he asks himself, and continues plowing.

Debate over whether or not Bradbury is, in the end, a science fiction writer, is fruitless when one considers this story or dozens like it. The only "science" in the story is the "atom war" somewhere far to the north, away from the ribbon of concrete. All other artifacts of man in the story—the automobile, a hubcap, a tire—provide successive ironies to the notion that while civilization may corrupt, it does not do so absolutely. A blownout tire may have brought death to the driver of a car, but it now provides Hernando with sandals; a shattered hubcap becomes a cooking pan. Hernando and his wife and child live in a prelapsarian world utilizing the gifts of the machine in primitive simplicity. These people recall the Noble Savage myth; they form a primary group possessing the idyllic oneness of true community. The strength of Hernando, then, is derived from the myth of the frontier; the quality and vigor of life derive from, indeed are dependent upon, the existence of the frontier.

Yet irony piles on irony: the highway—any highway—leads in two directions. The Americans in this fable form a seemingly endless flowing stream of men and vehicles. They ride northward toward cold destruction, leaving the tropical warmth of the new Eden behind them. Can we recreate the past, as Gatsby wondered. Perhaps, suggests Bradbury, if we re-incarnate the dreams of our youth and reaffirm the social ethic of passionate involvement. And nowhere does he make this moral quite as clear as in *Fahrenheit 451*.

Originally cast as a short story, "The Fireman," *Fahrenheit 451* underwent a number of transmutations before finding its final form. From the short story it became an unpublished novella, "Fire, Fire, Burn Books!" and was again transformed by twenty days of high speed writing into the novel.[1] An examination of a photocopy of the original first draft of "The Fireman," reveals how carefully Bradbury works. His certainty with words makes for extremely clean copy: three or four revisions on the first page; none on the second. He adds an adverb, "silently"; cuts an unnecessary sentence; sharpens the verb "spoke" to "whispered"; eliminates another sentence; anglicizes a noun. Nothing more. Yet the artistry is there, the clean-limbed expressive prose, the immediacy of the situation heightened by the terseness of the dialogue, the compounded adjectives, the brevity and condensation everywhere evident.

Inspection of his rewrite of the same page shows some further small but significant changes, changes that give Bradbury's prose its evocative poetic quality. Note the modifications in the following sentences: "Mr. Montag[2] sat among the other Fire Men in the Fire House, and he heard the voice tell the time of morning, the hour, the day, the year, and he shivered." This becomes sharper, more intense: "Mr. Montag sat stiffly among the other Fire Men in the Fire House, heard the voice-clock mourn out the cold hour and the cold year, and shivered." The voice now "mourns," not "tells," and the appeal to the senses is clarified, the general made specific as "some night jet-planes . . . flying" becomes "five hundred jet-planes screamed." These changes may be minor, to be sure, but they indicate the method of the writer at work. Titles which Bradbury provided to successive drafts indicate something of the way his mind moves: "The Fireman," "The Hearth and the Salamander," "The Son of Icarus," "Burning Bright," "Find Me in Fire," "Fire, Fire, Burn Books!" These metamorphosed into *Fahrenheit 451*, as anguished a plea for the freedom to read as the mid-twentieth century has produced.

Yet even *Fahrenheit 451* illustrates his major themes: the freedom of the mind; the evocation of the past; the desire for Eden; the integrity of the individual; the allurements and traps of the future. At the end of the novel, Montag's mind has been purified, refined by fire, and phoenix-like, Montag—hence man-kind—rises from the ashes of the destructive, self-destroying civili-zation. " 'Never liked cities,' said the man who was Plato," as Bradbury hammers home his message at the end of the novel. " 'Always felt that cities owned men, that was all, and used men to keep themselves going, to keep the machines oiled and dusted' " ("The Fireman," p. 197).

The leader of the book-memorizers at the end of the novel is significantly named Granger, a farmer, a shepherd guiding his flock of books along the road to a new future, a new Eden. "Our way is simpler," Granger says, "and better and the thing we wish to do is keep the knowledge intact and safe and not to anger or excite any-one, for then if we are destroyed the knowledge is most certainly dead. . . . So we wait quietly for the day when the machines are dented junk and then we hope to walk by and say, here we are, to those who survive this war, and we'll say Have you come to your senses now? Perhaps a few books will do you some good" (pp. 198-199).

This vision of the future which Bradbury provides at the end of *Fahrenheit 451* shows his essentially optimistic character. In fact, Bradbury seized upon the hatreds abroad in 1953 when the book was written, and shows that hatred, war, desecration of the individual are all self-destructive. Bradbury's 1953 vision of hatred becomes extrapolated to a fire which consumes minds, spirits, men, ideas, books. Out of the ashes and rubble revealed by this projected vision, Bradbury reveals one final elegiac redemptive clash of past, present, and future:

Montag looked at the mens' faces, old all of them, in the firelight, and certainly tired. Perhaps he was looking for a brightness, a resolve, a triumph over tomorrow that wasn't really there, perhaps he expected these men to be proud with the knowledge they carried, to glow with the wisdom as lanterns glow with the fire they contain. But all the light came from the campfire here, and these men seemed no different than any other man who has run a long run, searched a long search, seen precious things destroyed, seen old friends die, and now, very late in time, were gathered together to watch the machines die, or hope they might die, even while cherishing a last paradoxical love for those very machines which could spin out a material with happiness in the warp and terror in the woof, so interblended that a man might go insane trying to tell the design to himself and his place in it. They weren't at all certain that what they carried in their heads might make every future dawn brighter, they were sure of nothing save that the books were on file behind their solemn eyes and that if man put his mind to them properly something of dignity and happiness might be regained (p. 200).

What has been Ray Bradbury's contribution to science fiction? The question might well be rephrased: What has been Ray Bradbury's contribution to mid-twentieth century American literature? Neither question is easy to answer without risking the dangers of over-generalization. From the viewpoint of science fiction, Bradbury has proved that quality writing is possible in that much-maligned genre. Bradbury is obviously a careful craftsman, an ardent wordsmith whose attention to the niceties of language and its poetic cadences would have marked him as significant even if he had never written a word about Mars.

His themes, however, place him squarely in the middle of the mainstream of American life and tradition. His eyes are set firmly on the horizon-Frontier where dream fathers mission and action mirrors illusion. And if Bradbury's eyes lift from the horizon to the stars, the act is merely an extension of the vision all Americans share. His voice is that of the poet raised against the mechanization of mankind. Perhaps, in the end, he can provide his own best summary:

The machines themselves are empty gloves. And the hand that fills them is always the hand of man. This hand can be good or evil. Today we stand on the rim of Space, and man, in his immense tidal motion is about to flow out toward far new worlds, but man must conquer the seed of his own self-destruction. Man is half-idealist, half-destroyer, and the real and terrible thing is that he can still destroy himself before reaching the stars. I see man's self-destructive half, the blind spider fiddling in the venomous dark, dreaming mushroom-cloud whispers, shaking a handful of atoms like a necklace of dark beads. We are now in the greatest age of history, capable of leaving our home planet behind us, of going off into space on a tremendous voyage of survival. Nothing must be allowed to stop this voyage, our last great wilderness trek.[3]

II.

Anyone who has ever watched those classic "Flash Gordon" serials must have been puzzled by the incongruous meeting of the past and the future which runs through them. Planet Mongo is filled with marvelous technological advancements. Yet, at the same time, it is a world which is hopelessly feudal, filled with endless sword play and courtly intrigues. It is as if we travel deep within the future only to meet instead the remote and archaic past. This is not, however, a special effect peculiar to adolescent space operas. On the contrary, this overlapping of past and future is one of the most common features of science fiction. It is found, for example, in such highly acclaimed works as Frank Herbert's *Dune* and Ursula LeGuin's *The Left Hand of Darkness*, futuristic novels whose settings are decidedly "medieval." A similar effect is also created in such philosophical science fiction novels as Isaac Asimov's *Foundation* trilogy, Walter Miller's *A Canticle for Leibowitz*, and Anthony Burgess' *The Wanting Seed*. In each of these works a future setting allows the novelist an opportunity to engage in an historiographical analysis; in each the future provides the distance needed for a study of the patterns of the past. But of all the writers of science fiction who have dealt with this meeting of the past and the future, it is Ray Bradbury whose treatment has been the deepest and most sophisticated. What has made Bradbury's handling of this theme distinctive is that his attitudes and interpretations have changed as he came to discover the complexities and the ambiguities inherent in it.

Bradbury began to concentrate upon this subject early in his career in *The Martian Chronicles* (1951). In a broad sense, the past in this work is represented by the Earth—a planet doomed by nuclear warfare, a "natural" outgrowth of man's history. To flee from this past, Earthmen begin to look to a future life on Mars, a place where the course of man's development has not been irrevocably determined. But getting a foothold on Mars was no easy matter, as the deaths of the members of the first two expeditions show. To Captain Black's Third Expedition, however, Mars seems anything but an alien, inhospitable planet, for as their rocket lands in April of the year 2000, the Earthmen see what looks exactly like an early twentieth century village. Around them they see the cupolas of old Victorian mansions, neat, whitewashed bungalows, elm trees, maples and chestnuts. Initially Black is skeptical. The future cannot so closely resemble the past. Sensing that something is wrong, he refuses to leave the ship. Finally one of his crewmen argues that the similarity between this Martian scene and those of his American boyhood may indicate that there is some order to the universe after all—that perhaps there is a supreme being who actually does guide and protect mankind.

Black agrees to investigate. Setting foot on Martian soil, the Captain enters a peaceful, delightful world. It is "a beautiful spring day" filled with the scent of blossoming flowers and the songs of birds. After the flux of space travel it must have appeared to have been a timeless, unchanging world—a static piece of the past. But Black is certain that this is Mars and persists in his attempt to find a rational explanation. His logical mind, however, makes it impossible for him to accept any facile solutions. Eventually, though, despite his intellectual rigor, the Captain begins to succumb to the charms of stasis:

In spite of himself, Captain John Black felt a great peace come over him. It had been thirty years since he had been in a small town, and the buzzing of spring bees on the air lulled and quieted him, and the fresh look of things was a balm to his soul.[1]

As soon as he begins to weaken, he learns, from a lemonade-sipping matron, that this is the year 1926 and that the village is Green Town, Illinois, Black's own home town. The Captain now *wants* to believe in what he sees and begins to delude himself by theorizing that an unknown early twentieth century expedition came to Mars and that the colonizers, desperately homesick, created such a successful image of an Earth-like reality that they had actually begun to believe that this illusion *was* reality. Ironically, this is precisely what is done by Black and his crew. And it kills them.

Since by this time the Earthmen had become completely vulnerable to the seductiveness of this world of security and stasis, they now unreservedly accept "Grandma Lustig's" claim that " 'all we know is here we are, alive again, and no questions asked. A second chance' " (p. 41). At this point the action moves rapidly. The remainder of the crew abandons ship and joins in a "homecoming" celebration. At first Black is furious at this breach of discipline, but soon loses his last trace of skepticism when he meets Edward, his long-dead "brother." Quickly, he is taken back to his childhood home, "the old house on Oak Knoll Avenue," where he is greeted by an archetypal set of midwestern parents: "In the doorway, Mom, pink, plump, and bright. Behind her, pepper-gray, Dad, his pipe in his hand" (p. 43). Joyfully the Captain runs "like a child" to meet them. But later, in the apparent security of the pennant-draped bedroom of his youth, Black's doubts arise anew. He begins to realize that all of this could be an elaborate reconstruction, culled from his psyche by some sophisticated Martian telepathy, created for the sole purpose of isolating the sixteen members of the Third Expedition. Recognizing the truth too late, the Captain is killed by his Martian brother as he leaves his boyhood "home" to return to the safety of the rocket ship.

Bradbury's point here is clear: Black and his men met their deaths because of their inability to forget, or at least resist, the past. Thus, the story of this Third Expedition acts as a metaphor for the book as a whole. Again and again the Earthmen make the fatal mistake of trying to recreate an Earth-like past rather than accept the fact that this is Mars—a different, unique new land in which they must be ready to make personal adjustments. Hauling Oregon lumber through space, then, merely to provide houses for nostalgic colonists exceeds folly; it is only one manifestation of a psychosis which leads to the destruction not only of Earth, but, with the exception of a few families, of Mars as well.

On the surface, at least, Bradbury's novel, *Dandelion Wine* (1959), bears little resemblance to the classic science fiction of *The Martian Chronicles*. The setting is not Mars or some even more remote corner of the universe, but Green Town, Illinois, a familiar, snug American home town, obviously the Waukegan of the author's own childhood. The time is not the distant future but the summer of 1928. Neither are there any exotic alien characters, but instead, a cast of middle-Americans resembling more a Norman Rockwell painting than science fiction; and the novel's protagonist, rather than being a galaxy-spanning super-hero, is only Douglas Spaulding, a twelve-year-old boy more in the tradition of Tom Sawyer than Flash Gordon. In some ways, in fact, the novel seems to be anti-science fiction. A "time machine" is not, as one would expect, a marvel of science and technology, but an old man. And a so-called "happiness machine" built by the local inventor is a failure, whereas the true happiness machine is that foundation of Green Town life, the family. But despite the fact that it cannot be called science fiction, *Dandelion Wine* closely resembles *The Martian Chronicles* and much of Bradbury's other writing in that it is essentially concerned with the same issue—the dilemma created by the dual attractions of the past and the future, of stasis and change.

In *Dandelion Wine* Bradbury uses the experiences of his adolescent protagonist during one summer to dramatize this set of philosophical and psychological conflicts. At twelve, Douglas Spaulding finds himself on the rim of adolescence. On one side of him lies the secure, uncomplicated world of childhood, while on the other is the fascinating yet frightening world of "growing up." For Doug the summer of 1928 begins with the dizzying discovery that he is "alive." With this new awareness of self comes a desire to experience as much of life as possible. To aid him in this quest, to give him the speed needed to keep up with the fast moving flow of experience, Doug buys a new pair of "Cream-Sponge Para Litefoot Shoes" which will make him so fast that, as he tells the shoe salesman, " 'you'll see twelve of me.' "[2] " 'Feel those shoes, Mr. Sanderson,' " Douglas asks, " '*feel* how fast they'd make me? All those springs inside? Feel how they kind of grab hold and can't let you alone and don't like you just standing there?' " (p. 17). Clearly Doug is ready to move and to grow. In his new sneakers he welcomes the flux.

Soon, however, just when his shoes are getting broken in, Douglas learns that motion and change are not always good. As he is hiking with John Huff, his best friend, he is suddenly attracted by an opposite force:

Douglas walked thinking it would go on this way forever. The perfection, the roundness . . . all of it was complete, everything could be touched, things stayed near, things were at hand and would remain (p. 78).

Soon, this attraction to stasis was considerably increased when John informed Douglas that he and his family were leaving town. It is at this point that Doug comes to fully realize the dangers of movement and change:.

For John was running, and this was terrible. Because if you ran, time ran. . . . The only way to keep things slow was to watch everything and do nothing! You could stretch a day to three days sure, just by watching (p. 81).

Faced now with the realization that change has a negative, destructive edge, Doug attempts to bring about stasis. The boys play "statues," a game in which the players must remain stationary until released by the player who is "it." But Douglas takes the game far more seriously than John. He attempts to use it to keep John from leaving, and when his friend protests that " 'I got to go,' " Douglas snaps, " 'Freeze.' " Finally John flees, leaving Doug as the statue, listening to his friend's footsteps merging with the pounding of his own heart. " 'Statues are best,' " he thinks to himself. " 'They're the only things you can keep on your own. Don't ever let them move. Once you do, you can't do a thing with them' " (p. 83).

At this point the attractions of stasis have become greater than those of process and change. He is now drawn, with greater frequency, to "Summer's Ice House," just as he becomes more interested in the static world of his brother's statistical charts. His visits to hear the stories of olden times told by Colonel Freeleigh (himself rigidly confined to a wheelchair) become ever more frequent. And the inticements of a timeless, pastoral life become more difficult to resist, as the day when Doug accompanied Mr. Tridden, the conductor, on a last trolley ride to the end of the line (buses were being brought in to move poeple *faster*). This was a day devoid of movement, "a drifting, easy day, nobody rushing, and the forest all about, the sun held in one position . . ." (p. 76). Douglas is also increasingly drawn to the local penny arcade, a place which offers him the security that only repetition and stasis can bring. This was "a world completely set in place, predictable, certain, sure." Here, the various exhibits were frozen, activated only occasionally. Here the Keystone Kops were "forever in collision or near-collision with train, truck, streetcar," and here there were "worlds within worlds, the penny peek shows which you cranked to repeat old rites and formulas" (p. 147).

But just as he learned of the negative aspects of change, so Douglas, in his summer of discovery, becomes aware of the dangers of stasis. His friends believe that the ice house is the abode of "the Lonely One"—Bradbury's corny personification of death. Even pastoralism held dangers. As an intensification of this pastoral world, the ravine which cut through town was even more threatening and ominous than the ice plant. Emitting "a dark-sewer, rotten-foliage, thick green odor," this ravine goes beyond stasis, suggesting death and decay (p. 29). The pastoral mode evoked a similar feeling in old Helen Loomis, a woman who had enjoyed several "long green afternoons" in her garden with Bill Forester, a young newspaperman who, like Douglas, was fascinated by stasis. Wise from her ninety-five years of life, Miss Loomis gives Forester advice which might well apply to Doug as well:

You shouldn't be here this afternoon. This is a street which ends only in an Egyptian pyramid. Pyramids are all very nice, but mummies are hardly fit companions (p. 110).

What she is telling Forester is that stasis, although alluring, leads to petrification and death, a fact which Douglas, himself, was soon to learn in the arcade.

As he sees the Tarot Witch "frozen" in her "glass coffin," Douglas suddenly shivers with understanding. He now perceives the connections between stasis and non-being. The fortune teller is actually trapped in her glass tomb, brought to life only when someone slips a coin in the slot. This creates in Douglas the awareness that just as he is alive, so "someday, I, Douglas Spaulding, must die" (p. 145). Seeing the similarity in his and the witch's situations, he becomes obsessed with freeing her from the spell in which she has been cast by "Mr. Black," the arcade owner. Ironically, Douglas is successful in liberating her (he shatters the case) but he, himself, falls into a spell—a deep and mysterious coma. So as the cicadas herald those late summer midwestern days when time seems suspended, Douglas' condition approaches stasis.

Bradbury seems to be reiterating what he has said in *The Martian Chronicles*—that the past, or stasis, or both, is enticing but deadly, and that Douglas, like the colonists, must forsake the past and give himself up to change and progress. But it is not so simple and clear-cut. Douglas recovers and is once again ready to grow and develop. But what brings him out of his coma is a swallow of a liquid which Mr. Jonas, the junk man, has concocted out of pieces of the past (such as Arctic air from the year 1900). With this development, Bradbury's thesis seems to fall to pieces, for Douglas is saved for the future by the past. He is liberated from a static condition by bottled stasis. The ambiguous nature of his recovery is further compounded by the strange, anti-climactic nature of the last chapters of the novel in which Bradbury indulges in a nostalgic celebration of old-fashioned family life. This conclusion so detracts from the story of Doug and his rebirth that one can only conclude that the author was confused, or more probably ambivalent, about these past-future, stasis-change dichotomies.

It is evident, then, that in *Dandelion Wine,* Bradbury began to become aware of the complexity of his subject. Where in *The Martian Chronicles* he seemed confident in his belief that a meaningful future could only be realized by rejecting the past, in this later novel he appears far less certain about the relative values of the past and stasis. Perhaps in this regard Bradbury can be seen as representative of a whole generation of middle class Americans who have found themselves alternately attracted to the security of an idealized, timeless, and static past (as the current nostalgia vogue illustrates) and the exciting, yet threatening and disruptive future world of progress and change, especially technological change. One might see in his leaving the provincial security and simplicity of Waukegan, his Green Town, as a youth and traveling cross country into the modern, futuristic setting of Los Angeles just how this conflict might have taken hold of Bradbury's mind and imagination.

But one may also go beyond these personal and sociological explanations for his obsession with this subject and place it within an aesthetic context. As a genre, science fiction (and my comments on *Dandelion Wine* notwithstanding, Bradbury is primarily a science fiction writer) must deal with the future and with technological progress. This is its lifeblood and what gives it its distinctiveness. In order to enter the future, however, if only in a theoretical, purely speculative sense, one is forced to come to grips with the past. Change and progress call for a rejection and a sloughing off. This places a great stress upon the science fiction writer, for perhaps more than any other literary genre, science fiction is dependent upon traditions—its own conventions of character, plot, setting, "special effects," even ideas. It is as stylized an art form as one can find today in America. It is therefore ironic that such a conventionalized genre should be called upon to be concerned with the unconventional—with the unpredictability of change and process. In other words, this stasis-change conflict, besides being a function of Bradbury's own history and personality, also seems to be built into the art form itself. What distinguishes Bradbury and gives his works their depth is that he seems to be aware that a denial of the past demands a denial of that part of the self which is the past. As an examination of *I Sing the Body Electric*, his latest collection of short stories, will show, he has not been able to come to any lasting conclusion. Instead, he has come to recognize the ambiguity, the complexity, and the irony within this theme.

Of the stories in *I Sing the Body Electric* which develop the idea that the past is destructive and must be rejected before peace can be achieved, the most intense and suggestive is "Night Call Collect." In this grim little tale, eighty-year-old Emil Barton has been living for the past sixty years as the last man on Mars when he is shocked to receive a telephone call from, of all people, himself. In the depths of his loneliness Barton had tinkered with the possibilities of creating a disembodied voice which might autonomously carry on conversations. Now suddenly in the year 2097, long after he had forgotten about this youthful diversion, his past, in the form of his younger self, contacts him. Finding himself in a world peopled only by the permutations of his own self, the "elder" Barton tries desperately to break out of this electronic solipsism. He fails, however, and begins to feel "the past drowning him."[3] Soon his younger self even becomes bold enough to warn him, " 'All right, old man, its war! Between us. Between me' " (p. 128). Bradbury has obviously added a new twist to his theme. Instead of the future denying the past, it is reversed. Now the past, in order to maintain its existence, must kill off the present. Young Barton now tells his "future" self that he " 'had to eliminate you some way, so I could live, if you call a transcription living' " (p. 131). As the old man dies, it is obvious that Bradbury has restated his belief that the past, if held on to too tightly, can destroy. But there is an added dimension here. At the end of the story it is no longer clear which is the past, which is the present, and which is the future. Is the past the transcribed voice of the "younger" twenty-four-year-old, or is it the *old* man living at a later date in time? Or perhaps they are but two manifestations of the same temporal reality, both the "present" and the "future" being forgotten?

Of the stories in this collection one contradicts "Night Call Collect" by developing the idea that the past can be a positive, creative force. "I Sing the Body Electric" opens with the death of a mother. But, as in so many of Bradbury's writings, there is a possibility of a second chance. "Fantocinni, Ltd." offers "the first humanoid-genre minicircuited, rechargable AC-DC Mark V Electrical Grandmother" (p. 154). This time the second chance succeeds: the electric grandmother is the realization of a child's fantasy. She can gratify all desires and pay everyone in the family all the attention he or she wants. Appropriately, the grandmother arrives at the house packed in a "sarcaphagous," as if it were a mummy. Despite the pun, the machine is indeed a mummy, as the narrator makes clear:

We knew that all our days were stored in her, and that any time we felt we might want to know what we said at x hour at x second at x afternoon, we just named that x and with amiable promptitude . . . she should deliver forth x incident (p. 172).

The sarcaphagous in which this relic was packed was covered with "hieroglyphics of the future." At first this seems to be only another of those gratuitous "special effects" for which science fiction writers are so notorious. After further consideration, however, those arcane markings can be seen a symbol for the kind of ultra-sophisticated technology of which the grandmother is an example. Thus, both the future and the past are incarnated within the body of this machine. The relationship between the two is important, for what the story seems to suggest is that what the future (here seen as technological progress) will bring is the static, familiar, secure world of the past.

There is one other story in this collection which is important because in it is found one of Bradbury's most sophisticated expositions of the subtle complexities of this theme. "Downwind from Gettysburg" is, once again, a tale about a second chance. Using the well-known Disneyland machine as his model, Bradbury's story concerns a mechanical reproduction of Abraham Lincoln. In itself, this Lincoln-robot is a good thing. The past has been successfully captured and the beloved President lives again, if only in facsimile. Within this limited framework, then, the "past" is a positive force. But there are complications, for just as Lincoln gets a second chance, so does his murderer. Just as John Wilkes Booth assassinated a Lincoln, so does Norman Llewellyn Booth. Thus, as Bradbury had discovered through his years of working with this theme, the past is not one-dimensional. It is at once creative and destructive. It can give comfort, and it can unsettle and threaten. Clearly, then, this story is an important one within Bradbury's canon, for it is just this set of realizations which he had been steadily coming to during two decades of writing.

James Gunn

HENRY KUTTNER, C. L. MOORE, LEWIS PADGETT *ET AL.*

The year was 1942. The attack on Pearl Harbor was a few weeks in the past. The United States had declared war on Japan and Germany, and was in the midst of frantic military preparations. Men were volunteering for service; others were being drafted.

Even science fiction was affected. L. Ron Hubbard's *Final Blackout* had been serialized in *Astounding* in 1940. Robert Heinlein's prophetic atomic weapon story, "Solution Unsatisfactory" (published under the pseudonym of Anson MacDonald), appeared in 1941. These were only the leading edge of a wave of war-related stories; the science fiction magazines, too, were being retooled for war.

By 1942 John Campbell had been editor of *Astounding Science Fiction* for five years. Three major new writers had come into prominence in 1937 and 1938: Eric Frank Russell, L. Sprague de Camp, and Lester del Rey. Four more had been introduced in *Astounding* in 1939: Isaac Asimov, Robert Heinlein, Theodore Sturgeon, and A. E. van Vogt. Together with other writers (and a decade later, with other editors and magazines), they would begin

185

the development of what has become known as modern science fiction and the creation of what some have called science fiction's "golden age."

By 1942 Heinlein was well launched into his "future history" stories (he had completed all of them that would appear in *Astounding*) and had nearly perfected his major technical innovation—the naturalistic revelation of carefully constructed future societies. Asimov had brought his scientific mind to bear upon the explication and codification of science fiction concepts, had launched one major series (his robot stories), and had written the first two stories in his "Foundation" series (although they would not appear for some months). Sturgeon had completed a series of highly personal stories, mostly fantasy, and one significant science fiction story, "Microcosmic God." Van Vogt had created a major impact both with his superman and superpowers themes and with his breakneck, scenic style.

But by the beginning of 1942, or shortly thereafter, Heinlein had joined the Naval Air Experimental Station of the U. S. Navy Yard in Philadelphia as a civilian engineer, where L. Sprague de Camp, followed by Asimov, came to join him. Sturgeon had gone to the British West Indies in 1941, managed some mess halls and barracks for the Army, operated a gas station, and was to take a job as a bulldozer operator on an island where he remained until 1944. Van Vogt had become a clerk in the Canadian Department of National Defense but continued to write; after *Slan* appeared in 1940, however, little of significance was published (with the single exception of "The Seesaw") until "Recruiting Station" in March 1942.

As a direct result of the war, then, only three Heinlein stories (all under his Anson MacDonald pseudonym) appeared in *Astounding* in 1942 and none thereafter; only two Asimov stories were published in *Astounding* in 1942, one in 1943, three in 1944, and a scattering thereafter; only one Sturgeon story appeared in *Astounding* in 1942, and twelve in the years thereafter, beginning with "Killdozer!" in November 1944. Van Vogt continued his production with seven stories in 1942 and a substantial number in the years up to 1950.

But if some inputs into *Astounding* were dwindling, one was to start up in 1942. It would be a significant event in the evolution of science fiction: the publication of three stories over the name of an author never before published anywhere—Lewis Padgett —"Deadlock" (August); "The Twonky" (September); and "Piggy Bank" (December). In addition, C. L. Moore, a familiar name in fantasy though not unknown in science fiction, had a story, "There Shall Be Darkness" in the February issue.

The following year *Astounding* published eight stories by Padgett, one short story and two short-shorts by Henry Kuttner, a two-part serial by C. L. Moore, and a story by Lawrence O'Donnell; in 1944, one by Padgett, one by Moore, and one by O'Donnell; in 1945, seven by Padgett and one by O'Donnell; in 1946, six by Padgett and two by O'Donnell; in 1947, four by Padgett and one by O'Donnell; in 1948, one by Padgett; in 1949, two by Padgett; in 1950, three by O'Donnell; and in 1953, one by Padgett. These stories, as well as dozens of others published in other magazines, some under other names, were written, of course, by two authors, Henry Kuttner and Catherine Moore, who were at the time these stories appeared—and until Kuttner's death in 1958— Mr. and Mrs. Henry Kuttner.

As Lewis Padgett and Lawrence O'Donnell—and under their own names—they helped carry *Astounding* through the war years. More important, they contributed substantially to the evolution of science fiction during the formative early stages of the modern period.

The accidents and influences that bring two people together are always mysterious in retrospect. Thomas Wolfe noted in the opening sentence of *Look Homeward, Angel*:

A destiny that leads the English to the Dutch is strange enough; but one that leads from Epsom to Pennsylvania, and thence into the hills that shut in Altamount over the proud coral cry of the cock, and the soft stone smile of an angel, is touched by that dark miracle of chance which makes new magic in a dusty world.

The inexplicable workings of chance or the inevitable operations of destiny brought together an Indianapolis bank secretary and a sometime Los Angeles literary agent turned fantasy writer to make not just a marriage but at least two different major literary gestalts. Or, more precisely, fantasy introduced Henry Kuttner to Catherine Moore.

Catherine Moore was born in Indianapolis in 1911. Her childhood and adolescence were marred by periodic illness; her necessary withdrawals from a more active life—like H. G. Wells's famous broken leg—may have opened to her an inner world of books and stories, particularly Greek mythology, the *Oz* books, and Edgar Rice Burroughs. In 1931 she discovered *Amazing Stories*. "From that moment on," she has recalled, "I was a convert. A whole new field of literature opened out before my admiring gaze, and the urge to imitate it was irresistible."[1]

She attended Indiana University for a year and a half, but the Depression forced her to take a job as a secretary in a bank. She wrote in her spare time, and in 1933 produced and had published in the November 1933, issue of *Weird Tales*, her first story. It became a fantasy classic, "Shambleau." Over the next few years she continued to write romantic fantasies for *Weird Tales*, featuring such epic characters as Northwest Smith and Jirel of Joiry, but she also was having some success with science fiction, selling four stories to *Astounding* between 1934 and 1939.

Henry Kuttner was born in 1914 in Los Angeles, where his father ran a book store. His father died when Kuttner was five, and he spent his early years in San Francisco. He moved back to Los Angeles about the time he entered high school. Like Catherine Moore, he went from the *Oz* books to Edgar Rice Burroughs and then to *Amazing Stories* in 1926. Upon graduation from high school, he began working for a Los Angeles literary agency run by a cousin. His enthusiasm for *Weird Tales* fantasy brought him into contact with the Lovecraft circle of correspondents, and his first publications were in *Weird Tales*: first a poem, "Ballad of the Gods" in February 1936, and then "The Graveyard Rats" in March. He became a regular contributor to *Weird Tales* and to such hybrid magazines as *Strange Stories* and *Thrilling Mysteries*. Kuttner began to write science fiction stories in 1937, with publications in *Thrilling Wonder Stories*, *Marvel Science Stories*, and one in *Astounding*, "The Disinherited" (August 1938).

Five years into his career Kuttner seemed primarily a fantasy writer—certainly his fantasy writing represented not only the bulk of his production but the chief source of his reputation—and in 1939 when *Astounding* brought out its sister fantasy magazine, *Unknown*, Kuttner began to contribute stories immediately: one in 1939, two in 1940, 1941, 1942, and 1943. Moore contributed one story in 1940.

In 1938, through the Lovecraft circle, Kuttner had become acquainted with the Indianapolis writer, C. L. Moore, and had begun to visit Indianapolis on his trips between New York and Los Angeles. In 1939 he quit his job with the literary agency and moved in with his mother in New York City to write full time.

On June 7, 1940, in New York, Henry Kuttner and Catherine Moore were married. They lived there a year before moving to Laguna Beach, California. In 1942 Kuttner entered the Medical Corps and served until 1945 at Fort Monmouth, New Jersey. His wife lived nearby in Red Bank. After the war they bought a house at Hastings-on-Hudson, New York; in 1948 they could afford to move back to Laguna Beach. There Kuttner attended the University of Southern California, with the aid of the G. I. Bill; he earned a bachelor's degree in three and a half years, and had nearly completed a master's degree in English (he was going to write a thesis on the works of H. Rider Haggard) when he had a heart attack and died on February 4, 1958. Moore also attended Southern Cal; she earned a bachelor's degree in 1956 and a master's in 1963, also in English.

After her husband's death, Moore completed the screenplay for "Rappacini's Daughter" that they had been writing for Warner Brothers, and later wrote scripts for such television shows as "Maverick" and "77 Sunset Strip." She also picked up the teaching of Kuttner's writing course at U.S.C. and continued it two mornings a week for four years. She married Thomas Reggie in 1963, and lives in Los Angeles.

The marriage of Henry Kuttner and Catherine Moore was more than a wedding of man and woman; it also was a fusion of writers into a series of *personas* that may represent a unique experience in collaboration. In an introduction to a recent paperback edition of *Fury*, Moore wrote, "We collaborated on almost everything we wrote, but in varying degrees."[2] And in a private letter, she wrote, "Everything we wrote between 1940 and 1958, when Hank died, was a collaboration. Well, almost everything."

"It worked like this," Moore wrote in that introduction to *Fury*:

After we'd established through long discussion the basic ideas, the background and the characters, whichever of us felt like it sat down and started. When that one ran down, the other, being fresh to the story, could usually see what ought to come next, and took over. The action developed as we went along. We kept changing off like this until we finished. A story goes very fast that way.

Each of us edited the other's copy a little when we took over, often going back a line or two and rephrasing to make the styles blend. We never disagreed seriously over the work. The worst clashes of opinion I can remember ended with one of us saying, 'Well, I don't agree, but since you feel more strongly than I do about it, go ahead.' (When the rent is due tomorrow, one tends toward quick, peaceful settlements.)

Either separately or together, Kuttner and Moore used seventeen different pennames: the principal ones were Paul Edmonds, Keith Hammond, Hudson Hastings, Kelvin Kent, C. H. Liddell, Lawrence O'Donnell, Lewis Padgett, and Woodrow Wilson Smith. Donald B. Day, in his *Index to the Science Fiction Magazines 1926-1950*, lists another seven, most of which may have been "house" names.[3]

The Lewis Padgett pseudonym was adopted, probably, at the suggestion of Robert Heinlein, as a rate-raising device, not, as Sam Moskowitz has stated, "because of his tarnished reputation."[4] It was the Kuttners' first deliberately chosen communal name, and it was placed on stories that hoped to command the Kuttners' top going rate. "If the editor wouldn't pay," Moore has written in a private letter, "he had to use one of many other pseudonyms, and there were so many because we were producing so much copy in the 1940's that often we had two or three stories in the same issue of a magazine, and it looked rather stupid to use the Kuttner name three times in the table of contents. So either we or the editor would pick alternative names more or less out of thin air."

One of the names, Hudson Hastings, was picked because the Kuttners at that time were living in Hastings-on-Hudson. C. H. Liddell began as the author of "The Sky Is Falling" and "was simply the formal name of Chicken Little."

But the only important pseudonyms, Moore recalls, were Lewis Padgett and Lawrence O'Donnell. Neither name appeared outside the pages of *Astounding*, except for later reprints. O'Donnell "emerged gradually as the name we used for many of our more favorite stories. And gradually it became the one we used for those which were mostly mine. I didn't use C. L. Moore except in very rare cases, because I just didn't feel these were C. L. M. stories we were writing, but I could feel comfortable as Lawrence O'D."

As an illustration of how pseudonyms came into being, take 1943, the Kuttners' most prolific year in *Astounding*, when they had thirteen stories, including a two-part serial, plus two contributions by Kuttner to a department of short-short stories called "Probability Zero." In January Lewis Padgett was represented by "Time Locker," the first of the Gallegher stories, and Henry Kuttner had to use his own name on "Nothing But Gingerbread Left," the first story in *Astounding* under his name since 1938. In February Lewis Padgett had a story called "Mimsy Were the Borogoves" and Henry Kuttner had to be pressed into service again for the "Probability Zero" offering called "Blue Ice." The same situation prevailed in March, with a Lewis Padgett story entitled "Shock" and a Henry Kuttner short-short in "Probability Zero" called "Corpus Delicti." But a third Kuttner story that month demanded a new name: Lawrence O'Donnell was invented as author of "Clash by Night," which contained the first mention of the Venus undersea "keeps" and would provide setting and background for the later novel *Fury*. The Kuttners had stories, but no conflicts, in the April, May, June, October, November, and December issues; but another problem arose in the August issue: Padgett had a story called "Endowment Policy" and the Kuttners had a two-part serial beginning—it appeared under the name of C. L. Moore and was called "Judgment Night." Much later, so intimately had Moore become identified with her favorite pseudonym that she could not recall whether "Judgment Night" had not, in fact, appeared under the name O'Donnell.[5]

During the period between 1942 and 1947, Kuttner and Moore contributed forty-one stories to *Astounding*—forty-eight by 1955—including three two-part serials and one three-part serial. The significance of their contribution, however, lies not in the quantity nor in the continuation of the thrust of Campbell's new ideas about science fiction through difficult years, although these factors are meaningful. They were one (or two or four) of the finest writers to marry magazine science fiction to literary form, to do it sufficiently often to be noticeable and effective, and to do it—though perhaps without deliberate intent—with increasing skill.

They did it so effectively that two of their stories—one by Lewis Padgett and one by Lawrence O'Donnell—were selected by their fellow science fiction writers for inclusion in *The Science Fiction Hall of Fame.*[6] And their contributions to the wartime magazine period sustained the level of that "golden age" which had begun around 1938 or 1939.

The Kuttners built their reputations slowly: novels, though not the ideal form for science fiction, are the quickest and most spectacular routes to recognition. The Kuttners were primarily authors of short stories and novelettes. They produced only one significant novel, *Fury* (1947). But their shorter works created an immediate impact upon readers and writers alike, and made a substantial contribution to the development of science fiction.

Contributions to the development of science fiction can be categorized in several ways: in terms of content and technique; in terms of source; and in terms of the change, evolutionary or revolutionary.

Editors have exerted a disproportionate influence on the field because the science fiction magazines were virtually the only medium for science fiction in the United States between 1926 and 1946, and predominantly the medium between 1946 and 1960. A history of American science fiction cannot be written without substantial discussion of the contributions of Hugo Gernsback, John W. Campbell, Anthony Boucher, and Horace Gold, to mention only the major figures. The editors served not only as gate-keepers, deciding what would get through to the public, but in the case of Campbell, Boucher, and Gold they intervened in the creative process and actively helped shape science fiction to their desires through suggestions to authors, requests for particular kinds of stories or rewrites, and sometimes rewriting by others, including the editor himself.

But they could not do the writing, and sometimes they were surprised by unexpected contributions through which the writers themselves shaped the direction in which science fiction would go. Even though these new developments usually fit into the policy already set by the editor, or were recognized by him as a logical extension of that policy, sometimes they helped reshape that policy through innovations in content or technique.

In just this way Heinlein would bring to science fiction a method of constructing future societies and revealing them, from within, by the use of naturalistic detail; Asimov would bring his analytical mind to bear upon the myths and conventions of traditional science fiction, and would begin a process of codification and logical consideration exemplified in his robot series; van Vogt would bring to science fiction the narrative techniques of John Gallishaw and Thomas Uzzell, and his own "intensively recomplicated story," as James Blish has called it. And Theodore Sturgeon would pursue his own individual style and ideas wherever they led.

These same four authors would also pioneer in subject matter: Heinlein through his "future history" of the next two hundred years and his engineer-heroes; Asimov through his robot stories and his Foundation and its psychohistory; van Vogt with his supermen and superpowers, as well as his treatment of science as magic; and Sturgeon, ultimately, with his treatment of the varieties of love and sexual experience.

The ways in which a genre develops can be further divided into abrupt breaks with the past (Campbell's emphasis on an accurate representation of the scientific and engineering culture was something of a revolution, as was Gold's emphasis on the reactions of the average citizen, and the New Wave was an even greater departure in style, viewpoint, and subject matter) or a slow evolution. As Darko Suvin has pointed out in *Science Fiction Studies,* "A literary genre is a collective system of expectations in the readers' minds, stemming from their past experience with a certain type of writing, so that even its violations—the innovations by which every genre evolves—can be understood only against the backdrop of such a system."[7]

Evolutionary development comes about through increments of new areas of experience or imaginative concept. Edward Elmer (Doc) Smith, for instance, brought into science fiction the concept of universe-wide civilizations. Stanley Weinbaum brought realism to the romantic concept of aliens. Dr. David H. Keller added a concern for psychology, which the Kuttners would later reinforce. After 1946 when Groff Conklin lamented "the paucity of stories dealing with the social sciences and with the sciences of the mind," both subsequently were brought more fully into science fiction by a variety of writers, particularly, after 1949, in *Galaxy.*

Frederik Pohl and Cyril Kornbluth brought into science fiction (or brought back) the anti-utopia. Currently science fiction is expanding into biology and genetics.

What the Kuttners brought to science fiction, which broadened it and helped it evolve, was a concern for literary skill and culture. The Kuttners expanded the techniques of science fiction to include techniques prevalent in the mainstream; they expanded its scope to include the vast cultural tradition available outside science fiction, just as, in their ways, Heinlein would draw upon and bring into his fiction the engineering and military education he received at Annapolis, Asimov would open to science fiction the concepts and methods of the working scientist, and Hal Clement and Larry Niven would expand science fiction into the physical sciences in such works as *A Mission of Gravity* and *Ringworld*. The significance of the Kuttners' work rests in the fact that much of the development in science fiction over the past twenty years has come along the lines they pioneered.

This is not to say that everything the Kuttners wrote (not even the stories they wrote for *Astounding*) was without precedent; certainly man's cultural heritage and a concern for style were a part of science fiction in its beginnings, in the work, for instance, of Mary Shelley and Edgar Allan Poe, both of whom, directly or indirectly, benefited from a classical English education. And there was H. G. Wells. But those classical and literary traditions were lost in the science fiction ghetto created by Hugo Gernsback in 1926; they were replaced by newer pulp traditions of action and adventure, and eventually of scientific accuracy and informed speculation about one science after another, beginning with geography and mesmerism and progressing through chemistry, electricity, physics, and mathematics to computers, psychology, sociology, and biology.

Many areas of human experience, as contrasted with human knowledge, were considered unimportant or inappropriate to science fiction, either consciously—as in the case of sexual relationships and such other basic functions as eating and excreting—or unconsciously in areas in which writers were unaware or uneasy, such as cultural traditions and stylistic methods.

In the latter areas the Kuttners moved with growing skill and familiarity. Insofar as one can disentangle the gestalts they created, Moore seems to have contributed most of the unusual romantic involvements and perhaps all the classical references to myth, legend, and literature which served to expand and enrich the Kuttners' best work. Kuttner provided insights into the minds of children—he seemed to have a particular fondness for what has become known as the generation gap—and his literary references, perhaps appropriately, were almost entirely restricted to *Alice in Wonderland* and *Through the Looking Glass.*

I intend to examine a number of the Kuttners' stories, almost all of which were printed in *Astounding.* I believe that the magazine and the stories printed in it had the greatest influence on the development of the field between 1938 and 1950. Stories printed in other magazines usually were *Astounding* rejects, and even when original and effective (some were outside Campbell's definition and others slipped through one of the chinks in his editorial judgment) and possibly individually significant, they never had the cumulative impact of *Astounding* stories. I will proceed chronologically, examining each story for subject, theme, and technique.

Kuttner had one story in *Astounding* in 1938 (August), "The Disinherited"; Moore had four prior to their marriage: "The Bright Illusion" (October 1934), "Greater Glories" (September 1935), "Tryst in Time" (December 1936), and "Greater than Gods" (July 1939).

As fantasy writers, the Kuttners were attracted first to the new *Unknown,* introduced by Campbell as a companion fantasy magazine to *Astounding* with the issue of March 1939. Kuttner's "The Misguided Halo" appeared in the August issue. In April 1940, two months before their marriage, came Kuttner's "All Is Illusion"; in October, Moore's "Fruit of Knowledge"; and in December, Kuttner's "Threshold." In 1941 *Unknown* (it would change its name to *Unknown Worlds* with its October issue) published Kuttner's "The Devil We Know" (August) and "A Gnome There Was" (October); in 1942, "Design for Dreaming" (February) and "Compliments of the Author" (October); and in 1943, when *Unknown Worlds* discontinued publication, probably because of the paper shortage, "Wet Magic" (February) and "No Greater Love" (April).

But after their marriage the Kuttners turned most of their efforts toward science fiction, particularly during the 1942-1945 period when Kuttner was serving in the Medical Corps in New Jersey. "There Shall Be Darkness" (February 1942) by Moore was the first, followed by "Deadlock" (August 1942), "The Twonky" (September 1942), and "Piggy Bank" (December 1942), all by Lewis Padgett.

"The Twonky" was a memorable story frequently anthologized and adapted for other media. What makes it distinctive is its domestic setting and matter-of-fact tone; into this situation is introduced a console radio-record player. Kerry Westerfield, a likeable professor at the university, does not know that it is actually a Twonky, manufactured by a workman from the future who was caught in a temporal snag and, while under partial amnesia, created a Twonky with the materials at hand in a radio factory. The Twonky analyzes Westerfield, performs services for him—such as lighting his cigarette and washing the dishes—and then begins to censor his reading and his personal habits. Westerfield's reactions run through amazement, interest, and finally consternation. In the end, the Twonky blocks his friend's memory, destroys his wife when she starts toward it with a hatchet, and then disintegrates Westerfield when he attacks it, saying, "Subject basically unsuitable. Elimination has been necessary." And then, "Preparation for next subject completed." The story ends with a newly married couple looking over the house and admiring the console.

The story is pleasantly and efficiently told, with some effective references to music and literature (including *Alice in Wonderland*). "The Twonky" suggests one other observation: without its introductory exposition about the Twonky's origin, "The Twonky" would have a Kafkaesque mainstream quality; explanations seem to be one aspect which distinguishes science fiction from mainstream stories. The mainstream cherishes its ambiguity.

"Piggy Bank" includes significant mythological references, as well as an unusual plot for science fiction: Ballard, a robber baron who has climbed to power with a stolen, secret process for manufacturing diamonds, finds his empire threatened by a series of seemingly unstoppable diamond thefts probably conducted by a criminal gang encouraged by a rival baron. He instructs his technological genius, Gunther, who makes the diamonds for him and protects the secret for his own survival, to make him a diamond-studded, invulnerable gold robot conditioned for self-preservation through flight, thus providing Ballard with a piggy bank containing all the wealth he will need in any emergency. When Gunther delivers the robot, Ballard calls it "Argus" because "his eyes had diamond lenses, specially chosen for their refractive powers":

He was blazingly beautiful, a figure out of myth. In a bright light he resembled Apollo more than Argus. He was a god come to Earth, the shower of gold that Danae saw.[8]

Secure at last, Ballard has Gunther killed in such a way that he tricks from Gunther the telephone number of the man who is to make public the patent number of the diamond-making process. But Ballard's business rival begins to assault his commerical castle, and Ballard must obtain some of the diamonds from Argus. The phrase, "implanted in Argus," fails to stop the robot from fleeing, and a posthumous note from Gunther informs Ballard that the key phrase will not work unless Gunther has made a daily adjustment. Argus cannot be captured by any of Ballard's ingenious traps; at last he finds himself ruined in the presence of riches. In final desperation, surrounded by his rival's guards, he shouts at Argus the phrase relayed through his rival from Gunther—the phrase that will immobilize Argus but make all its diamonds worthless—the patent number of the artificial diamond process.

A critic might quibble with the plot. Like the Doomsday machine in "Dr. Strangelove," the fact that Gunther needed to re-indoctrinate Argus every day should not have been kept secret if Gunther wished to continue living; but the writing and the concept are excellent, and the imagery is refreshing. In "Piggy Bank," also, we see at work a narrative method which Kuttner perfected, if he did not invent—a method which James Blish described in *The Issue at Hand*:

Padgett stories for years have begun in just this way: The narrative hook, almost always dealing with incipient violence, madness, or both; enough development of the hook to lead the story into a paradox; then a complete suspension of the story while the authors lecture the reader on the background for a short time, seldom more than 1,000 words. The lecture technique is generally taboo for fiction, especially in the hands of new writers, and only two science fiction writers have managed to get away with it and make the reader like it, Heinlein being the other.[9]

I'm not sure I would go along with all the specifics of Blish's outline, but I agree with its thrust; the Kuttners were masters of plot, and their manipulation of exposition was masterly. In the expository section of "Piggy Bank," incidentally, the Kuttners (the story was largely Kuttner's) set down a background for a world similar to that which Pohl and Kornbluth would describe in greater detail ten years later in the more famous *The Space Merchants*:

The stranglehold of the robber barons was still strong. Each one wanted a monopoly, but, because they were all at war, a species of toppling chaos was the result. They tried desperately to keep their own ships afloat while sinking the enemy fleet. Science and government were handicapped by the Powers, which were really industrial empires, completely self-contained if not self-supporting units. Their semanticists and propagandists worked on the people, ladling out soothing sirup. All would be well later—when Ballard, or Ffoulkes, or All-Steel, or Unlimited Power took over. . . .[10]

In the Kuttners' big 1943 year, three of the thirteen stories —"Time Locker" (January), "The Proud Robot" (October), and "Gallegher Plus" (November)—belonged to Kuttner's series about the drunken inventor Gallegher (Galloway in the magazine version of "Time Locker") which later were collected into a book entitled *Robots Have No Tails*. A significant two-part serial by Moore, "Judgment Night," was published in August and September. Kuttner's "Clash by Night" introduced, for the first time, the concept of a Venus on which the land and its various life forms were so deadly that man had built his cities under impervium domes in the oceans. It contained, also, one of the early suggestions that an atomic accident might consume the Earth. Earth had been turned into another sun:

A star—all that remained of Earth, since atomic power had been unleashed there two centuries ago. The scourge had spread like flame, melting continents and leveling mountains.[11]

The concept would be used again by Kuttner, not only in *Fury*, the novel built upon the same background, but in the two-part 1947 serial, "Tomorrow and Tomorrow." In response to the catastrophe on Earth, scientists on Venus had outlawed atomic research and adopted a peculiarly modern "Minervan Oath":

. . . to work for the ultimate good of mankind . . . taking all precautions against harming humanity and science . . . requiring permission from those in authority before undertaking any experiment involving peril to the race . . . remembering always the extent of trust placed in us and remembering forever the death of the mother planet through misuse of knowledge. . . .[12]

However accidental the choice of the O'Donnell pseudonym, in the first of these stories some of the characteristics are apparent which would be developed and enlarged in later work to be published under that name: the use of chapter epigraphs, literary quotations, and mythological references (in this case to Greek gods Mars, Minerva, and Aphrodite); relatively complex characterization (in "Clash by Night," Captain Scott is torn between two different kinds of life and between his loyalty to his Free Companions and the military life and his knowledge that it is meaningless and doomed); and conflict and complication which are not altogether linear. The usual Kuttner story, even the customary Padgett narrative, is slick and controlled; "Clash by Night" approaches the texture of real life. Moore, in a private letter, attributes this first O'Donnell story to Kuttner, but internal evidence suggests that she may have had a significant hand in it.

In 1943 *Astounding* also published one of the Kuttner classics, the story which placed seventh for inclusion in *The Science Fiction Hall of Fame*, "Mimsy Were the Borogoves." "Mimsy . . ." introduced one of Kuttner's favorite notions: children are aliens. This quiet, controlled story begins with a scientist in the future stuffing into a time-travel device some of the toys which had helped his son "pass over from Earth"; Scott, the son of Dennis and Jane Paradine, discovers the faulty device, extracts the toys, and, along with his younger sister, Emma, begins to play with them. The toys teach Scott and Emma how to perceive and manipulate different kinds of space and relationships because, unlike adults, they're "not handicapped by too many preconceived ideas." Eventually, while their parents puzzle out what the children are doing, learning, and becoming, the children discover the way to pass over into a larger world through a strange physical parallel to the equation described in the *Through the Looking Glass* quatrain beginning " 'Twas brillig. . . ."

Science fiction and fantasy have discovered many ways to achieve conviction; science fiction, in particular, has struggled for verisimilitude. One fantasy technique is the final triumphant display of the key artifact, as in many a tale of horror: "He unwrapped the scrap of dirty yellow silk and I saw, nearly blinding me with its radiance, the diamond eye of the Hindu idol!" or "There in his hand was the tiny figure of a man only three inches high, *and he was alive!*" Science fiction refined and sophisticated the technique. Kuttner used it almost unchanged in "The Third Eye"—also called "Don't Look Now"—the frequently anthologized and dramatized 1948 *Startling Stories* tour-de-force which ends with the Martian opening his third eye and looking after the man leaving the bar. In "Mimsy . . ." Kuttner does it more subtly. A series of references to *Through the Looking Glass* leads to the revelation that Alice Liddell also had found a box of toys from the future (and the reader realizes that the opening section describes *two* time travel experiments) and that she had told Charles Dodgson the songs and verses which he sprinkled through the book he would later write.

Kuttner brought in other references: Hughes' *High Wind in Jamaica*, the nature of education, the spawning patterns of eels and salmon. And the quiet tone builds to a final climax in which the sensible father sees his son and daughter disappear like smoke. We feel his horror and his wife's horror yet to come, as well as the potential horror of the children when they arrive in a larger world where there are no adults and where they will be alone, possibly helpless, and afraid.

The next year, 1944, *Astounding* published only three stories by the Kuttners, but they all were important. "When the Bough Breaks" by Lewis Padgett plays upon the notion introduced in "Mimsy . . ." that children are aliens. Almost as soon as Kuttner has introduced Joe and Myra Calderon (Joe is a favorite Kuttner character, a reasonable, rational university professor) as the new parents of the infant Alexander, he insinuates that "babies are a great trial. Still they're worth it." But then goblin-like men from the future arrive at their door and acclaim Alexander as a mutant, the father of their race, and a long-lived "x-free superman" of the future. They have traveled through time to his childhood so that they can remove the frustrations Alexander suffered as a child and begin his education early enough that he can attain still greater feats of intellect and insight. Joe and Myra are unable to discipline Alexander, at first because of the powerful gadgets of the dwarfs from the future and then because of the growing powers of the infant superman. His parents can only watch nervously as Alexander grows more powerful but not more mature. He teases and torments his parents through his abilities of teleportation, telekinesis, and energy control, with "a child's normal cruelty and selfishness." One dwarf informs them:

'. . . tolerance for the young is an evolutionary trait aimed at providing for the superman's appearance. . . . Infants are awfully irritating. They're help-less for a very long time, a great trial to the patience of parents—the lower the order of animal, the faster the infant develops.'[13]

Joe and Myra realize they can look ahead to nineteen more years of torment as Alexander progresses socially from well-trained monkey to bushman to super-powerful cannibal and eventually to practical joker. Driven beyond endurance, they allow Alexander to play with a blue ovoid his dwarf mentor has forbidden him, and Alexander destroys himself.

Besides the insights into infant irritation and parental pa-tience, the story is enriched with references to biology ("partheno-genesis, binary fission") and mythology ("Deucalion and what's her name—that's us. Parents of a new race"; "I feel more like Prometheus. . . . He was helpful, too. And he ended up with a vulture eating his liver.") And the story includes comments about riddles, the nature of humor, and comic strips. Moore estimates that "When the Bough Breaks" was seventy per cent Kuttner.

"The Children's Hour" in the March issue was pure Moore, although published under the name of O'Donnell and apparently the first in which the O'Donnell pseudonym was used by choice rather than necessity. The story is a rich exploration of three months lost from the memory of a soldier named Lessing. Through hypnosis by a camp officer, Lessing begins to remember a strange and wonderful girl he had met and loved two years ago, a "glamorous" girl named Clarissa, whose presence made "a world a little brighter than human." Eventually, as he works his way back to their meetings and at last to their final parting, he realizes that Clarissa was a superbeing growing toward maturity on an infinity of worlds. "After that, the destiny of *homo superior* has no com-mon touching point with the understanding of *homo sapiens*. We knew them as children. And they passed. They put away childish things."

The narrative itself would be unexceptional without the decription of scene and situation which creates images in much the way Moore built them in the fantasy adventures of Northwest Smith:

In atmospheres of oxygen and halogen, in lands ringed with the shaking blaze of crusted stars beyond the power of our telescopes—beneath water, and in places of cold and darkness and void, the matrix repeated itself, and by the psychic and utterly unimaginable power and science of *homo superior*, the biological cycle of a race more than human ran and completed itself and began again. . . .[14]

Significantly, the story reflects more than the events it relates: an insight into the child's world ("Everything shone, everything glistened, every sound was sweeter and clearer; there was a sort of glory over all he saw and felt and heard. Childhood had been like that, when the newness of the world invested every commonplace with particular glamour.") and into the shared experience of mythology and literature, with quotations from Longfellow and Shakespeare and a comparison (again) to Danae when Lessing sees Clarissa standing in an impossible golden shower and compares her with Danae whom Zeus visited in a shower of gold.

The third story of 1944 would have made any writer's year; it became an instant classic. It was clearly Moore, and, in fact, was published under her own name: "No Woman Born." The story line is simple and effective: a lovely woman, a singer and actress, has been so horribly burned in a theater fire that her brain has had to be transferred into a metal body. Harris, her manager, is going to see her for the first time since the accident, a year before; he is reluctant because she had been so beautiful and now is cold and unfeeling metal. Maltzer, the scientist who had overseen the secret collaboration of artists, sculptors, designers, and scientists that had constructed her new body, is worried about how Deirdre will appear to the public and how she, in turn, will react to that reaction. This concern builds throughout the novelette—through Deirdre's ability to project an image of herself as a beautiful woman, her desire to perform in public again, her triumphant return to the stage with a single dance and a single song, Maltzer's apprehension that Deirdre is worried, and his final attempt at suicide as punishment for creating her beautiful, fragile, and vulnerable, without weapons to fight her enemies. In a final scene, Deirdre flashes across the room with superhuman speed to save Maltzer from throwing himself out the window. She tells him and Harris that she is worried, true, not because she is defenseless but because she is superior to humanity, with weapons, strength, new skills, and even new senses; her concern is that she will grow away from humanity, that she will change.

The story is distinguished by a skillful use of what Henry James created and called the technique of the central intelligence: Harris plays the same role for "No Woman Born" that Strether plays for *The Ambassadors*. Even more than the technical excellence of the story, its observations, texture, and extensions round it into three dimensions. Deirdre is a real woman (I find myself identifying her with the author), and Maltzer is an understandably concerned creator with a Frankenstein complex. The descriptions of Deirdre, so essential to conviction, provide what James called "the specifications": golden metal, bare skull with the delicate suggestion of cheekbones; a crescent-shaped mask across the frontal area where her eyes would have been, filled in with something translucent and aquamarine; a body clad in a fine metal mesh shaped like a longer Grecian chlamys; and arms and legs formed from diminishing metal bracelets—"she looked, indeed, very much like a creature in armor, with her delicately plated limbs and her featureless head like a helmet with a visor of glass, and her robe of chain-mail. But no knight in his armor ever moved as Deirdre moved, or wore his armor upon a body of such inhumanly fine proportions." Other comparisons help extend the story into different areas of experience: James Stephens' poem with its lines, "There has been again no woman born / Who was so beautiful; not one so beautiful / Of all the women born—" In addition, certain perceptions emerge about the nature of humanity, not only the power of the human soul to impress human form on metal but the nature of creation: "The thing we create," Maltzer says, "makes living unbearable." And the final opening up of the story at the end, with the speculation as to what Deirdre will become before her brain wears out in another forty years or so. She thinks of herself as unique, like the Phoenix; there never will be another like her, and she wonders, in a moving final paragraph, how she will change:

Her voice was soft and familiar in Harris' ears, the voice Deirdre had spoken and sung with, sweetly enough to enchant a world. But as preoccupation came over her a certain flatness crept into the sound. When she was not listening to her own voice, it did not keep quite to the pitch of trueness. It sounded as if she spoke in a room of brass, and echoes from the walls resounded in the tones that spoke there.
'I wonder,' she repeated, the distant taint of metal already in her voice.[15]

The next year, 1945, was another big year in *Astounding*: eight stories, all of them competent but none outstanding. Four of them—"The Piper's Son," "Three Blind Mice," "The Lion and the Unicorn," and "Beggars in Velvet"—belonged to Kuttner's "Baldies" series about mutant telepaths trying to remain a part of human society through restraint and good manners while they cope with paranoia among themselves: effective stories, competently done, sensibly conceived, but seldom touched with greatness or special insights.

"What You Need" (October) and "Line to Tomorrow" (November) demonstrate Kuttner's ingenuity with stories about time, one of his favorite subjects. In these two stories he is concerned with the problems of foreknowledge. In "Line to Tomorrow" a character named Fletcher finds himself listening to a telephone conversation between a student, who is doing research in what seems to be approximately Fletcher's period, and his professor in the future. Fletcher overhears and writes down what seems to be a cure-all and an equation that demolishes an entire laboratory when a scientist tries to apply it; he finally overhears enough to deduce that the student is a decade or so in his own future and that when Fletcher reaches that time period he will go mad. "What You Need" begins with a man entering a shop which advertises, "We have what you need"; continues with a commercial transaction with the proprietor who sells his customers objects, such as a pair of scissors, which they will need desperately at some time in the future; and ends with the proprietor selling his customer slick shoes that doom him to death, because otherwise he would kill the proprietor and stop him from reshaping the world into a better place. "The future is a pyramid shaping slowly, brick by brick, and brick by brick Talley had to change it. . . ."[16]

Eight more stories appeared in *Astounding* in 1946, one of them a two-part serial, in spite of the fact that the Kuttners were venturing into other fields. They were turning out magazine-length novels (about 40,000 words) for both *Startling Stories* and *Thrilling Wonder Stories*; these were primarily adventure stories, with a strong element of fantasy and some scientific explanation. Their first of this type had been "Earth's Last Citadel," a 40,000-word serial for *Argosy* in 1943. In 1945 they published a 20,000-word short novel, "Sword of Tomorrow," in the fall issue of *Thrilling Wonder Stories*; in 1946, a 40,000-word novel, "The Dark World," in the summer issue of *Startling Stories* and an 18,000-word short novel, "I Am Eden," in the December issue of *Thrilling Wonder Stories*. In addition, Duell, Sloan & Pearce published the first two Kuttner mystery novels in 1946: *The Brass Ring* and *The Day He Died*.

But the influential stories were those published in *Astounding*. Of the eight, two deserve special notice. "The Fairy Chessmen," a two-part serial in the January and February issues, should be discussed in conjunction with another two-part serial in the January and February issues a year later, "Tomorrow and Tomorrow." Both begin with similar scenes in which a man with overpowering responsibilities fears that he is beginning to lose his sanity. In "The Fairy Chessmen," the protagonist is Robert Cameron, Civilian Director of Psychometrics in Low Chicago. (Life on the surface is no longer possible in a United States which has been at war for decades with "the Falangists.") Cameron fears he is losing his mind when reality begins to change around him; the story opens with a great line: "The doorknob opened a blue eye and looked at him."[17] In "Tomorrow and Tomorrow," Joseph Breden has nightmares about blowing up the atomic pile of which he is a guardian; he lives in a world the antithesis of "The Fairy Chessmen": a Global Peace Commission, set up after an abortive World War II, has kept peace for one hundred years, but the price of peace has been a stern maintenance of the status quo, including a ban on new research.

The stories have more similarities than differences: both involve mutations caused by proximity to radiation; both include interaction with strange, extra-temporal forces (in "Chessmen" a genetically bred and conditioned warrior from the future named Ridgeley, whose nation has been defeated in his own time, has escaped by means of one-way time travel to Cameron's world and is manipulating the war on both sides, while in "Tomorrow" a mutant called "the Freak" perceives alternate worlds created by decisions made during World War II); and both progress by means of plots and counter-plots. Both have some nice touches, including in "Chessmen" effective description of Low Chicago; and both have well calculated surprises at the end. In "Chessmen" Cameron solves his problem, but now fears that what he must do will bring about Ridgeley's world. Before his aide can propose an alternative to a world continually at war by directing man's need for an Enemy toward the stars, the hostile universe, Cameron goes mad; the final sentence repeats the first. In "Tomorrow" Kuttner suggests that the world should have its atomic war and then get on to a beneficent, peaceful world where progress is possible (compare H. G. Wells's utopian novels). But the two short novels, though readable enough, do not represent major additions to the science fiction canon, possibly because they never suggest universals.

"Vintage Season," published in the September 1946, *Astounding* under the name of Lawrence O'Donnell, may be the ultimate expression of Catherine Moore's art. An immediate sensation when it appeared, the novelette still retains its evocative appeal, as evidenced by its inclusion in *The Science Fiction Hall of Fame*, volume II, where it was ranked sixth among the novelettes. The narrative is relatively simple: a young man named Oliver Wilson rents his house to three foreigners, Omerie, Klia, and Kleph Sancisco; they are perfectly dressed but as if for a part, they are arrogantly assured, and they look "expensive." The complication comes through Oliver's fiancée, who wants him to get out of his lease and accept a better offer from another "foreigner." The substance of the story involves the Sanciscos, who move into the house with him and conduct themselves strangely, and Oliver's growing involvement with them and gradual understanding of what they are: time-travelers, dilettantes of the future making a sort of pilgrimage of the seasons—Canterbury in autumn in the 14th century, Christmastime in Rome at the Coronation of Charlemagne in 800, and May in Oliver's house and time. The time-travelers have rules, and Kleph breaks one when she tells him:

Now this month of May is almost over—the loveliest May in recorded times. A perfect May in a wonderful period. You have no way of knowing what a good, gay period you live in, Oliver. The very feeling in the air of the cities— that wonderful national confidence and happiness—everything going as smoothly as a dream. There were other Mays with fine weather, but each of them had a war or a famine, or something else wrong. . . .[18]

At the end all the Sancisco's friends from the future gather in the three front bedrooms of the house to watch a small meteor strike the city. The city burns; Oliver falls ill; the character who has been largely an observer becomes the central figure as he awakens to find the future's great composer of music and visual images, Cenbe, finishing his composition from the inspiration of the city's destruction, with Oliver's death-marked face one of the major motifs. Fatally ill, Oliver writes down a message about the time-travelers who might be captured and forced to warn about impending disasters, but six days later the house is dynamited as part of a futile attempt to halt the relentless spread of the Blue Death.

The impact of the story comes from two elements: the gay mood of the pilgrims in time contrasted with the cataclysmic events involving the protagonist and his city; and the distancing effect from contemporary man—which lies at the heart of all good science fiction—achieved through Oliver's inability to understand the Sanciscos: what they do and why, their pleasures, their lives, their values, and their attitudes toward his present. As he observes Cenbe:

. . . suddenly Oliver realized from across what distances Cenbe was watching him. A vast distance, as time is measured. Cenbe was a composer and a genius, and necessarily strongly empathetic, but his psychic locus was very far away in time. The dying city outside, the whole world of *now* was not quite real to Cenbe, falling short of reality because of that basic variance in time. It was merely one of the building blocks that had gone to support the edifice on which Cenbe's culture stood in a misty, unknown, terrible future.[19]

Oliver had succumbed to the lure of the delightful and the unknown, including Kleph, who had seemed more human than the others but was only weaker and more foolish; he now realizes that "all of them had been touched with a pettiness, the faculty that had enabled Hollia to concentrate on her malicious, small schemes to acquire a ringside seat while the meteor thundered in toward Earth's atmosphere. They were all dilettantes, Kleph and Omerie and the others. They toured time, but only as onlookers. Were they bored—sated—with their normal existence?" Stories are great as they exhibit uniqueness of idea; specificity of character, setting, and action; suitability of diction and style; and universality of theme. All of these qualities can be found in "Vintage Season."

Similar statements, though more qualified, might be made about the Kuttners' 1947 *Astounding* serial, *Fury*, another story by O'Donnell. The novel was eighty-per-cent Kuttner. The setting, a watery Venus still in its ravening Jurassic period, has been rendered improbable, perhaps impossible, by recent scientific observations and unmanned rocket explorations. But the story-line, the driving of a decaying humanity out of its undersea paradise onto the hostile surface, retains its universality. The Kuttners attack the problem that defeats most utopias, how to make people do what is good for them.

The story begins seven hundred years after the undersea Keeps were created, six hundred years after Earth was turned by atomic holocaust into a star, and three hundred years after "Clash by Night." The Keeps are ruled by immortals—tall, slim, aristocratic mutants who outlive normal humanity by centuries and can make their plans for the long term. For lack of a challenge, because life is too easy, the Keeps have become "the tomb, or womb, or both for the men of Venus."

To a couple of immortals, at the cost of the mother's life, is born a child. Turning insanely on the infant, the father has the child operated upon and converted, by endocrinological tampering, into someone who will grow up fleshy, thick, and bald—obviously not an immortal. The child grows up to be Sam Reed; as a street urchin he comes under the tutelage of a master criminal named the Slider and learns to live ruthlessly and savagely, using others before they can use him. He lives with fury, in constant rebellion against the shortness of his life measured against his needs and ambitions, not knowing that he is immortal. The plot brings him into contact with his own Harker family of immortals (he has an affair with a woman who may be his great-great-grandmother); with Ben Crowell, a one-thousand-year-old immortal who can predict the future and has become the Logician at the Temple of Truth; and with Robin Hale, an immortal who is the last surviving Free Companion and wishes to persuade the people of the Keeps to go landside. Sam uses Hale to work a stock swindle based on conquering landside, but in the moment of his triumph his mistress, bribed by the Harkers, gives him dreamdust. Normally dreamdust is fatal, but Sam is nursed through forty years of unconsciousness. He awakens to the realization that he, too, is immortal. The remainder of the novel consists of Sam's efforts to force the people of the Keeps to the land surfaces, deadly with Venusian life forms though they are; his plans culminate in a simulated rebellion which turns radioactive the impervium domes of the Keeps.

Woven through the plot is the kind of insights seldom found in science fiction novels: immortals view life differently (they can take up occupations that require fifty or one hundred years of preparation; they have time to let their enemies die); a workless society provides limited alternatives (a person can be a technician, an artist, or a hedonist); an unrelenting search for pleasure must go continually further for satisfaction (deadly "happy clocks" and "dreamdust"); foreknowledge has built-in difficulties (which is why the utterances of oracles are always cryptic).

The novel is rounded with literary touches which satisfy the reader looking for some extension of the work beyond the here-and-now (or there-and-then): epigraphs, a prologue and an epilogue, quotations, mythological references. In the prologue the word "fury" is applied to the deadly, teeming land surface of Venus; later the word describes Sam Reed. After Sam awakens, a character comments, "Someone had fed him dream-dust forty years ago. *The voice is Jacob's voice, but the hand is the hand of Esau.*"

Finally, wounded, defeated through treachery, Sam is spirited away by Ben Crowell, who tells him:

'. . . Up till now we've needed you, Sam. Once in a long while a fella like you comes along, somebody strong enough to move a world. . . . There's nothing you wouldn't do, son, nothing at all—if it would get you what you want. . . . If you hadn't been born, if Blaze hadn't done what he did, mankind would be in the Keeps yet. And in a few hundred years, or a thousand, say, the race would have died out. . . . But now we've come landside. We'll finish colonizing Venus. And then we'll go out and colonize the whole universe, I expect. . . . All you could think of was repeating the thing that made you a success—more fighting, more force. . . . You had the same drive that made the first life-form leave water for land, but we can't use your kind any more for a while, Sam. The race has got immortality, Sam, and you gave it to 'em. . . .'[20]

Ben Crowell puts Sam to sleep where he will stay until he and his "fury" may be needed again:

'I hope you die in your sleep. I hope I'll never have to wake you up. Because if I do, it'll mean things have gone bad again. . . . Maybe we'll need a man like you again, Sam. I'll wake you if we do. . . .'[21]

The novel concludes with an epilogue which, in spite of its gimmickery, opens up the novel for further speculation and suggests eternal principles at work rather than the special circumstances which so often weaken the endings of science fiction novels: "Sam woke—"

By mid-1947 the Kuttners' contributions to *Astounding*—and to the genre—were almost over. In addition to the two serials, three more stories would be published that year, one in 1948, two in 1949, three in 1950, and one in 1953. Other stories appeared in the *Magazine of Fantasy and Science Fiction* in 1951, 1955, and 1956, and in *Galaxy* in 1952. Two worth special mention are "Private Eye" in the January 1949, *Astounding* and "Two-Handed Engine" in the August 1955, *Magazine of Fantasy and Science Fiction*. Both are mature considerations of crime prevention worked out through the experiences of a single criminal. In "Private Eye" science has discovered how to pick up visual and aural impressions from matter so that investigators can, in effect, look into the past and trace a person's actions before he committed a crime, thus documenting motive and premeditation. The story is about Sam Clay, who sets up a crime so carefully that he cannot be convicted. But he discovers as he is committing the murder that he likes the job he has taken as a coverup, that he doesn't want to be a murderer, and that the chain of events he has initiated cannot be stopped. Freed, he is blackmailed by the one-time fiancée for whom he had planned the crime: he kills her, with clear intent and motive, and triumphantly satisfies the big, floating, staring eye he used to see during his unhappy childhood, with its legend: THOU GOD SEEST ME. "Two-Handed Engine" envisions a human utopia of self-repairing and self-constructed machines after a devastating war, which is also a time of ultimate individualism with no deterrent to crime. In an effort to restore the human conscience, the machines have been instructed to create "Furies"—giant, indestructible robots—as externalized consciences to follow persons convicted of murder until, at a moment known only to the Furies, they carry out his execution. The narrative concerns a man hired to kill another after he has been convinced that false data can be fed into the computer to re-direct a Fury. But a Fury comes after him anyway. Finally he confronts the computer scientist who had tricked him, and the computer scientist kills him while the Fury is watching. Desperately, knowing he will be pursued by a Fury, the scientist codes false information into the computer—and it works. Yet he finds himself pursued by something even worse, an internalized conscience. The Furies may not be incorruptible, but they have succeeded in the task they were assigned.

Both stories were very nearly fifty-fifty collaborations; both are rich plum-puddings of stories. In "Private Eye" the fullness comes in large part from psychology; in "Two-Handed Engine," from legend and literature. Even the titles are revealing: "Private Eye" is a psychological pun; "Two-Handed Engine" is a quotation from Milton:

> But that two-handed engine at the door
> Stands ready to smite once, and smite no more. . . .

The Kuttners' decline in production for *Astounding* is easily explained. In 1948 they had returned to California and had started their college studies. The two mystery novels they had published in 1946 would lead to five more: *Man Drowning* for Harper in 1951 and four mysteries for Pocket Books between 1956 and 1958. In addition, they produced nine novels or short novels for *Startling Stories* and *Thrilling Wonder Stories* between 1947 and 1952.[22] These stories alone represented a production of nearly 300,000 words. Probably they were easy words, compared at least with the difficult, tightly woven words of the Kuttners' *Astounding* stories. Interesting reading in their way, they usually feature a heroic man precipitated into strange circumstances and required, in the end, to do battle against strange, unearthly powers. "The Mask of Circe," for instance, begins in traditional Edgar Rice Burroughs and A. Merritt fantasy style: a man named Talbott is sitting in the north woods listening to a story told by Jay Seward, a restless, haunted man with a bronze face—"it might have been a mask hammered out of metal, with the tall Canadian pines a background and the moonlight silvering it with strange highlights." They sit in a "moon-drenched clearing," and Seward says, "Tonight something's going to happen. Don't ask me what." Seward had been doing psychological research on ancestral memories and had unleashed within himself the memories of Jason; a voice kept calling for Jason to return to the sea. One night he did return, leaping to the deck of a ghostly Argos, and found himself at last the pivotal figure in a battle between Hecate, the last of the alien beings who became gods on Earth, and Apollo, the beautiful, powerful machine created by the gods which draws upon the sun for atomic power. In the end Jason-Seward prevails, with the help of the Golden Fleece, which Hephaestus had created before his death to destroy Apollo by bottling up within him the sun's energy.

Such stories achieve their tone, in part, through the use of elevated diction. As A. Merritt's *The Moon Pool* speaks of "shafts of radiance," "cylindrical torrents," "amber," "amethyst," "molten silver," "phosphorescence," "coruscations," and "incandescence," so, too, in "The Mask of Circe" a "Nubian face" is ebony, not black; hemispheres are milky; water is opalescent; walls are mirror-silver; glow is crepuscular; and the glare of gold is intolerable. The air of the alien and the ineffable is achieved by mating contradictory adjectives: in *The Moon Pool* the narrator's wife disappears into the pool in the arms of the dweller, and "her eyes stared up to me filled with supernal ecstasy and horror"; in "The Mask of Circe" the Kuttners write of Apollo's "beautiful, hideous face." Yet they departed from the Burroughs-Merritt fantasy tradition by frequently providing a rational explanation for their mysteries—the walls of Jericho, for instance, leveled by supersonic vibrations.

The Kuttners' significant work, however, was their science fiction, particularly that written for *Astounding*, although several noteworthy stories escaped Campbell, such as "Absalom," another child-father conflict of superpowers (*Startling Stories*, Fall 1946); "Call Him Demon," in which a child destroys a meat-hungry alien with strange mental powers by feeding him the child's grandmother (*Thrilling Wonder Stories*, Fall 1946); and "Don't Look Now" (*Startling Stories*, March 1948).

The Kuttners' range of subjects, in their production for *Astounding*, at least, was somewhat limited. Like a dog with a favorite bone, they would pick up an idea, chew on it for awhile, bury it, and then dig it up again and again to begin the process all over. Psychology, for instance, seemed to be much on their minds, for their stories are filled with men going mad, fearful that they are going mad, or suffering from paranoid symptoms or serious neuroses, as in "The Piper's Son," "Tomorrow and Tomorrow," "The Fairy Chessmen," "Line to Tomorrow," "Private Eye," "No Woman Born," *Fury*, "Endowment Policy," "The Children's Hour," "The Cure," and others. Other favorite subjects included androids, robots, and what we now call cyborgs, as in "Android," "No Woman Born," "The Twonky," "Home There's No Returning," "Piggy Bank," and "The Proud Robot"; foreknowledge and time travel, as in "Vintage Season," "Line to Tomorrow," "The Cure," "What You Need," "The Fairy Chessmen," "Mimsy Were the Borogoves," "Time Locker," and "When the Bough Breaks"; superman and superpowers, as in "The Children's Hour," "Margin for Error," "The Piper's Son," "Absalom," "The Fairy Chessmen," "When the Bough Breaks," "Mimsy Were the Borogoves," and others; crime and punishment, as in "Private Eye," "Two-Handed Engine," "Time Locker," "Piggy Bank," and others. Several favorite possible events sometimes provided central themes but more often background: atomic catastrophe in "Tomorrow and Tomorrow," *Fury*, "The Piper's Son," "Two-Handed Engine," "Margin for Error"; meteor and plague in "Vintage Season"; and children as aliens, often inhuman, sometimes monsters, in "Call Him Demon," "When the Bough Breaks," "Mimsy Were the Borogoves," "Absalom," and "The Piper's Son."

The Kuttners did not deal with such themes as "the wonderful journey," or man and the future (in any extrapolative sense, with the possible exception of *Fury*, "Judgment Night," and—in lesser ways, because they are not extrapolative but thematic— "The Fairy Chessmen" and "Tomorrow and Tomorrow"); cataclysm (they dealt entirely with precataclysm or post-cataclysm, and never in a cataclysmic vein); and only in a limited way with man and his environment, man and alien, and man and religion.

The Kuttners concerned themselves principally with man and society; how is man going to function in the new worlds that will be created by changes in technology, science, and social restructuring? To this theme they brought perceptions and techniques refined by their fantasy writing. Every writer seeks to convince his reader that what he is reading is, in some sense, real. The fantasy writer tries to achieve this conviction through psychological or mythic truth; the naturalistic writer, through verisimilitude. Even the romantic or the satiric writer believes that he is reflecting reality. Tobias Smollet asserted, "Every intelligent reader will, at first sight, perceive I have not deviated from nature in the facts, which are all true in the main, although the circumstances are altered and disguised to avoid personal satire." Jean-Jacques Rousseau wrote, "In an imaginary picture, every human figure must have traits common to men, or the picture is worthless." Fanny Burney explained in her preface to *Evelina,* "The heroine of these memoirs, young, artless, and inexperienced is 'no faultless monster, that the world ne'er saw,' but the offspring of Nature, and of Nature in her simplest attire."

The fantasy writers of the early twentieth century, it is true, had no such belief. They overwhelmed the reader with the sweep of their imaginations, the pace of their adventures, and the color of their descriptions; in fact, the more fantastic the writers wrote them, as in one all-time A. Merritt favorite, *The Ship of Ishtar,* the better their readers liked them. Science fiction struggled in the other direction, toward realism and credibility, and achieved its ends through different means—perhaps, thereby, contributing to the fabled loss of Sam Moskowitz's "sense of wonder," for something that is explained is no longer a miracle: the rainbow, God's covenant with man that there will never be another Flood, becomes only another natural phenomenon when science explains that it is caused by the refraction of sunlight by raindrops.

In its search for credibility, scinece fiction tried pseudo-scientific explanations or explanations by analogy (as in "Doc" Smith's epics), scientific logic (as in Isaac Asimov's robot stories), extrapolation from present possibilities or trends (as in a host of rocketry and atomic bomb stories), naturalistic detail (as in Robert Heinlein's early novels and juveniles), ordinary heroes or anti-heroes (as in Pohl and Kornbluth's *The Space Merchants* and other *Galaxy* stories), to cite some of the most important methods.

Science fiction is most obviously distinguished from the best of mainstream literature by its thinness, its orientation toward plot to the exclusion of other qualities of literature. What the Kuttners brought to science fiction from fantasy were the qualities of literature: the quest for conviction through characterization and individualization, through setting, through symbol and myth. Fantasy always has been close to mainstream literature, if not indistinguishable from it; in our times, at least, both are concerned with private visions rather than the public—or shared—visions of science fiction. The mixture of the two brought back from beyond the grave of years what might be called literary science fiction, or science fiction which attempted to meet the standards of mainstream literature. It was not an easy task, for elements on both sides are antagonistic. At best, an uneasy balance could be struck: too much science fiction convention, too much explanation, and the characters seem manipulated by the story. The non-initiated reader is lost. Too much concern for style, for myth, for the individual, and the heart of science fiction—the idea—is buried beyond recall. In the 1940's the Kuttners provided the best mixture.

They were not without predecessors: Stanley Weinbaum, John Campbell writing as Don A. Stuart, and, of course, the man who deserves more than anyone the name of father of science fiction, H. G. Wells. The Kuttners had contemporaries: Theodore Sturgeon; sometimes Clifford Simak and Lester del Rey; Jack Williamson and Ed Hamilton in their later styles; James Blish; Damon Knight; Phil Klass writing as William Tenn, to name the most obvious. Most of all, they had successors.

It is tempting to say that the Kuttners drove science fiction writers out of their impervium magazine domes onto the literary landside where they had to face ravening readers and critics. But the Kuttners were professionally quiet and gentle; they never drove anyone. What they did was show the way, making their toves slithy and arranging them so that they would gyre and gimbel, and if other momes could follow they would, like the Kuttners, rath outgrabe.

Thomas D. Clareson

THE COSMIC LONELINESS OF ARTHUR C. CLARKE*

S ince the publication of *Interplanetary Flight: An Introduction to Astronautics* (1950) and *The Exploration of Space*
(1951)—the latter a Book of the Month Club selection in the
summer of 1952—Arthur C. Clarke has undoubtedly become the
most widely-known spokesman for those advocating space travel.
Indeed, he has been called "one of the truly prophetic figures of
the space age."[1] Yet despite such early awards as the 1961
Kalinga Prize in recognition of his success in popularizing space
flight, the incident best measuring the impact of his dream of
man's journeys to the moon, the planets, and—ultimately—the
stars did not occur until 1971. Then, during the Apollo 15 mis-
sions, astronauts David Scott and James Irwin named a crater near
Hadley Rille for *Earthlight,* Clarke's early novel (1951, 1955)[2] in
which he used a twenty-first-century lunar colony as setting and
suggested that the moon will become the hub of the habitable

---

*A portion of this paper was published as "[Arthur C. Clarke]: The
Early Novels," *Algol*, 12 (November 1974), 7-11. Although Clarke had published in the British amateur magazines before the war, his first American
publication was 1946.

216

solar system because of its mineral wealth.

Acknowledging that "the explosive development of astronautics" during the 1960's had made some of his books "very out of date," Clarke declared that *The Promise of Space* (1968) was "an entirely new book" which replaced many of the earliest ones and should remain "largely valid through the 1970's"; similarly, *Report on Planet Three and Other Speculations* (1972) contained his "later thoughts on a number of subjects."[3] As a result his non-fiction has a special value for the student of his fiction because in it one can trace the persistence and evolution of his themes as he continually explores and re-works ideas and situations which inform his short stories and novels. As in *The Challenge of Space* (1959),[4] one may learn that he has used "much of the material" in three essays "to provide the background" of three early novels, *Earthlight, The Sands of Mars* (1951, 1952), and *Islands in the Sky* (1952).[5] In one of those articles, "Vacation in Vacuum," one discovers the "Sky Hotel," which develops into the resort hotel on Titan in "Saturn Rising" (*F&SF*, March 1961) and, finally, into the hotel satellite of *2001: A Space Odyssey*. Again, much later, Clarke pointed out that in the essay "The Star of the Magi" (1954) readers of his fiction would "recognize . . . the origins" of his prize-winning story, "The Star" (*Infinity*, November 1955).[6]

Although it is everywhere apparent that his main concern involves man's encounter with alien intelligence, at the heart of his vision—most obvious throughout his non-fiction and early novels—remains the certainty that the exploration of space and the colonization of the planets of innumerable suns will bring a new Renaissance freeing mankind from the short-sighted prejudices and limitations of earth-bound, modern civilization. Repeatedly he invokes images fusing his voyagers "Across the Sea of Stars" with those explorers who opened up the Earth, as he does in *Prelude to Space* (1951), which celebrates preparations for the voyage of the *Prometheus* to the moon and climaxes with the departure of that first ship. In an epilogue, some years after the establishment of a lunar colony, the narrator muses:

. . . Once again the proud ships were sailing for unknown lands, bearing the seeds of new civilizations which in the ages to come would surpass the old. The rush to the new worlds would destroy the suffocating restraints which had poisoned almost half the [twentieth] century. The barriers had been broken, and men could turn their energies outwards to the stars instead of striving among themselves.

Out of the fears and miseries of the Second Dark Age, drawing free—oh, might it be forever!—from the shadows of Belsen and Hiroshima, the world was moving towards its most splendid sunrise. After five hundred years, the Renaissance had come again. The dawn that would burst above the Apennines at the end of the long lunar night would be no more brilliant than the age that had now been born.[7]

Or again, in *The Challenge of Space,* in a different but frequent mood:

. . . For a man 'home' is the place of his birth and childhood—whether that be Siberian steppe, coral island, Alpine valley, Brooklyn tenement, Martian desert, lunar crater, or mile-long interstellar ark. But for Man, home can never be a single country, a single world, a single Solar System, a single star cluster. While the race endures in recognizably human form, it can have no abiding place short of the Universe itself.

This divine discontent is part of our destiny. It is one more, and perhaps the greatest, of the gifts we have inherited from the sea that rolls so restlessly around the world.

It will be driving our descendants on toward a myriad unimaginable goals when the sea is stilled forever, and Earth itself a fading legend lost among the stars.[8]

Although Clarke spreads the human drama across future millenia, he often strikes a contrapuntal note by warning that "Everyone recognizes that our present racial, political, and international troubles are symptoms of a sickness which must be cured before we can survive on our own planet—but the stakes may be higher than that. . . . The impartial agents of our destiny stand on their launching pads, awaiting our commands. They can take us to that greater Renaissance whose signs and portents we can already see, or they can make us one with the dinosaurs. . . . If our wisdom fails to match our science, we will have no second chance."[9] Out of the conflict revealed by these admonitions came one of his finest short stories, "If I Forget Thee, O Earth" (1951), in which a son of the lunar colony witnesses for the first time the rising of an Earth poisoned for centuries to come by a nuclear holocaust.

And when Clarke wonders whether or not the Solar System will, indeed, "be large enough for so quarrelsome an animal as *Homo sapiens*,"[10] one conjures up the second of his stories to be published in America, "Rescue Party" (*Astounding,* May 1946), in which alien representatives of a galaxy-wide Federation come to save mankind just before the sun goes into nova. Finding an empty Earth, they learn that man has built a fleet of ships to save himself. The captain muses about such "very determined people" and jests that one must be polite to them because they are outnumbered only "about a thousand million to one": "Twenty years afterward, the remark didn't seem funny." Both narratives bear one of the distinguishing marks of Clarke's story-telling. Not unlike O'Henry, he likes a quick climax—often a single punchline— which may surprise but always opens new perspectives.

Any misgivings that Clarke may have, rise from his doubts concerning the uses made of the new technologies. As early as 1946 he wrote:

We must not, however, commit the only too common mistake of equating mere physical expansion, or even increasing scientific knowledge, with 'progress'—however that may be defined. Only little minds are impressed by sheer size and number. There would be no virtue in possessing the Universe if it brought neither wisdom nor happiness. Yet possess it we must, at least in spirit, if we are ever to answer the questions that men have asked in vain since history began.[11]

Somewhat later he approached this basic theme more affirmatively when he asserted that "mere extension of the life span, and even improved health and efficiency, are not important in themselves. . . . What is really significant is richness and diversity of experience, and the use to which that is put by men and the societies they constitute."[12] Still in the 1950's, while speculating about man's encounter with alien intelligence, he used that central concern to say something of man himself:

. . . Most disconcerting of all would be the discovery that Man alone is a myth-making animal, forever impelled to fill the gaps in his knowledge by fantasies. (Yet if this be the price we have had to pay for the whole realm of art, which is always an attempt to create the nonexistent, we need not be ashamed. We will be better off than beings who possess all knowledge, but know nothing of poetry and music.)[13]

This emphasis upon both man's humanity and the need for it to shape the workings of society leads to Clarke's judgment of H. G. Wells, a judgment which seems a valid appraisal of Clarke himself:

. . . Wells saw as clearly as anyone into the secret places of the heart, but he also saw the universe, with all its infinite promise and peril. He believed—though not blindly—that men were capable of improvement and might one day build sane and peaceful societies on all the worlds that lay within their reach.[14]

When he adds that "we need this faith now, as never before in the history of our species," he has completed the context which gives importance to that "greater Renaissance" brought about by the advent of space flight. In 1951 Clarke captured the significance of that awakening when he concluded *The Exploration of Space* with the imagined verdict that "an historian of the year 3,000" might pass on the twentieth century:

It was, without question, the most momentous hundred years in the history of Mankind. . . . To us a thousand years later, the whole story of Mankind before the twentieth century seems like a prelude to some great drama, played on the narrow strip of stage before the curtain has risen and revealed the scenery. . . . Man realised at last that the Earth was only one of many worlds; the Sun only one among many stars. The coming of the rocket brought to an end a million years of isolation. With the landing of the first spaceship on Mars and Venus, the childhood of our race was over and history as we know it began. . . .[15]

". . . the childhood of our race was over . . .": there is a delightful irony in that line because of the widespread popularity of *Childhood's End* (1953), Clarke's only work—fiction or non-fiction—in which *"The stars are not for Man."*[16] Billed as "a towering novel about the next step in the evolution of man," it belongs, most simply, to that group of stories in which vastly superior aliens intrude into the affairs of men—a plot having perhaps its widest vogue during the decade or so after World War II. In this instance the Overlords, who possess the form of Satan, terminate the Soviet-American race for the moon, end the threat of nuclear holocaust, and in fifty years bring about a seeming utopia. (At their appearance one hears briefly what has become for Clarke an ever more important theme: ". . . the stars—the aloof, indifferent stars—had come to him. . . . The human race was no longer alone.") Creating an 'Earthly Paradise,' is not, however, the final purpose of the Overlords; they were sent, their leader explains, to act as midwives while the human race evolved psychically preparatory to uniting itself with the cosmic Overmind.

The most dangerous threat to this development, he continues, lay in the scientific investigation of "paranormal phenomena." Left to itself, such study might have unleashed forces capable of spreading "havoc to the stars." The Overlords are racially incapable of taking this evolutionary step and do not comprehend the forces at work; yet while the Overmind triggers and guides the change, they must act as guardians, protecting man from himself, until the last generation of children is ready for the transformation.

The novel ends as a solitary adult watches the children, now joined into a single intelligence, undergo a metamorphosis which not only releases them from their human form but dissolves the Earth itself into the energy necessary to complete the change. All of this in the presence of what seems to be "a great cloud . . . a hazy network of lines and bands that keep changing their positions . . . a great burning column, like a tree of fire . . . an auroral storm . . . the great misty network . . ."[17] Like other galactic races which have completed their probation, mankind has become a part of the Overmind. Although David Samuelson questions the artistic effectiveness of much of *Childhood's End,* he notes that "we feel the tug of the irrational, in familiar terms. The Overmind clearly parallels the Oversoul, the Great Spirit, and various formulations of God, while the children's metamorphosis neatly ties in with mystical beliefs in Nirvana, 'cosmic consciousness,' and 'becoming as little children to enter the Kingdom of God.' "[18] One might add that its resolution recalls—but does not duplicate—stories by the followers of Madame Blavatsky and John Fiske in the late nineteenth century which sought reconciliation between traditional beliefs and new scientific data, thereby often insisting that the next step in evolution must involve some higher potential of the human spirit. The essentially traditional mysticism of that resolution, as well as the emphasis upon the children as "successors" to mankind with whom their parents would "never even be able to communicate," may well account for much of the appeal of the novel, particularly in the classroom. A typical academic reading, that of L. David Allen, concludes that "basically, *Childhood's End* is a religious vision of the way that mankind might develop and the desirability of that direction."[19]

Apparently many individuals have felt that such a transformation—"apotheosis"[20]—more than compensates for the loss of the stars. Clarke did not. He prefaced the original, paperback edition with the warning that "The opinions expressed in this book are not those of the author," and in a recent letter explained that he had inserted the "disclaimer in *CE* so people wouldn't think I'd recanted the views expressed in *The Exploration of Space*, etc!"[21] In view of his continuing attack upon orthodox religion—it surfaces frequently in *Childhood's End* itself—such a disavowal suggests a deep conflict in Clarke which may even have affected the artistry of the novel, leading, for example, to Samuelson's inference that "not fully in control of his materials, Clarke has attempted more than he can fulfill."[22] In contrast, Allen believes that Clarke brought to the "sweeping vision" of the novel "a sense of detailed reality . . . more concrete, detailed, and complex" than *2001: A Space Odyssey*.[23] Most importantly, the disavowal emphasizes the uniqueness of *Childhood's End* in the canon of Clarke's work. Its final sequence contradicts all else that he has said about the future of humanity.

"Earth and the Overlords," the first of the three parts of *Childhood's End*, was originally published as a magazine novelette, "Guardian Angel" (*Famous Fantastic Mysteries*, April 1950); it alone appeared separately. The basic action of the two versions remains the same, although in a climax typical of so many of Clarke's stories, the novelette ends upon the suggestion that man's "Guardian Angel" is, indeed, the Devil. Not yet satisfied, Clarke closed the narrative with fragments of an earlier dialogue telling something of Karellen and thereby opened an otherwise closed incident:

'. . . and he put up a terrific fight before they made him take this job. He pretends to hate it, but he's really enjoying himself.'
    '. . . immortal, isn't he?'
    'Yes, after a fashion, though there's something thousands of years ahead of him which he seems to fear—I can't imagine what it is.'
    Armageddon?[24]

Clarke ignored that ending in the subsequent development of *Childhood's End*. Thus in the novelette it simply provided an amusing—startling?—twist on another story of the first contact between humanity and aliens. Once again, as so often occurs in science fiction, an idea rather than the quality of human experience, had fascinated the author.

Variations in language and detail show Clarke's eye for revision, but the most significant difference between the versions of the story occurs because of the omission of a single speech originally in the novelette. In sketching the long-term plans of the Overlords, Karellen remarks:

'Then there will be another pause, only a short one this time, for the world will be growing impatient. Men will wish to go out to the stars, to see the other worlds of the Universe and to join us in our work. For it is only beginning—not a thousandth of the suns in the Galaxy have ever been visited by the races of which we know. One day, Rikki, your descendants in their own ships will be bringing civilization to the worlds, that are ripe to receive it— just as we are doing now.

. . . .

'It is a great vision,' he said softly. 'Do you bring it to all your worlds?'
'Yes,' said Karellen, 'all that can understand' (p. 128).

Here, then, is the basic dream: man will one day become an active participant in the galactic community. Yet nothing of this passage remains in the finished novel. For whatever reasons, sometime between 1950 and 1953, even while he was popularizing space flight and advocating the journey to the stars in his other writing, both fiction and non-fiction, Clarke set aside that dream while completing *Childhood's End* in a fashion that could not be predicted from the text of "Guardian Angel."

In light of his immediate disclaimer, his production of one of the generally recognized 'classics' of modern science fiction speaks well for his ability to be convincing despite any personal disbelief in what he portrays. (Its reception also says something about his audience. While the majority continue to see it as a religious vision, surely one may read that final transformation as an escape from, a denial of the human condition. Nor should one forget that the metamorphosis solves a basic problem which Clarke raised in a number of his early works. Not only do the Overlords bring about utopia, they also close off the promise of space except for a few flights to the moon to establish a lunar observatory. For Clarke, when the abolition of armed forces increases "the world's effective wealth," when standard of living rises to a point where the necessities are provided free as a public service, when neither the arts nor science contributes anything fresh or expands man's knowledge, and when the earth becomes a vast playground as humanity attempts to escape the boredom of utopia, only a single question remains: *"Where do we go from here?"* Not coincidentally the 'Earthly Paradise' of *Childhood's End* calls to mind those decadent societies of the far future against which his young protagonists rebel in works like *Against the Fall of Night* (1948, 1953) and *The Lion of Comarre* (1949, 1968). Indeed, Jan Rodricks' stowing away aboard a flight to the home planet of the Overlords echoes that rebellion. With the challenge of interstellar space eliminated by the Overlords, Clarke provides in the metamorphosis of the children an alternate answer—one with which he apparently was never in sympathy intellectually. Thus its uniqueness.)

Other than *Childhood's End*, the longer narratives among his early works divide themselves into two groups, the first strongly didactic, reflecting Clarke's desire to sell astronautics to the public. *Prelude to Space*, written within three weeks during the summer of 1947, celebrates preparations for the voyage of the *Prometheus* to the moon in 1978 and, as noted, climaxes with the departure of that ship. In the 'Epilogue' Dirk Alexson, the historian who must produce an enduring record of that flight, reflects upon the successful colonization of the moon and the coming of a new Reniassance. Wisely the shifting narrative focus stays primarily with Alexson, thereby making more acceptable the introduction of an abundance of technical detail as he learns about the project. This includes far more than the mechanics of the technology, however, for he readily understands the importance of the program to the future. He discerns, for example, that the men who are "not ashamed of wanting to play with spaceships" are *"visionaries, Poets if you like, who also happen to be scientists"*; in the course of their play, they "will change the world, and perhaps the Universe." They are the Space Dreamers.[25]

Another character summons up what has become a familiar image in Clarke's rebuttal to those who would spurn the venture into space because, properly run, there is no better world than Earth: "The dream of the Lotus Eaters . . . is a pleasant fantasy for the individual—but it would be death for the race" (p. 105). Finally, on the eve of the flight as the Director-General of the project muses over a book of poetry, one senses that the fictional mask has dropped and that Clarke speaks for himself as much as any imagined character. The passage ends on an elegiac tone out of keeping with the optimism of the novel but anticipatory of a chord which has sustained Clarke's finest fiction:

The eternal night would come, and too soon for Man's liking. But at least before they guttered and died, he would have known the stars; before it faded like a dream, the Universe would have yielded up its secrets to his mind. Or if not to his, then to the minds that would come after and would finish what he had now begun (p. 176).

Prelude to Space has little plot action because there are too many things to describe and talk about, including over-views imagining the ship's departure from the atmosphere and summarizing the diverse, essentially uninformed public attitudes toward space flight. It is on the eve of the launching, through the Director-General that Clarke insists, "We will take no hunters into space." The principal incident involves the failure of a religious fanatic to sabotage the *Prometheus*. In contrast, *Earthlight* (1951, 1955) introduces a spy from Earth into the moon colony of the twenty-second century on the eve of an interplanetary war between Earth and the Triplanetary Federation. (That name alone underscores his intimacy with the older magazine science fiction.) Earth's ex-colonies on Mars, Venus, Mercury, and the moons of Jupiter and Saturn comprise the Federation; the issue concerns raw materials, for only Earth has access to the heavy elements essential to the technologies of all the worlds. Clarke has explained that *Earthlight* had its beginning as early as 1941 when he wondered whether or not he could out-do "the splendid battle sequence in E. E. Smith's classic space opera *Skylark Three* [1930]."[26] So much attention is given to descriptions of the moon colony and the lunar surface and to an extended account of a battle between spaceships and a lunar fortress that the spy does not reveal who had been leaking information to the Federation until twenty years afterward.

The battle is not an end in itself because the fortress masks a mining operation which, for the first time, obtains heavy elements from the deep interior of the moon; thus, as noted, the moon becomes the hub of the solar system, her "inexhaustible wealth" supporting all of the inhabitable planets. Again idea dominates. One incident, the sinking of a tractor beneath surface dust—related to the main story-line only in that it allows characters with whom the reader is familiar to observe the battle—served as the genesis of *A Fall of Moondust* (1961). All of this is played out against the backdrop of *Nova Draconis*, the first supernova in this Galaxy since the Renaissance. Its appearance permits reflections upon the fragility of life, but unfortunately it does not attain a unifying symbolic value. Its presence, however, does emphasize how long the phenomenon has teased Clarke's imagination.

The Sands of Mars (1952) makes use of familiar patterns. Its protagonist, a famous science fiction writer, has been invited to be the sole passenger aboard the new spaceliner *Ares* so that he can write a book about its initial voyage. One journeys with him from a space station to Port Lowell, the principal domed city of the Martian colony. When he decides to throw in with the Martian pioneers rather than to return to Earth, his task becomes that of selling the colony to an Earth already weary of supporting it. The novel gains a unity because the point of view remains almost entirely with the protagonist, but apparently in an attempt to make the characters more complex, Clarke has added to the plot the contrived romance between the protagonist's protégé (actually his son by a young woman he loved at the university) and the daughter of the "Chief Executive" of the colony. More appropriate adventures occur: discovering a project so secret that most of the colonists know nothing of it; crashing into a geological fault in an unexplored area after a sandstorm of hurricane force; finding an unknown species of animal life which brings to mind Tweel of Stanley Weinbaum's "A Martian Odyssey." Project Daw, as it is called, detonates Phobos, the Martian moon, transforming it into a miniature sun. Not only does it bring heat to the barren world, but its light will promote the growth of a recently discovered plant capable of releasing the oxygen from those metallic oxides which form the Martian sands. In short, Mars has been reborn.

However readable these novels are, beyond the circle of science fiction aficionados they have their chief importance, as Clarke suggested of *Prelude to Space,* as a means of spreading the "Zeitgeist of Astronautics."[27] They are as much propaganda pieces as is *The Exploration of Space.* Yet they may also say something of the essential nature of science fiction. Even in *Prelude to Space,* the protagonists leave familiar settings to venture into unknown worlds, whether extraterrestrial or not. As in

Earthlight and *The Sands of Mars* especially, much attention may be given to their technologies. (One recalls Clarke's frequently cited remark that a sufficiently advanced technology is indistinguishable from magic.) However, the true sense of wonder spoken of by him and many others lies in the exploration of those exotic, often hostile worlds. The protagonists may return or not—often they have come home; often they have created new homes. In Clarke intellectual curiosity may replace such reliable devices as those devastating catastrophes so popular with a writer like John Wyndham, but the result is the same. The issue is man's ability to survive in and comprehend those far lands, whether they are beyond Eden or beyond Jupiter. This mixture of familiarity and otherness, reality and fantasy, has led David Young to refer to science fiction as "our most viable version of the pastoral."[28]

The degree to which he is correct may be seen even more clearly in a second group of Clarke's early narratives. In an introduction to *The Lion of Comarre and Against the Fall of Night* (1968), while acknowledging the emotional impact of Olaf Stapledon's *Last and First Men* (1930), and John W. Campbell's "Twilight" (1934), upon him as an individual and subsequently upon his early fiction, he wrote:

. . . And, undoubtedly, much of the emotional basis came from my transplantation from the country (Somerset) to the city (London), when I joined the British Civil Service in 1936. The conflict between a pastoral and an urban way of life has haunted me ever since.

He went on to say of the two stories:

Though they are set eons apart in time, they have much in common. Both involve a search, or quest, for unknown and mysterious goals. In each case the real objectives are wonder and magic, rather than any material gain. And in each case the hero is a young man dissatisfied with his environment.[29]

One discerns an indebtedness to Stapledon, but *Against the Fall of Night* (1948) and *The Lion of Comarre* (1949) are the earliest of those works in which Clarke responds to Campbell's melancholy vision of the twilight of humanity seven million years in the future. Having been served and cared for too long by perfect machines which will operate flawlessly until the end of time, the childlike remnant of mankind awaits extinction because it has forgotten the knowledge behind those machines and has lost the intellectual curiosity needed to learn again. Taken as a group, these works are restatements of Clarke's refusal to accept Campbell's pessimism.

Begun in 1937, the year after Clarke's move to London, and not completed until 1946—after five drafts—*Against the Fall of Night* has retained a devoted audience, although flawed by its brevity and a reliance upon unembellished conventions from magazine science fiction. Clarke's feeling for it led him to expand it as *The City and the Stars* (1956), the only instance in which he has completely revised a published story. Its point of departure echoes Campbell. The immortal populace of Diaspar, the only city remaining amid the deserts of Earth, lives contentedly amid wondrous machines which fulfill their every need and desire. The people have never viewed the world beyond the walls of the city and know of the desert—the nothingness—only by legend; indeed, they are afraid to venture out of Diaspar. Much of their fear stems from a supposed fact of history: half a billion years ago the Invaders drove man from the stars; since then he has confined himself to his dying planet. (Like Triplanetary Federation, the term Invaders links Clarke to the space opera of the 1930's.)

Only Alvin, the young protagonist, the only child born to the immortals in seven thousand years, possesses curiosity and a desire for knowledge. Refusing to accept the "gracious decadence" of Diaspar, he seeks and finds a way into the outer world, where he finds the "Land of Lys," a vast oasis of forest and grass-covered plains protected by mountains from the desert. When asked why he left the city, he explains that he was lonely. The tall, golden haired inhabitants—very unlike the people of Diaspar—are both mortal and telepathic; they welcome him because during the four hundred million years since communication between the two cultures was ended by mutual consent, they have aided the handful of individuals who escaped from the closed city, seeking to "regenerate" mankind. His discovery precipitates a crisis, for he wishes Lys and Diaspar to cooperate, and they are unwilling to do so.

To suggest that *Against the Fall of Night* is an account of Alvin's search for self identity is to read the novel as another exercise in psychological realism. It is instead an attempt to make a symbolic statement about the destiny of mankind. Alvin functions to destroy man's false concept of history—his fear of the

Invaders and their supposed blockade of Earth—thereby liberating both cultures from their self-imposed confinement. As soon, however, as the escape from the prison of the city becomes a quest for meaning, the narrative surrenders to an assortment of conventions and devices from magazine science fiction. Too much happens too quickly. Whereas Alvin largely controls the action of the first half of the story, one feels that from this point onward he is manipulated by his discoveries. Nothing is fleshed out. To summarize briefly: he learns that from space, accompanied by marvelous robots, came a mystic who taught his followers to await the return of the "Great Ones." Since the robots survive, one helps Alvin discover the interstellar ship left near Diaspar and now buried beneath the sands. Seeking the "Great Ones," they fly to the central sun of the Galaxy, but find its planet devoid of life. Although there are ruins, Alvin, lonely and filled with despair, does not know where else to search for intelligence; he has observed the "stars scattered like dust across the heavens," but realizes "that what is left of Time is not enough to explore them all."[30] Only then does Clarke intrude a solution.

The "burst of power" of Alvin's ship summons the creature Vanamonde "across the light-years." He is "a pure mentality"—a mind free from physical limitations—whose creation by the "Empire" (the "Great Ones") consumed the efforts of all the races of the Galaxy for half a billion years. He sets straight the record of history. Man never battled with Invaders for control of the stars. Before he passed the orbit of Persephone, "the stars reached him" —with devastating effect, for everywhere he found "minds far greater than his own." In dismay he turned in upon himself, studying genetics and the mind. Only after he had mastered such things as telepathy and immortality did he return to space to take his place in the "Empire," whose supreme achievement was the creation of Vanamonde. Yet Vanamonde was a second effort; the first had been the so-called "Mad Mind," which, for whatever reasons, ravaged—destroyed—portions of the universe until brought under control and imprisoned in an artificial star. It will one day gain its freedom; thus, after the creation of Vanamonde, the Empire abandoned this Universe for another.

Here may well be a vision comparable to that of Stapledon's *Last and First Men*, but so sudden is the revelation, so vast the time span (how many billion years?) and cosmic sweep of the Empire, that all which has gone before in the novel dwindles in significance. Alvin, Diaspar, the Earth: "I have made no reference to the Earth itself, for its story is too small a thread to be traced in the great tapestry" (p. 207). Nevertheless, because of the cooperation of the two cultures and the coming of Vanamonde, a Renaissance is assured. "Man had rediscovered his world," reflects Alvin, "and he would make it beautiful while he remained upon it. And after that—" (p. 212). Clarke undoubtedly improved upon the artistry of the work when he revised it as *The City and the Stars*, but the theme remains the same.

Similarly, in *The Lion of Comarre*, the young protagonist, who wishes to be an engineer and dreams of flight to the stars, rebels against a world grown stagnant. Just as Alvin was the only child born to the immortals in seven thousand years, so Richard Peyton III is the genetic reincarnation of Rolf Thordarsen, the builder of legendary Comarre, associated with the Decadents. Weary of "this unending struggle for knowledge and the blind desire to bridge space to the stars," these men believed that the aim of life was pleasure and chose to build cities "where the machines will care for our every need as soon as the thought enters our minds. . . .": "It was the ancient dream of the Lotos Eaters . . . the cloying promise of peace and utter contentment" (pp. 15, 61). Peyton finds the city in the Great Reserve of Africa, resists the attempt of the "Thought Selectors" to entrance him in a dream world while he is asleep, and encounters a master robot which has a will and consciousness of its own. From that meeting will come "The Third Renaissance," when man and machine will share the future as equals. Peripheral to the group, "The Road to the Sea" (1950) projects a future in which mankind has retained the use of a few wonderful machines, although forgetting the knowledge behind them. Man has forsaken the great cities and "returned to the hills and forest."[31] Seeking to learn something of the new country into which his village has been required by law to move, as it must every three life-times, a young artist searches for the ancient city of Shastar. There he encounters descendants of those men who long ago had traveled to the stars; they have returned only in order to evacuate Earth—which faces destruction from a force reminiscent of the "Mad Mind" of *Against the Fall of Night*. Even a cursory glance indicates how closely these narratives are inter-related at all levels from imagery and incident to theme.

To emphasize the creative relationship of science and man-kind, however bright a future it may portend, may well overlook those concerns which lead to Clarke's finest fiction. In *The City and the Stars*, while embellishing an early description of the mystic who came from the stars, Clarke accuses him of suffering from a disease that afflicted "only *Homo sapiens* among all the intelligent races of the Universe . . . religious mania." He then declares:

The rise of science, which with monotonous regularity refuted the cosmologies of the prophets and produced miracles which they could never match, eventually destroyed all these faiths. It did not destroy the awe, nor the reverence and humility, which all intelligent beings felt as they contemplated the stupendous Universe in which they found themselves.[32]

Unlike those nineteenth century writers, like John Fiske, who protested the astronomical difficulties they encountered in main-taining their beliefs, Clarke, obviously, is not afraid of the distances between the stars. Nor does he need to impose some deductive system upon the nature of things because, for him, the interaction of life, intelligence, and the galactic universe itself is mystery enough. However else one interprets these early stories, they celebrate intelligence *per se*, and in so doing anticipate his essay, "Science and Spirituality," in *Voices from the Sky* (1965):

Of all these questions, the place of intelligence in this gigantic universe of a hundred thousand million suns is the most important, the one that most teases the mind. During the past decade, the idea that life was a very rare and peculiar phenomenon, perhaps existing only upon our planet, has been completely demolished; within ten years we may know.[33]

Throughout Clarke's fiction there is no want of life or intel-ligence; they abound in a multitude of forms on a multitude of planets: "For what is life but organized energy?"[34] In *Against the Fall of Night* and *The City and the Stars*, while wandering the blighted universe, Vanamonde had found "on countless worlds . . . the wreckage that life leaves behind"; in *Childhood's End*, the first child to travel psychically goes beyond the range of the Overlords' ships and finally travels in another universe to a planet lighted by six colored suns—a planet that never repeats the same orbit: "And even here there was life."[35] But there is the other side of the coin, those stories like "Transcience" (*Startling Stories,* July 1949) which are dominated by a note of sadness.

In "Transcience"—whose indebtedness to the mood of Campbell's "Twilight" Clarke has acknowledged—an omniscient narrator paints three scenes. A hominid encounters the ocean for the first time. While building castles in the sand, a small boy from a village watches the departure of the last great ocean liner, not yet realizing that "tomorrow would not always come, either for himself or for the world." In the far-distant future, another child is interrupted at play to be taken aboard a spaceship into exile from Earth, for "something black and monstrous eclipsed the stars and seemed to cast its shadow over all the world." During what time is left only the sea and the sand will remain: "For Man had come and gone."[36]

Most often Clarke has maintained an omniscient narrator so that he can, as noted, switch the perspective quickly in order to gain some desired effect. Consistently, however, he has achieved his highest artistry in those stories unified by a first-person narrator recalling personal experience, as in "The Star" (1955). A Jesuit, the astrophysicist of an expedition returning to Earth from the so-called Phoenix Nebula, finds himself troubled by the report he must make of what was actually a super-nova. The "burden of our knowledge" has caused his faith to falter. On the farthest planet of what was a solar system, the crew of his ship found a Vault prepared by a people who knew that they were doomed and were trapped because they had achieved only interplanetary flight, not star-flight. "Perhaps," he writes, "if we had not been so far from home and so vulnerable to loneliness, we should not have been so deeply moved":

Many of us had seen the ruins of ancient civilizations on other worlds, but they had never affected us so profoundly. This tragedy was unique. It is one thing for a race to fail and die, as nations and cultures have done on Earth. But to be destroyed so completely in the full flower of its achievement, leaving no survivors—how could that be reconciled with the mercy of God?

. . . There can be no reasonable doubt: the ancient mystery is solved at last. Yet, oh, God, there were so many stars you could have used. What was the need to give those people to the fire, that the symbol of their passing might shine above Bethlehem?[37]

Or again, "Before Eden" (1961), in which the first astronauts to land on Venus discover a responsive, though mindless, plant. After conducting appropriate tests, Graham Hutchins, "the happiest biologist in the solar system," reflects:

> . . . This world around them was no longer the same; Venus was no longer dead—it had joined Earth and Mars.
> For life called to life across the gulfs of space. Everything that grew or moved upon the face of any planet was a portent, a promise that Man was not alone in this universe of blazing suns and spiraling nebulae. If as yet he had found no companions with whom he could speak, that was only to be expected, for the light-years and the ages still stretched before him, waiting to be explored. Meanwhile, he must guard and cherish the life he found, whether it be upon Earth or Mars or Venus.[38]

Pressed by the inexorable deadline for their departure, Hutchins and his companion postpone a little longer—for a few months until they can return to Venus with a team of experts and with the eyes of the world upon them—this meeting which "Evolution had labored a billion years to bring about." The mindless plant absorbs their wastes collected into a plastic bag and thereby contaminates the planet so that Hutchins' pictures and specimens are the "only record that would ever exist of life's third attempt to gain a foothold in the solar system. Beneath the clouds of Venus, the story of creation was ended" (p. 150).

For Clarke, these stories give expression to the central drama of the universe. He might be speaking for himself when he says of the alien visiting prehistoric Earth in "Moon-Watcher" (1972): "Centuries of traveling through the empty wastes of the universe had given him an intense reverence for life in all its forms."[39] Yet as the very language of these stories indicates, this reverence is accompanied by an anxiety which re-echoes through his finest fiction, perhaps reaching something of a climax in his essay, "When Aliens Come," in *Report on Planet Three*:

> . . . perhaps the most important result of such contacts [radio signals] might be the simple proof that other intelligent races do exist. Even if our cosmic conversations never rise above the 'Me Tarzan—You Jane' level, we would no longer feel so alone in an apparently hostile universe.[40]

Such a view surely echoes something of that horror felt especially during the decades at the turn of the century when science told man that he dwelt alone in an alien universe. That is why the apocalyptic moment of first contact is so important to Clarke; it dramatizes—resolves—what may be called his cosmic loneliness.

"The Sentinel" (1951) captures the melancholy of that loneliness. Perhaps more than any other single story it has proved seminal to the development of his artistry. That it provided the symbolic monolith which structures *2001: A Space Odyssey* measures but does not determine its importance. Once again Clarke makes use of a first-person narrator, one who recalls a discovery which he made twenty years earlier. From the first he fuses vividly his memories of the lunar landscape and what it was like to live aboard a surface vehicle in *Mare Crisium* during the summer of 1996. Because he is reflecting upon past action, one soon realizes that what is important is the implication of such a discovery on a moon proved barren by twenty years' further research. He guesses that early in prehistory Earth was visited by "masters of a universe so young that life as yet had come only to a handful of worlds. Theirs would have been a loneliness we cannot imagine, the loneliness of gods looking out across infinity and finding none to share their thoughts."[41] And so they left a sentinel—a signaling device to let them know when man had reached the moon.

In November 1950, Clarke first dramatized that "Encounter in the Dawn."[42] An alien astronaut gives various tools, including a flashlight of some kind, to a prehistoric man already possessing a flint-tipped spear. This may be called the astronauts' story. That their own worlds are being destroyed by a series of explosions—whether super-novae or atomic bombs, one cannot be finally certain—well illustrates how a number of ideas and images wove themselves through Clarke's imagination. As he is about to depart, the astronaut muses:

. . . In a hundred thousand of your years, the light of those funeral pyres will reach your world and set its people wondering. By then, perhaps, your race will be reaching for the stars. . . . One day, perhaps, your ships will go searching among the stars as we have done, and they may come upon the ruins of our worlds and wonder who we were. But they will never know that we met here by this river when your race was very young.[43]

Despite the increasing number of references in his non-fiction to a possible meeting during some period of the Earth's past, he did not re-work the plot until *2001: A Space Odyssey* (1968), where it becomes the first section of both the film and the novel. This version may be called Moon-Watcher's story, the story of the man-apes, particularly since the "super-teaching machine"[44] —the monolith—is substituted for the physical presence of the astronauts. The emphasis upon the education—the awakening—of Moon-Watcher and his companions completely submerges the sense of cosmic loneliness. Thus, not until the four short tales—"First Encounter," "Moon-Watcher," "Gift from the Stars," and "Farewell to Earth"—first published in *The Lost Worlds of 2001* (1972) did Clarke give the encounter its fullest development thematically.

Again the narrative focus is upon one of the astronauts, Clindar. A member of one of ten landing parties making a census of the Earth, he finds a small group of hominids. Possessing no tools and living "always on the edge of hunger," they have not yet been "trapped in any evolutionary *cul-de-sac*"; "they could do everything after a fashion." Whether because Clindar "looked straight into a hairy caricature of his own face" or because he saw one of the young males contemplating the moon in a manner suggesting "conscious thought and wonder," he decides to intervene in an attempt to tip the scales "in favor of intelligence." Left to themselves the near-apes would have little chance of survival, for "the universe was as indifferent to intelligence as it was to life." And so he gave them an "initial impetus" by teaching them to hunt and use clubs.

As his ship departs, he realizes that nothing may come of his efforts because many factors could destroy "the glimmering pre-dawn intelligence, before it was strong enough to protect itself against the blind forces of the Universe." Nevertheless, he and his companions install a signaling device on the moon to inform them if the descendants of Moon-Watcher reach their satellite. Then they will be worthy of a second visit. For "only a space-faring culture could truly transcend its environment and join others in giving a purpose to creation": Clarke makes no more succinct statement of his central dream. Yet it is a dream hard-pressed by anxiety, "for if the stars and the Galaxies had the least concern for mind, or the least awareness of its presence, that was yet to be proved."[45]

Without exception Clarke's recent major works—*2001: A*

Space Odyssey (1968), "A Meeting with Medusa" (1971), and *Rendezvous with Rama* (1973)—have dealt with the concept of first contact, but none has significantly modified the philosophical stance presented in the encounter between Clindar and Moon-Watcher. *2001: A Space Odyssey* suggests that those who left the Sentinel have now evolved into beings "free at last from the tyranny of matter," thereby bringing to mind Vanamonde.[46] Bowman journeys to the eighth moon of Saturn, Japetus, an artificial satellite which proves to be a kind of "Star Gate" through which he passes; he finally undergoes a metamorphosis changing him into a "Star-Child"—certainly an echo of the visions of Olaf Stapledon. In *Rendezvous with Rama,* Clarke pays explicit tribute to H. G. Wells's "The Star" adapting its basic plot to his own ends, for the new celestrial body plunging through the solar system proves to be a giant spaceship. Most attention is given to its exploration, although there is opportunity for political confrontation in the General Assembly of the United Planets when the citizens of Mercury launch a missile at Rama because it invades their solar space and supposedly threatens to become another planet. Instead it draws energy directly from the sun and departs, leaving the protagonist indignant because "the purpose of the Ramans was still utterly unknown":

They had used the solar system as a refueling stop, a booster station—call it what you will; and then had spurned it completely on their way to more important business. They would probably never know that the human race existed. Such monumental indifference was worse than a deliberate insult.[47]

Because the Ramans seem always to do things in threes, there is the final suggestion of further flights.

In contrast, "A Meeting of Medusa" attains the highest artistry of his recent works; it combines an innovative plot with an effective character study, and it gains unity by focusing solely upon Howard Falconer, though not told from the first person. He is a cyborg who flies a hot-air balloon through the upper atmosphere of Jupiter. And he discovers life in the form of a gargantuan creature like a jellyfish, a medusa. When it begins to handle his balloon, he flees. There is the final suggestion that he will act as an ambassador between humanity and the "real masters of space," the machines; the awareness of his destiny makes him take "a sombre pride in his unique loneliness."[48] Certainly "A Meeting with Medusa" suggests that Clarke may have found a new perspective from which to consider the old concerns.

For Clarke, man has chosen the right path, employing his intelligence and technology to reach out toward the stars. "Though men and nations may set out on the road to space with thoughts of glory or of power," he wrote in 1965, "it matters not whether they achieve those ends. For on that quest, whatever they lose or gain, they will surely find their souls."[49] Somewhere amid the blazing suns and swirling nebulae, if only in the artifacts of a civilization long dead in the vastness of time, man will find that he has become part of a community of intelligence which alone gives meaning to the indifferent splendor of the Universe. Until then he must dream of the stars and, like Clarke, be haunted by a sense of cosmic loneliness until he finds the Sentinel.

Thomas L. Wymer

THE SWIFTIAN SATIRE OF KURT VONNEGUT, JR.

"It is no exaggeration to say that Vonnegut's audience has been slow in learning how to read his stories."[1]   Max Schulz, recognizing this fact, tries to show us how by analyzing Vonnegut as a Black Humorist, as the product of a modern pluralistic universe, "an illogical world," "a world devoid of a discursive value system" (p. 5). "The unconfirmed thesis" is a strategy which exemplifies "the desperate shifts to which one kind of novelist in the sixties has been forced by his honest reponse to the existential implications of the times" (p. 7).   In *God Bless You, Mr. Rosewater* Vonnegut employs this tactic, Schulz says, by posing "the problems of the obsolete man in a technological society . . . while carefully refraining from any normative judgment" (p. 13).   His great virtue is "his willingness to resist the temptation to formulate answers," and his ability to "courageously live with irresolveables" (p. 27).

What we get, in effect, is an explanation of Vonnegut in the standard terms of modernism, a view typical of a number of studies since the publication of *Slaughterhouse-Five*.   This approach, however, often needlessly separates modern writers from older literary traditions which provide frameworks in terms of

238

which they can be clearly understood. Vonnegut, I shall try to show, is an unusually able satirist who, in a manner typical of Swift, although not necessarily in deliberate imitation of him, does lead us to normative judgments about the evils he attacks. Such norms as he does not provide, though they may be explained in terms of the modern writer's supposedly courageous refusal to give answers, are thoroughly consistent with the traditional ends and rhetoric of the satiric mode.

The problems of reading Vonnegut show striking parallels with those encountered in reading Swift. The major difficulty can be described as the problem of the second irony. Maynard Mack has pointed out how the satirist, in order to attack some evil— Mack calls the attack the thesis layer—will establish a satiric voice, a persona, to represent the "more or less ideal norm" against which the evil is measured—the norm is the antithesis layer. There are such standard personae as the *vir bonus* or good, plain man who reacts to evil with gentlemanly good sense; the *naïf* or *ingénu*, the simple heart who reacts with the bewilderment of innocence; and the satirist as hero, or public defender, who reacts with righteous rage.[2] Swift, however, has a way of throwing peculiar curves. In "A Modest Proposal" the persona analyzes the Irish problem with all the clarity, humanity, and reasonableness of the perfect *vir bonus* until he suggests that the Irish use their children as commodities like cattle to solve their economic woes. As a technique it is of maximum effectiveness in calling attention to the problem, while it calls forth from the reader the indignant affirmation of the value of human life, which is the first prerequisite to the discovery of any solution.

Another more subtle example is the narrator of *A Tale of a Tub* who, in "A Digression Concerning Madness," effectively attacks as madmen all conquerers, establishers of new schemes in philosophy, contrivors and propogators of innovations in religion and politics, all who in their pride attempt "to reduce the notions of all mankind exactly to the same length, and breadth, and height of their own." But the attack on rationalism turns into praise, apparently honest on the persona's part but ironic on Swift's, of a kind of Epicureanism, the search for happiness, which is to be found in not thinking at all, in the "perpetual possession of being well deceived; the serene peaceful state of being a fool among knaves." The persona thus becomes the voice not of an ideal norm but of an opposing extreme which is equally fallacious.

The trap one easily falls into with Swift is the failure to perceive the irony of the antithesis. The parallel problem in Vonnegut is revealed in the kinds of judgments made about the question of whether Billy Pilgrim and his Tralfamadorian solution are to be identified with Vonnegut. Almost all the possible responses have appeared in the criticism, and they can be schematized as follows. First, one can recognize the thesis layer but accept the antithesis layer as a valid norm: "the serene and peaceful state of being a fool among knaves" is a laudable ideal; Tralfamadorians are better than human beings and Billy is right to emulate them.[3] Second, one may accept the antithesis layer as the author's position but find that position disturbingly inadequate and question the author's judgment: Swift was himself mad; Billy is to be identified with Vonnegut, but his solution is puerile.[4] Third, one may see both thesis and antithesis as deliberately ironic, and call this an indication of the author's hopelessness: Swift and Vonnegut have given in to despair, or they are not satirists but Black Humorists.[5] Fourth, one may see both ironies, recognize the author as a master satirist, and examine his works in an attempt to explain their rhetorical structures and to understand the artist behind the masks. All of these approaches have been applied to Swift, the last yielding the greatest fruit; all but the last have been applied to Vonnegut.[6]

Such an approach demands a further examination of the nature of satire, especially why satirists like Swift seem to attack everything and leave us nowhere to stand. Often we have simply failed to see a norm that is developed in more subtle ways than we expect, but often the presentation of such a norm is not of primary importance. This is especially true when the satirist attacks a set of evils which are the results of a failure to exercise the simplest virtues, the merest humanity. That England was failing to do so is the crowning irony of "A Modest Proposal," for instance, where the moral norm is characteristically understated while the work illustrates, to paraphrase Schulz, the desperate shifts to which one kind of satirist has been forced to bring his audience to exercise its moral imagination. Vonnegut has probably done more than anyone to call to the attention of the English-speaking world the nightmare that was Dresden. That fact alone is enough to suggest that he, too, might be trying to similarly trick us into exercising our moral imaginations.

J. Michael Crichton describes a response to Vonnegut which is remarkably close to that produced in the attentive reader by Swiftian satire, while his apparent lack of understanding or awareness that the technique is Swiftian leads to an error which illustrates how Swift can help us with Vonnegut:

It is a classic sequence of reactions to any Vonnegut book. One begins smugly, enjoying the sharp wit of a compatriot as he carves up Common Foes. But the sharp wit does not stop, and sooner or later it is directed against the Wrong Targets. Finally it is directed against oneself. It is this switch in midstream, this change in affiliation, which is so disturbing. He becomes an offensive writer, because he will not choose sides, ascribing blame and penalty, identifying good guys and bad.[7]

This an excellent description of a classic sequence of proper responses to Swiftian satire—until the last sentence. Crichton fails to recognize that Vonnegut does not choose sides among those he attacks because his technique is the Swiftian one of presenting equally false theses and antitheses. The critic then confuses that refusal to take sides with a refusal to blame, which permits him to unconsciously contradict himself. It is a new twist on a problem all satirists come to know well: as Swift described it in the preface to *The Battel of the Books,* "Satyr is a sort of Glass, wherein Beholders do generally discover every body's Face but their Own." The reader has cooperated with the satirist in coming to admit, "I am at fault," but it is the reader alone who has managed to turn this into, "But I am not to blame," while Vonnegut's purpose is most typically to show how we are all to blame. How that purpose reveals itself through patterns of irony can be shown with any of Vonnegut's novels, but for the sake of economy I shall concentrate on *Slaughterhouse-Five,* referring for supportive evidence to others of Vonnegut's works.

In *Slaughterhouse-Five*[8] there are two central thematic concerns: first, the presentation of the horror of war and its dehumanization of man, for which theme the central character Billy Pilgrim serves as the major example of victim; second, a kind of solution to this problem, a world view associated with extraterrestrial beings called Tralfamadorians, for which Billy Pilgrim becomes the major spokesman. The first theme, the thesis layer, is quite clear and needs no explanation; the antithesis layer again offers major difficulties.

A Tralfamadorian explains to Billy that time does not change. "It does not lend itself to warnings or explanations. It simply *is*. Take it moment by moment, and you will find that we are all, as I've said before, bugs in amber" (p. 74). Free will is therefore nonsense. The Tralfamadorians, living in an eternal now with all time spread before them, know that the universe will suddenly disappear when one of their test pilots, experimenting with new fuels, presses a starter button. Why won't they prevent it? "He has *always* pressed it, and he always *will*. We *always* let him and we always *will* let him. The moment is *structured* that way." What can be done about wars? "There isn't anything we can do about them, so we simply don't look at them. We ignore them. We spend eternity looking at pleasant moments . . ." (p. 101).

Tony Tanner sees the issue clearly:

Billy becomes completely quiescent, calmly accepting everything that happens as happening exactly as it ought to (including his own death). He abandons the worried, ethical, tragical point of view of western man and adopts a serene conscienceless passivity. . . . Here I think is the crucial moral issue in the book . . . how are we to regard his new vision? (pp. 312-313)

Tanner goes on to point out the weakness of such a view, the question of whether we can afford to ignore the ugly moments in life, but he also sees the opposed question of whether conscience can "cope with events like the concentration camps and the Dresden air raid." Perhaps we need "fantasies to offset such facts." He tries to balance the two views:

Vonnegut has, I think, a total sympathy with such quietistic impulses. At the same time his whole work suggests that if man doesn't do something about the conditions and quality of human life on Earth, no-one and nothing else will. Fantasies of complete determinism, of being held helplessly in the amber of some eternally unexplained plot, justify complete passivity and a supine acceptance of the futility of all action. Given the overall impact of Vonnegut's work I think we are bound to feel that there is at least something equivocal about Billy's habit of fantasy, even if his attitude is the most sympathetic one in the book (p. 314).

Tanner is an excellent reader whose sensitivity helps reveal the possible error which throws him off the track. The fact that "total sympathy" turns into "at least something equivocal" illustrates the disorienting effect of the Swiftian technique, but Swift's pattern is suggested even more clearly. Tanner's confusion turns on the opposition between the apparent judgment of Vonnegut the man and the "whole work," its "overall impact." That opposition is there, but how we understand it depends on whether or not we trust Vonnegut the artist. Tanner does not. Put the case that Vonnegut the artist knows what he is doing; then it follows that the work as a whole is the most reliable measure of Vonnegut's purpose, while any discrepancies between "the overall impact" and Vonnegut *the man in the novel* (his major appearances are not in preface or epilogue but in the first and last chapters) would have to be explained by seeing that man as a satiric persona. This suggestion is plausible enough on a purely theoretical level; how accurate it may be must depend again on close analysis of the ways in which irony operates in the novel.

For the portion of the novel that deals with the war experience Billy functions as the satiric persona of the *naïf*. Totally victimized, he bears effective mute witness to the insane and dehumanizing cruelty that is war. But his function as *naïf* wears thin. If we discount Billy's prediction of his own death in 1976, the portion of his life covered by the novel extends to 1968. Billy has reached the age of forty-six. By this time he has for some twenty years been married to the rich, fat daughter of the owner of the Ilium School of Optometry, "a girl nobody in his right mind would have married" (p. 102). From the Buick and $30,000 a year his father-in-law guaranteed him in 1948 he has moved up by 1967 to $60,000 a year and his own Cadillac, complete with right-wing bumper stickers (p. 49). He is a president of the local Lions Club who applauds speeches by marine majors advocating "bombing North Vietnam back into the stone age," and he admits proudly that he is a veteran and has a son who is a sergeant in the Green Berets (p. 52). "Everything was pretty much all right with Billy" (p. 135). In short, he blindly supports in every way consistent with his age and position all those forces which had brought him to Dresden. He is, in fact, a familiar Vonnegut type, the agent-victim.

Tony Tanner describes this type as it appears most clearly defined in *Sirens of Titan*:

[Malachi] comes to a crucial perception—'that he was not only a victim of outrageous fortune, but one of fortune's cruellest agents as well.' Himself used and abused, he uses and abuses others. It is man's status as agent-victim which preoccupies Vonnegut; and once one of his characters comes to see this double aspect of human life and action he usually, like Malachi, becomes 'hopelessly engrossed in the intricate tactics of causing less rather than more pain.' And once again the desire to be beyond other people's schemes is voiced (p. 299).

Strangely enough, when his discussion turns to *Slaughterhouse-Five*, Tanner does not seem to recognize the agent-victim type in Billy, but he still helps clarify the road down which Vonnegut leads us. First we are led to see how culture, society, the universe itself seem to deny our freedom by categorizing us in terms of artificial systems and using us (the thesis layer). Then we are led to recognize how we contribute to that process because we are users and victimizers as well, the actual agents of our own victimization (the antithesis layer). Finally, we are presented with the question of whether it is possible to break out of this cruel self-destructive pattern. Vonnegut's answer, Tanner and most of the critics tell us, is No.

Vonnegut does, I think, suggest a more positive possibility, but it is important to realize that his "answer," although it will clearly imply a moral norm, will not be exactly a "solution." It is Miles Rumford who says in the passage Tanner quotes that the attempt to cause less rather than more pain is "hopeless"; it is also Rumford who, recognizing the injustice of a "free" society in which both exploiters and exploited are dehumanized, attempts to "save" mankind by engineering a war which results in death on a planet-wide scale; he goes on to create a totalitarian society in which human beings are rendered "equal" by being brutally reduced to their lowest common denominator. Vonnegut is acutely aware of how man's solutions to his problems have so often caused incalculable pain (Dresden and its more recent analogue, Vietnam, seem constantly to be in Vonnegut's mind in this connection). It is this awareness which accounts in large part for his characteristic use of the thesis-antithesis pattern, for the limited nature of his

moral judgments, and for his tendency to focus more on expressing the folly of others' solutions than on offering his own. But, as
we shall see, he does come to imply a moral basis for his judgments
as he deliberately exposes follies.

The process of undercutting and exposing the folly of the
Pilgrim-Tralfamadorian position is built into the structure of
Slaughterhouse-Five. It is constructed, we are told on the title
page, "somewhat in the telegraphic schizophrenic manner of tales
of the planet Tralfamadore." The technique is explained in
greater detail later on by a Tralfamadorian: these tales are laid out
"in brief clumps of symbols":

[each] is a brief, urgent message—describing a situation, a scene. We Tralfamadorians read them all at once, not one after the other. There isn't any
particular relationship between all the messages, except that the author has
chosen them carefully, so that, when seen all at once, they produce an image
of life that is beautiful and surprising and deep. There is no beginning, no
middle, no end, no suspense, no moral, no causes, no effects. What we love
in our books are the depths of many marvelous moments seen all at one
time (p. 76).

Immediately following these lines we are told that Billy goes
through a time warp and finds himself at the age of twelve quaking
in fear on the edge of the Grand Canyon: "His mother touched
him, and he wet his pants" (p. 77).

The connections between the two scenes are not particularly
subtle. The "image of life that is beautiful and surprising and
deep" takes us by way of the puns to the Grand Canyon, but
Billy's terror hardly marks this as a marvelous moment. The point
is carried further when little Billy next takes "a peewee jump of
only ten days" to Carlsbad Caverns, where he is "praying to God
to get him out of there"; a ranger turns out the lights in order to
give the terrified child the beautiful surprise of total darkness.
This instant undercutting of the Tralfamadorian concept of the
novel should alert us to the fact that Vonnegut has chosen his
messages carefully, but in a way which parodies the other-worldly
form he has created. Tralfamadorians use the schizophrenic manner to build up impressions of beautiful, unrelated images; Vonnegut parodies the form by juxtaposing ironically contrasting
scenes. And the irony directs us to read the novel's messages not

like Tralfamadorians, who see them "all at once, not one after another," but like human beings. In fact, the center of the novel's satiric thrust is its exposure of the sad fact that most people behave more like Tralfamadorians than like human beings, while the fundamental "ought" is one repeated throughout Vonnegut's works since its initial statement in his first novel, *Player Piano*: "The main business of humanity is to do a good job of being human beings" (p. 273).

As soon as one begins reading the novel like a human being, the observable relationships between scenes become so numerous that only a few can be pursued here. One of the major relating devices is a series of recurrent images: colors like blue and ivory, orange and black, nacreous pink; images like roses and mustard gas; the first dirty photograph in the western world; a barbershop quartet. All these images are associated with Billy's war experiences. Blue and ivory, for instance, recall a series of war scenes: shortly after his capture Billy sees "corpses with bare feet that were blue and ivory" (p. 56); on the prison train he lay "at an angle on the cornerbrace, self-crucified, holding himself there with a blue and ivory claw" (p. 69); as he debarks from the prison train he notices a dead soldier, "His bare feet were blue and ivory" (p. 128). These images recur, however, over twenty years later, all directly referring to Billy: in 1967 on the night of the Tralfamadorian kidnapping, there are three references to Billy's blue and ivory feet (pp. 62, 63, 65); and again in 1968, "His bare feet were blue and ivory" (p. 24). The black and orange combination appears first in 1944: "The locomotive and the last car of each train were marked with a striped banner of orange and black, indicating that the train was not fair game for airplanes—that it was carrying prisoners of war" (p. 60). The connection here is more immediate, for the next scene takes us by time jump to 1967, the night after the wedding of Billy's daughter: "The wedding had taken place that afternoon in a gaily striped tent in Billy's backyard. The stripes were orange and black" (p. 62).

The color images serve to undercut not only the Tralfamadorian concept of the novel but the philosophical view which underlies that concept. The Tralfamadorians advise Billy "to concentrate on the happy moments of his life, and to ignore the unhappy ones—to stare only at pretty things as eternity failed to go by" (p. 168). It is a selective approach to time that emphasizes the unrelatedness of events, the discontinuity of time. The ironic effect of the novel, however, runs counter to that view, insisting instead that time past is contained within time present, that Dresden is still happening while we ignore it. The recurrent images illustrate how Billy's whole existence is shot through with reminders of the unhappy moments. The fact that Billy so seldom seems to recognize these reminders illustrates his monumental blindness, his incredible lack of moral awareness, characteristics which continually recur. In 1944 for instance, "Billy found the afternoon stingingly exciting. There was so much to see—dragon's teeth, killing machines, corpses with bare feet that were blue and ivory. So it goes" (p. 56). In 1967 the morning before the Tralfamadorian kidnapping he is "stopped by a signal in the middle of Ilium's black ghetto":

The people who lived there hated it so much that they had burned down a lot of it a month before. . . . There was a tap on Billy's car window. A black man was out there. He wanted to talk about something. The light had changed. Billy did the simplest thing. He drove on (p. 51).

The simplest thing is precisely what the Tralfamadorians habitually do: whenever an unpleasantness intrudes on their happy moments, they close their eye (p. 115). A major irony which Billy's behavior exhibits is that, except for the power to control time jumps, Billy had become an excellent practicing Tralfamadorian long before he ever heard of such creatures. And his embracing of their world view is rendered suspect by the fact that their view is an excuse for and justification of the way he has been living all along, like a Tralfamadorian machine: "Tralfamadorians, of course, say that every creature and plant in the Universe is a machine" (p. 133). But the only reason he needs such a philosophical view is the fact that his mechanization began to break down; he began around 1964 to show increasingly disturbing symptoms of being human, symptoms which Tralfamadorianism manages to "cure."

The key scene is the wedding party of Billy's daughter. A barbershop quartet of optometrists sing "That Old Gang of Mine," and Billy finds himself weeping:

. . . he could find no explanation for why the song had affected him so grotesquely. He had supposed for years that he had no secrets from himself. Here was proof that he had a great big secret somewhere inside, and he could not imagine what it was (p. 149).

For one of the few times in his life Billy examines his own response and pursues it to a memory. He remembers four of his guards emerging from his slaughterhouse bomb shelter the morning after the Dresden holocaust, looking at the scene of utter desolation:

The guards drew together instinctively, rolled their eyes. They experimented with one expression and then another, said nothing, though their mouths were open. They looked like a silent film of a barbershop quartet (p. 153).

Shortly before this scene our narrator had described a story by Kilgore Trout about a robot whose occupation was dropping jellied gasoline on human beings. The robots, we are told, "had no conscience, and no circuits which would allow them to imagine what was happening to the people on the ground" (p. 144). In spite of Billy's mechanistic behavior, his memory of the quartet reveals the secret that, unlike the robots, he does have such circuits. His memory, however, stirs his conscience on a very elementary level, and it is at this point that the time warp theory is introduced to Billy by Trout, who notices Billy's upset and tells him he must have seen through a "time window": "Most of Trout's novels, after all, dealt with time warps and extra-sensory perception and other unexpected things. Trout believed in things like that, was greedy to have their existence proved" (p. 150). With the aid of Trout's theory Billy manages not to achieve anything like moral awareness. Billy's memory triggers a time jump to the Tralfamadorian zoo where he is telling Montana Wildhack about what it was like in Dresden just after the bombing—a very closely connected and unTralfamadorian time jump. He begins with the quartet of guards and describes the scene in cold detail. We are treated to the stunned odyssey of a hundred American POW's through the ruins, past charred bodies, the desolation momentarily relieved by a strafing run by American fighter planes trying "to hasten the end of the war," and we come to rest with the prisoners in an outlying inn where a blind German innkeeper feeds and beds them. The last line of the chapter quotes the inn-keeper: " 'Good night, Americans,' he said in German. 'Sleep well' " (p. 156). Billy is only telling a story. Vonnegut is address-ing us, and doing so in a way designed to inspire most unTralfama-dorian feelings of guilt.

Perhaps the most heavily loaded scene of the novel occurs appropriately enough near the end. It is a May afternoon two days after the end of the war. Billy, still in Dresden, is lying in "a coffin-shaped green wagon" which he and some friends had found abandoned with horses, and then ridden around in. The others leave, Billy falls asleep, and we are told that if he had had the Tralfamadorian power to choose his times, "he might have chosen as his happiest moment his sun-drenched snooze in the back of the wagon" (p. 168). But Billy's happiness has a price; he hears voices and looks over the edge of the wagon:

A middle-aged man and wife were crooning to the horses. They were notic-ing what the Americans had not noticed—that the horses' mouths were bleed-ing, gashed by the bits, that the horses' hooves were broken, so that every step meant agony, that the horses were insane with thirst. The Americans had treated their form of transportation as though it were no more sensitive than a six-cylinder Chevrolet (p. 169).

The scene becomes emblematic of the purpose of the novel:

Billy asked them in English what it was they wanted, and they at once scolded him in English for the condition of the horses. They made Billy get out of the wagon and come look at the horses. When Billy saw the condition of his means of transportation, he burst into tears. He hadn't cried about anything else in the war (p. 170).

By emblematic I mean that Billy functions as a kind of Everyman, perhaps the average reader, the typical blind and insensitive west-ern man who pays little attention to the suffering around him and probably had no knowledge whatever of Dresden before reading Vonnegut's novel. The man and wife are identified as "doctors, both obstetricians," a detail which helps reveal the wagon's func-tion as a perverse womb symbol, coffin-shaped to suggest the death to come from a false peace built upon indifference. The doctors, in attempting to deliver Billy from his indifference by making him look at the suffering horses, reflect Vonnegut's attempt to wake us to the world of suffering which we all ignore and to which we contribute.

The importance of this scene is reinforced by the reference to it at the conclusion of the novel which focuses on a scene two days before, the day the war ended:

> Billy and the rest wandered out into the shady street. The trees were leafing out. There was nothing going on out there, no traffic of any kind. There was only one vehicle, an abandoned wagon drawn by two horses. The wagon was green and coffin-shaped.
>   Birds were talking
>   One bird said to Billy Pilgrim, 'Poo-tee-weet?'

We end with symbols of rebirth centering on the bird's song; that song, however, is not a statement of rebirth but a question. We know how Billy will answer; he will climb into the womb, not out of it; the attempt to deliver him will result in the pointless sentimentality of his crying, and then he will forget the incident, remembering only the happy moment before. In short, Billy's birth will be aborted. The question that is not answered, however, is directed at us: is it possible for man to learn, in the terms the question was raised in *Sirens*, "the intricate tactics of causing less rather than more pain"; can man break out of the cruel self-destructive pattern in which he seems to be trapped?

How Western man will answer that question we can only speculate, but if some of the critics are any indication we have small basis for optimism. McNelly, for instance, maintains that "earthlings can find stoical, hopeful acceptance in the pattern presented by Tralfamadore" (p. 198). Somer sees Billy as the crowning success in Vonnegut's struggle to create "a hero who can survive with dignity in an insane world" (p. 230). In fact, Billy's stance of "heroic" acceptance is expressed in the situation of his being imprisoned with a voluptuous, guilt-free, sexually hyperactive movie queen, a classic adolescent wet dream.

A major thesis of the novel is that killing on a massive scale happens not simply because of the lovers of violence like Paul Lazzaro or Roland Weary, nor because of the rationalizers of violence like Professor Rumford, but also because of the Billy Pilgrims, the nice, plain, innocent, blind fools who lend passive support to that killing. Vonnegut builds up additional incidents to support this implication. The victims of his passive infliction of pain are not confined to horses; he has troubles on the prison train because his *sleep* is violent: "Nearly everybody, seemingly, had an atrocity story of something Billy Pilgrim had done to him in his sleep" (p. 68). Billy boards a plane in 1968 knowing it will crash, but says nothing because "he didn't want to make a fool of himself by saying so" (p. 133). Vonnegut also uses a real historian, British Air Marshal Sir Robert Saundby: speaking of Dresden, he says, "Those who approved it were too remote from the harsh realities of war to understand fully the appalling destructive power of air bombardment in the spring of 1945" (p. 162). Indeed, if we could imagine that Tralfamadorian test pilot who destroys the universe as having a "human" face, we would see neither the sadistic leer of a Roland Weary nor the insane hate of a Paul Lazzaro, but the vacant grin of Billy Pilgrim.

Far from championing passive or blind acquiescence, Vonnegut insists on the importance of awareness, the necessity of human beings understanding how they cause pain, how they commit atrocities in their sleep. An excellent case in point is the conclusion to *Sirens of Titan*. By this time Malachi, having won the love of Beatrice, has achieved his goal of causing less rather than more pain, and has been living a contented life on Titan. Finally, however, Beatrice dies (at the age of seventy-four) and Salo, an earlier version of a Tralfamadorian, returns Malachi to Earth, dropping him off at a busstop. It is snowing and the bus is delayed two hours, during which time Malachi freezes to death. Both deaths point up the possibilities and fundamental limitations of being human: one may, after all, live happily but not ever after. The major irony surrounding Malachi's death, however, is directed toward something else. As Salo and Malachi exchange farewells:

The complaint of a vaguely disturbed sleeper came from the open bedroom window near by. 'Aw, somebody,' the sleeper compalined, '*afo wa, de-yah ummmmmmmmmmm*' (p. 317).

A few lines later:

'*Sim-faw!*' cried the sleeper menancingly, to anyone who might menace his sleep. '*Soo! A-so! What's a mabba? Nf.*'

And after the spaceship leaves Malachi alone:

> '*Fraugh!*' cried the sleeper, as though he suddenly understood all.
> '*Braugh!*' he cried, not liking at all what he suddenly understood.
> '*Sup-foe!*' he said, saying in no uncertain terms what he was going to do about it.
> '*Floof!*' he cried.
> The conspirators presumably fled (p. 318).

The purpose of this seemingly irrelevant bit of action is symbolic, and the language bristles with ironic second meanings. The sleeper is mankind, locked within himself, complaining and vaguely disturbed, but angry at anyone who would wake him. Declaring his understanding of everything in nonsense syllables, he belligerently defends himself against imaginary foes, but remains asleep while something beautiful dies outside for the simple want of a warm place to sit.

The sleeper metaphor is an appropriate one with which to end the novel, since it also begins it. There the narrator introduces himself as a man of a century in the future telling "a true story from the Nightmare Ages" to his contemporaries in an attempt to explain what people were like "in olden times":

> Mankind, ignorant of the truths that lie within every human being, looked outward—pushed ever outward. What mankind hoped to learn in its outward push was who was actually in charge of all creation, and what all creation was about.
> Mankind flung its advance agents ever outward, ever outward. Eventually it flung them out into space, into the colorless, tasteless, weightless sea of outwardness without end.
> It flung them like stones.
> These unhappy agents found what had already been found in abundance on Earth—a nightmare of meaninglessness without end. The bounties of space, of infinite outwardness, were three: empty heroics, low comedy, and pointless death.
> Outwardness lost, at last, its imagined attractions.
> Only inwardness remained *terra incognita*.
> This was the beginning of goodness and wisdom.

This passage offers a conceptual framework with which we are to view the absurd actions which follow. The theme of the novel is not the meaninglessness of life but the revelation of how human attitudes and the actions based on those attitudes create meaninglessness, of how outwardness paradoxically locks us within a nightmare of meaninglessness without end.

The nature of inwardness is explored primarily by the revelation of the nature of its opposite. But part of the importance of the sleeper metaphor is the way in which it reveals that inwardness, though it can be mistaken for withdrawal (Billy Pilgrim is a perfect example), is not to be confused with it. It is outwardness which cuts the self off from meaningful contact with any other. Outwardness involves a preoccupation with the notions of purpose, of knowing, of mastering, of knowing who masters. Man confronts the universe with a set of demands, all of which seem to be concerned with how man functions within or is controlled by a system. The universe does not answer these questions or answers them in ways that make man appear to be a mere mechanism, and we conclude that the universe is absurd and human life meaningless. Vonnegut's point is that the answers are meaningless because the *questions* are absurd. In seeking to answer them, we reduce ourselves to objects and contribute to our dehumanization, which is why our "solutions" typically intensify the problem.

Vonnegut's recognition of this pattern places him in the middle of one of the richest veins of modern thought: with Heidegger, who explains how Western man came to conceive of himself as not in but set over against nature and thus alienated himself from Being, and how we have become so accustomed to conceiving of our will as the elevation of ourselves over another, as an act of conquest, that "the idea that all willing should be grounded in letting-be offends the understanding."[9] With Buber, who explores the nature of love in terms of the distinction between the "I-it" and the "I-Thou" relationships. I am not claiming here any direct influence. These ideas so permeate existentialist thought and have come to permeate even popular expression so much (the complaint about treating women as sexual objects), that it may be impossible to determine the specific source of such ideas for Vonnegut. In fact, these concepts are pervasive enough to be thought of as among the most common terms in which modern man tries to assert his humanity. Buber's thought especially represents the modern version of the humanistic tradition, a tradition which has long provided satirists with a normative background, the standards of sanity against which the world's madness is measured.

A clear example of how meaninglessness is fostered by the questions we ask is developed in a conversation the narrator of *Cat's Cradle* has with a bartender and a whore. The bartender recalls having recently read that science had discovered "the basic secret of life":

> 'I saw that,' said Sandra. 'About two days ago.'
> 'That's right,' said the bartender.
> 'What *is* the secret of life?' I asked.
> 'I forget,' said Sandra.
> 'Protein,' the bartender declared. 'They found out something about protein.'
> 'Yeah,' said Sandra, 'that's it' (p. 31).

The irony points up how irrelevant the secret of life, *as science defines it*, is to our actual living and to our sense of life's value. Perhaps the difference between outwardness and inwardness can best be expressed in philosophical terms as the difference between epistemology and axiology, between the perception of fact and the perception of value.

The nature of that difference is especially revealed in *Cat's Cradle* by its two sets of major image patterns. The first is the cat's cradle itself, which is linked with a highly empirical sort of epistemology, with the conception of the universe as mechanism and the perception of patterns which are, in terms of value, meaningless. That "bunch of X's between somebody's hands" contains *"No damn cat, and no damn cradle"* (p. 137); it bears no vital relationship to human experience. The image is especially associated with Felix Hoenikker, who is a total failure as a human being. He is a perfect curiosity machine whose discovery of ice-nine is linked to his preoccupation with the arrangements of objects in space, like cannonballs on a court-house lawn, oranges in a crate, or molecules of water. His son Newt remarks of him, "Sometimes I wonder if he wasn't born dead. I never met a man who was less interested in the living. Sometimes I think that's the trouble with the world: too many people in high places who are stone-cold dead" (p. 63). The phrase "stone-cold dead" is part of the second image pattern, the metaphors which associate such lifeless objects as stones and blocks of ice with human beings. Typically they are presented in an ironic context which suggests, as in Felix's case, that they are not doing a good job of being human, or that they are being reduced to objects; and the fact that the novel ends with the whole planet reduced to a block of ice suggests that this, rather than the cat's cradle, is the dominant metaphor of the novel. The implications of the cat's cradle are epistemological, relating to fact and suggesting the meaninglessness of the observation of empirical patterns. The implications of the ice block images are moral, relating to value and suggesting that the reduction of human beings to objects is a debasement of a greater value they either possess or ought to possess.

The metaphor is extended to express how such patterns of debasement are perpetuated, become a kind of legacy: "Angela, Franklin, and Newton Hoenikker had in their possession seeds of *ice-nine*, seeds grown from their father's seed—chips, in a manner of speaking, off the old block" (p. 51). Angela is used by a government agent who marries her in order to acquire the secret of *ice-nine*. Newt is similarly used by a Russian agent, although he can be manipulated sufficiently without marriage. And Franklin's model shop is used as a front for a criminal ring. But more than being used, Frank is a truer chip, since he shares in the activity of reducing others to objects. While his father does it as the theoretical scientist, Frank is the engineer. The only thing he can do well is model making, and his skill is consummate. The narrator is awed by one of Frank's model railroad layouts:

The details were so exquisitely in scale, so cunningly textured and tinted, that it was unnecessary for me to squint in order to believe that the nation was real—the hills, the lakes, the rivers, the forest, the towns, and all else that good natives everywhere hold so dear (p. 68).

This passage recalls a similarly ironic statement by another engineer in *Player Piano*: "If only it weren't for the people, the goddamned people . . . always getting tangled up in the machinery. If it weren't for them, earth would be an engineer's paradise" (p. 313). Frank's model is just such a paradise, a full-scale model of which he tries to build on San Lorenzo, but of course he fails—there are people there.

One could multiply examples showing how every character in the novel is used as a vehicle for the moral protest implicit in the ironic presentation of people reducing themselves and being themselves reduced to objects. But these scientists, engineers, militarists, patriots, industrialists, and so forth are all associated with the more obvious thesis layer. Of more importance to the critical understanding of Vonnegut's satiric technique is the antithesis layer, those characters who are the major spokesmen for attack, the narrator and Bokonon. Most critics again identify the antithesis layer with Vonnegut, but the dehumanizing patterns revealed in the thesis layer carry over into the antithesis layer, revealing again the agent-victim pattern.

The narrator functions as a reliable ironic observer for most of the novel until, in a manner typical of Swift, he becomes himself the object of satire. The first clear indication of a break in his clarity of vision occurs when he falls in love with a picture of Mona Monzano. There is no way in which a love based only on a picture can be anything but a subject-object, an I-it relationship. If we are deceived into sympathy with the romantic nonsense of love at first sight, we are finally disabused when the narrator tries to possess his love object. He is promised her hand in marriage and completes his first Boko-maru with her. Afterward he declares, "I don't want you to do it with anybody but me from now on. . . . As your husband, I'll want all your love for myself" (p. 170). Mona refuses and he has to back down, but the point is clear: he would have used Mona as his own stack of cannonballs if she had let him.

This display of weakness on the narrator's part is important in setting up the attitude necessary for evaluating his final act. He presumably follows Bokonon's advice, the last words of the novel:

If I were a younger man, I would write a history of human stupidity; and I would climb to the top of Mount McCabe and lie down on my back with my history for a pillow; and I would take from the ground some of the blue-white poison that makes statues of men; and I would make a statue of myself, lying on my back, grinning horribly, and thumbing my nose at You Know Who.

The page before this the narrator tells of a conversation he had with Newt: "I spoke of meaningful, individual heroic acts. I praised in particular the way in which Julian Castle and his son had chosen to die." Newt answers, "Well, maybe you can find some neat way to die, too." The narrator remains blind to the irony of Newt's remark, and most of the critics have also seen the ending as "a neat way to die." Robert Scholes, in fact, calls it "the best response" (p. 44). I would suggest, however, that

Bokonon's advice epitomizes the "empty heroics, low comedy, and pointless death" which were used to characterize outwardness in *Sirens*.

The narrator's errors in love show that he is in his own way as guilty of the dehumanization of others as those he ironically attacks. He can see this process in others, in Frank for instance:

And I realized with chagrin that my agreeing to be boss had freed Frank to do what he wanted to do more than anything else, to do what his father had done: to receive honors and creature comforts while escaping human responsibilities. He was accomplishing this by going down a spiritual oubliette (pp. 183-184).

But he cannot see it in himself. By blaming "You Know Who," which on one level implies God, he absolves himself of responsibility, flushing himself down a spiritual oubliette. And he does it, in a brilliant metaphoric stroke by Vonnegut, by turning himself into a block of ice, reducing himself to an object, a veritable monument to human stupidity, unknowingly showing how all agents of dehumanization ultimately become their own victims. And the ambiguity of "You Know Who" is a final satiric masterstroke: "You Know Who" is both the narrator himself and each one of us. Vonnegut is no modern comic Prometheus, flippantly thumbing his nose at the great S.O.B. in the sky. Like all good satirists his eyes are on the Earth where all posturing is comic and where the folly of man is sufficient cause for the world's evil.

This view of the narrator's death does much to explain another major symbol associated with him. The first words of the novel are "Call me Jonah," a variation on the opening words of *Moby Dick*. The narrator explains that his real name is John, but that it might as well be Jonah, "not because I have been unlucky for others, but because somebody or something has compelled me to be certain places at certain times, without fail." Since we have shown him to be an unreliable persona, we should not be surprised to see more significance to the Jonah symbol than he. For instance, when Jonah, fleeing from the presence of the Lord, is caught in a storm at sea, the mariners "said every one to his fellow, Come, and let us cast lots, that we may know for whose cause this evil is upon us. So they cast lots, and the lot fell upon Jonah" (1:7). Jonah is one of the archetypal agent-victims, one part of the

Jonah figure which John never sees in himself.

John, unlike Jonah, appears to be seeking the truth in his attempt to write a book on the day the first A-bomb dropped. But at the end of the novel when by destroying himself he declares his lack of understanding, it is clear that, like Jonah, he has all along been fleeing from the truth. Unlike Jonah, however, John is stuck in the whale, frozen forever because he never realizes his folly and there appears to be no God to set him free.

Jonah goes on to do the work of the Lord, but in a manner similar to John, as an unreliable messenger. According to God's command, he goes to Nineveh, declaring that the city will be overthrown in forty days for its wickedness. Surprisingly, however, the city and its king believe him, city-wide mass repentance and fasting are declared, and God relents. The great joke, however, is that this makes Jonah angry. He came all this way to carry God's message, and now God has made a liar of him. The fact is Jonah did not understand the message he carried. For him it was simply that Nineveh would be destroyed; for the king:

> But let man and beast be covered with sackcloth and cry mightily unto God: yea, let them turn every one from his evil way, and from the violence that is in their hands. Who can tell if God will turn and repent, and turn away from his fierce anger, that we perish not? (3:8-9)

And Jonah is not simply angry; he stalks sullenly out of the city, camps near the wall, and waits "till he might see what would become of the city" (4:5). What he gets for his pains is a case of sunstroke and the wish to be dead—all because he has been embarrassed, his conception of truth has been proved wrong, and, as God says, "sixscore thousand persons that cannot discern between their right hand, and their left" (4:11) have been permitted to live. It is little wonder the novel's third word is "Jonah": he is an almost perfect Vonnegut "hero."

Vonnegut's message cannot, of course, be absolutely identified with that of the *Book of Jonah*. The novel seriously questions the nature and existence of God and provides us with no clear answer to these questions. But Jonah does help clarify the kind of answer Vonnegut is willing to give. His narrator says early in the novel, "Anyone unable to understand how a useful religion can be founded on lies will not understand this book, either" (p. 16).

Similarly, a religion which leads men "to turn everyone from his evil way, and from the violence that is in their hands" is to that extent useful, lie or not. But in keeping with the thesis-antithesis pattern, Bokonon, while effectively exposing some of the follies of organized religion, also perpetuates others. Vonnegut goes beyond *Jonah* in showing how religion, by preaching the notion that "somebody or something has compelled me to be certain places at certain times," can provide man with an excuse for denying his own responsibility, thus flushing himself down a spiritual oubliette. That is precisely the weakness of Bokononism and what makes it not Vonnegut's answer but another in a long line of "gimcrack religions." Its' notions of patterns like karasses and wampeters operating in a world governed by the principle of dynamic tension, analogous to the cat's cradle, are a set of pseudo-explanations as irrelevant to real living as DNA is to the secret of life. For all its pretentions to belief in the sacredness of man, Bokononism attempts to shelter man from a knowledge of himself by diverting his attention from his own inwardness; as another attempt to "engineer" happiness, it fails as miserably as Frank's, and the Hook becomes a fitting symbol of Bokonon's reduction of man to an object, his contribution to the dehumanization of man.

It could be argued that Bokonon is superior to such objections because he knows he is lying, but calling himself a liar is his self-deceptive pretext for denying his responsibility for anything he says, another version of the familiar spiritual oubliette. This is a theme, moreover, which Vonnegut has dealt with in his most explicitly moral novel, *Mother Night*. There the main character is, in fact, a satirist who discovers that knowing he lies does not excuse him and that the pose of ironic detachment does not release him from involvement in the world or from responsibility for what he says and does.

The fact that the narrator of *Cat's Cradle* is himself guilty of a variation on the very evils he attacks brings us back to *Slaughterhouse-Five* and to one of the seeming barriers to the recognition that Vonnegut's purpose is to ridicule Tralfamadorians as types of human inhumanity: the fact that he so often in his voice as narrator repeats the phrase which is the Tralfamadorian response to death, "So it goes." There are a number of important functions which that phrase serves. It appears applied indiscriminately to such matters as dead champagne, dead lice, dead soldiers, the death of the Universe, of characters in Trout's novels, of 135,000 Dresden residents, of Jesus, and the death of the novel. This is not a simple expression of indifference; it is a *reductio ad absurdum* which parodies indifference, much as the description of the disarray on Belinda's dressing table in Pope's *Rape of the Lock*, "Puffs, powders, patches, Bibles, billetdoux," both expresses and parodies the disorder of her sense of values. Similarly "so it goes" functions ambiguously as the sign of the persona's indifference and as Vonnegut's ironic comment on Tralfamadorian indifference, a device of double irony common in Swift. Indeed, there is a bit of Billy Pilgrim in every man, and Vonnegut also uses the persona to acknowledge his own share of man's common inhumanity. And perhaps, as Tanner sensed, there is a certain degree of necessary distancing from the horror of war which the phrase provides; we have noted the necessity of both not being indifferent and not being sentimental. That balance is adroitly achieved when Vonnegut steps out of his satiric persona and gives his answer to the novel's question, thereby separating himself from Billy and the Tralfamadorians (it is analogous to Swift's practice when, after having presented his outrageous proposal as a modest one, he concludes, "Therefore let no man talk to me of other expedients," and proceeds to list a set of alternatives so practical and humane that it becomes clear that the ironic mask has been dropped). Vonnegut again uses the bird's song to set up the question. We know Billy's answer, but Vonnegut's is clearly different:

Everything is supposed to be very quiet after a massacre, and it always is, except for the birds.

And what do the birds say? All there is to say about a massacre, things like 'Poo-tee-weet?'

I have told my sons that they are not under any circumstances to take part in massacres, and that the news of massacres of enemies is not to fill them with satisfaction or glee.

I have also told them not to work for companies which make massacre machinery, and to express contempt for people who think we need machinery like that. (p. 17)

These two short paragraphs are set off not only by double-spacing but also by their style; free of irony or whimsy, they have the ring of an oracular declaration, a commitment. Still, as an answer it may strike some as insufficient, but its limitations are, I think, carefully considered. Billy Pilgrim demonstrates in one figure two major follies: the supposition that we can transcend the limitations of our humanity and the insistence that those limitations are necessarily so great as to deprive us of any responsibility for our humanity. Vonnegut's commitment demonstrates how moral responsibility operates within these extremes.

The moral vision suggested here is modern since it is derived from a conception of human freedom, but that conception, far from freeing us of moral norms, creates new ones. Being free in Vonnegut's existential terms becomes itself not a factual situation but a possibility that ought to be achieved; freedom is moreover characterized by its mutality: the deprivation of another's freedom ultimately victimizes oneself. One cannot therefore save or forcibly change another person or the world. But each person is responsible for what he himself does, both in directly denying and in lending active or passive support to those who deny the freedom of others. The sense of this obligation, however, in order to be consistent with freedom, must come from within, which means that the only way the world can be saved is the hard way, by the commitment of enough individual human beings to the task of finding a way to resist without destroying, of causing less pain without flying from responsibility; the task of becoming, in short, better human beings. That commitment is expressed in what Vonnegut says he has told his sons, his contribution to a modern children's crusade. No man can stop people from killing, but he can himself at least stop encouraging it.

Vonnegut has often been attacked for being simple-minded, even by those who detect his moralistic tendencies. The "Be kind" of *Rosewater* or the "love whoever is around to be loved" of *Sirens* reveal for Tanner "a detectable strain of sentimental sententiousness" (p. 300). Yet such formulations appear in contexts which insist that simple love, though important, is not enough. The follies of mistaken or misdirected love are among the most common targets of Vonnegut's irony. The repeated exposure of such follies, however, has a cumulative effect which gives his irony its distinctive flavor not of anger but of sadness. As incredibly insensitive and stupid as his human beings may be, he communicates a profound consciousness of how really difficult it is to love properly, how impossible it seems not to exhibit some share in man's stupidity. It tempts one to give up the struggle. But the "answers" of despair or mere laughter or retreat into fantasy are not Vonnegut's; they are among the responses of our time which he critically examines and discards. Essential to being human is the capacity to face oneself, to make moral judgments in the knowledge that one is without certainty, to create value through the agony of personal commitment. As difficult and even dangerous as it is to try to be decent, he says, in effect, human beings have to try, have to start somewhere. He sticks his own neck out early in *Slaughterhouse-Five* with his own commitment; the rest of the novel attempts to set us up to face the same question: "Poo-tee-weet?"

NOTES

Notes for *The Worlds of Jack Williamson*

[1] Williamson, *H. G. Wells: Critic of Progress* (Baltimore: The Mirage Press, 1973), p. 7.

[2] Williamson, *After World's End*, in *The Legion of Time* (1938; rpt. Reading, Pa.: Fantasy Press, 1952), pp. 138-139.

[3] Williamson, as in *Darker Than You Think* (1938; rpt. New York: Berkley, 1969).

[4] Williamson, *Bright New Universe* (New York: Ace Books, 1967), p. 114.

[5] Williamson, *H. G. Wells*, p. 36; an excellent introduction to historical and critical approaches to Darwin and evolutionary theory is A. G. N. Flew's *Evolutionary Ethics* (London: Macmillan and Company, Ltd., 1967).

[6] *Ibid.*, p. 42; see Charles Darwin, *The Origin of Species*, 6th ed. (London: J. Murray, 1872), pp. 234, 428. (Williamson's note.)

[7] See Flew, pp. 27-30; e.g.: ". . . precisely in so far as it is true that the future both of mankind and of the entire evolutionary process on this planet—indeed in the whole solar system—is in our hands, to that extent there can be no question of finding any guarantee of future progress, either in the actual course of evolution before the emergence of man, or in its hypothetical development supposing there were to be no further human participation" (p. 28).

[8] Williamson makes a puzzling statement about his reconstruction of Wells's works: he says that he will "consider in some detail first his imaginative exploration of the cosmic limits, next his study of the human limits, and finally his usually pessimistic evaluations of progress achieved.

"Any separation of the novels and stories into such categories is, of course, arbitrary. The scheme is imposed upon the fiction, *not discovered in it*" (p. 50; my italics).

If Williamson means by that last phrase that schemes do not come ready to hand in fiction, that critical structures cannot totally capture the experience and meaning of a work, that the author may not have deliberately had these schemes in mind when writing, that the critic does pull the meaning of works together by his schemes—if he means these things, then I agree. But if Williamson is suggesting that there is little valid, objective, descriptive truth and accuracy in what critics draw from literature, that all opinions are equally defensible, that the perhaps epiphanic methods of artistic creation cannot be measured by the reader's mind, then he is simply and philosophically incorrect.

[9] Williamson, *H. G. Wells*, p. 128; Edward T. Hall, *Silent Language* (New York: Doubleday, 1959), p. 170.

[10] Williamson, *H. G. Wells*, p. 92.

[11] For instance, Williamson, *H. G. Wells*, p. 27; *Bright New Universe*,

pp. 26-27.

[12]Williamson, *The Cometeers* (1936, 1950; rpt. New York: Pyramid Books, 1967), pp. 66-67, 92.

[13]The Romans knew Pluto ('Hades,' 'the Underworld') also as Orcus ('Death,' 'the Underworld') as place or force. Orco in Latin may mean 'to Hades.' Pluto, as Hades, is hard and inexorable. By virtue of the helmet given him by the Cyclops, he can move in this world, dark, unseen, hated by mortals.

[14]Williamson, *The Cometeers*, p. 113.

[15]*Ibid.*, pp. 116-117; Jay Kalam hints that he found one of Arrynu's female androids beautiful and destructive, and he seems to wish he could have had a fully human love relationship—his recalling is wistful and full of regret. He says that he almost disgraced the Legion, an extreme statement from one of his reserved, thoughtful, and iron character (p. 148).

[16]Jay Kalam refers to the controller of the Cometeers, "the authority of that shining emperor" (p. 153).

[17]*Ibid.*, p. 128.

[18]Williamson, *H. G. Wells*, p. 75; a reference to Huxley's "Preface" in *Evolution and Ethics and Other Essays* (New York, 1898), p. viii. (Williamson's note; the date seems to be erroneous.)

[19]Williamson, *Darker Than You Think*, p. 167.

[20]Williamson, *Dragon Island* (New York: Simon and Schuster, 1951).

[21]Williamson, *The Legion of Time*, p. 100.

[22]See Flew, chap. IV, pp. 31-51.

[23]Williamson, "With Folded Hands," a 1947 story in *The Pandora Effect* (New York: Ace Books, 1969), pp. 77-125.

[24]Williamson, *The Humanoids* (1948, 1949; rpt. New York: Lancer Books, 1969).

[25]Williamson, *H. G. Wells*, p. 98.   [26]*Ibid.*, p. 98.

[27]*Ibid.*, pp. 89-90.

[28]Williamson, *Darker Than You Think*, pp. 148-149.

[29]Williamson, *H. G. Wells*, p. 135.

[30]Williamson, *The Reign of Wizardry* (1940; rpt. New York: Lancer Books, 1973), p. 253.

[31]Williamson, *Seetee Shock* (1949, 1950; rpt. New York: Simon and Schuster, 1950).

[32]*Ibid.*, p. 232.

[33]Williamson, *H. G. Wells*, p. 117.

[34]Mircea Eliade, *The Sacred and the Profane: The Nature of Religion* (1957; rpt. New York: Harper Torchbooks, 1961), pp. 12, 22, 32.

[35]Tripus, 'tripe', 'three-faced': it has three of everything that goes into making up a face (pp. 75-76).

[36]Williamson, *Bright New Universe*, p. 86; Sledge, the humanoids' inventor in "With Folded Hands," was therefore not religious. The "religion" of James Cave is backed by Williamson's usual devices of symbolic names and puns. Cave's alien cancer is cured by one of the aliens, causing one character

to say, " 'James Cave was resurrected' " (p. 154). The false man, Caine, was the father of Adam, and he is called "JC" in both roles. Such intellectual punning, accidental or otherwise, is not excruciating in *Bright New Universe* (as it is in many other authors' works in this genre) because the vision is comic, though serious.

[37] As Adam says early in the book, contact is "the only game in town" (p. 8).

[38] *Ibid.*, p. 12.

Notes for *Olaf Stapledon's Dispassionate Objectivity*

[1] Stapledon, *Last and First Men* (London: Methuen, 1930; rpt. *Last and First Men & Star Maker*, New York: Dover, 1968), p. 13.

[2] Stapledon, *Last Men in London* (London: Methuen, 1932; rpt. *Last and First Men & Last Men in London*, London and Baltimore: Penguin, 1972), p. 577.

[3] Stapledon, *Star Maker* (London: Methuen, 1937; rpt. *Last and First Men & Star Maker*, New York: Dover, 1968), p. 249.

[4] Stapledon, *Odd John* (London: Methuen, 1935; rpt. *Odd John & Sirius*, New York: Dover, 1972), p. 86.

[5] Stapledon, *Sirius* (London: Secker & Warburg, 1944; rpt. *Odd John & Sirius*, New York: Dover, 1972), p. 309.

Notes for *Clifford D. Simak: The Inhabited Universe*

[1] Clifford Simak, "Face of Science Fiction," *Minnesota Libraries*, 17 (December 1953), 197-201.

[2] Simak, "The World of the Red Sun," in Isaac Asimov, ed., *Before the Golden Age* (Garden City, New York: Doubleday & Company, Inc., 1974), p. 197.

[3] John W. Campbell, Jr., "Twilight," in Robert Silverberg, ed., *Science Fiction Hall of Fame* (Garden City, New York: Doubleday & Company, Inc., 1970), p. 35.

[4] For a discussion of the importance of this theme in science fiction, see Thomas Wymer, "Perception and Value in Science Fiction," *Extrapolation*, 16 (May 1975), 103-112; and Thomas D. Clareson, "Many Worlds, Many Futures: Contemporary Science Fiction," in Thomas D. Clareson, ed. *Many Worlds, Many Futures* (Kent, Ohio: Kent State University Press).

[5] The "Hellhounds" are quite content to let the galaxy be destroyed because that will cause it to contract to the point at which there will be another "big bang." Being capable of existing outside time and space, they can then dominate the new galaxy.

[6] Simak, *Cosmic Engineers* (New York: Gnome Press, 1950), p. 206.

[7] This view is perhaps most thoroughly expressed in Donald A. Woll-

heim, *The Universe Makers: Science Fiction Today* (New York, Evanston, and London: Harper and Row, 1971).

[8] Simak, "Sunspot Purge," *Astounding Science Fiction*, 26 (November 1940), 62.

[9] Many of the remarks attributed to Simak come from taped interviews which he and I have had; in this instance, the interview took place during Torcon, the World Science Fiction Convention held in Toronto over the Labor Day weekend, 1972.

[10] Simak, "Hunch," *Astounding Science Fiction*, 31 (July 1943), 11-12.

[11] Simak, *City* (New York: Ace Books, Inc., 1952), pp. 77-78.

[12] Simak, *Time & Again* (New York: Ace Books, Inc., 1951), pp. 32-33: an indictment of man's brutality, emphasizing that he wiped out the creatures of earth "except for the ones he allowed to live for the service that they gave him" (pp. 28-29).

[13] Simak, *Goblin Reservation* (New York: Berkley, 1968), pp. 28-29, 129.

[14] Simak, *Out of Their Minds* (New York: G. P. Putnam's Sons, 1970), p. 180.

[15] Taped interview between Clifford Simak and Thomas Clareson, Torcon, Labor Day weekend, 1972.

[16] Simak, "Shotgun Cure," *Magazine of Fantasy and Science Fiction*, 20 (January 1961), 40.

[17] Simak, *Ring Around the Sun* (New York: Simon and Schuster, 1953), p. 144.

[18] Taped interview between Clifford Simak and Thomas Clareson, Minneapolis, Minnesota, 12 October 1974.

[19] Simak, "The Big Front Yard," in Isaac Asimov, ed., *The Hugo Winners* (Garden City, New York: Nelson Doubleday, Inc., 1962), pp. 175, 184.

[20] Simak, "All the Traps of Earth," in *All the Traps of Earth and Other Stories* (Garden City, New York: Doubleday & Company, Inc., 1972), p. 49.

[21] Simak, *Destiny Doll* (New York: Berkley, 1971), pp. 220-221.

[22] Simak, *Time Is the Simplest Thing* (Garden City, New York: Doubleday & Company, Inc., 1961), p. 69.

[23] Simak, *All Flesh Is Grass* (Garden City, New York: Doubleday & Company, Inc., 1965), pp. 112-113.

[24] Simak, *The Werewolf Principle* (New York: G. P. Putnam's Sons, 1967), p. 213.

[25] Simak, *Why Call Them Back from Heaven?* (Garden City, New York: Doubleday & Company, Inc., 1967), p. 172.

[26] Simak, "The Golden Bugs," *Magazine of Fantasy and Science Fiction*, 18 (June 1960), 121.

[27] Simak, "The Thing in Stone," in Donald A. Wollheim and Terry Carr, eds., *World's Best Science Fiction 1971*, p. 196.

[28] P. Schuyler Miller, "The Reference Library," *Analog Science Fiction*, 89 (June 1972), 168.

[29] Taped interview between Clifford Simak and Thomas Clareson, Minneapolis, Minnesota, 12 October 1974.

[30] Simak, *A Choice of Gods* (New York: Berkley, 1972), p. 50.

[31] Simak, "The Marathon Photograph," in Robert Silverberg, ed., *Threads of Time* (New York: Thomas Nelson, Inc., 1974), pp. 150-151.

[32] Taped interview between Clifford Simak and Thomas Clareson, Minneapolis, Minnesota, 12 October 1974.

[33] Simak, "Epilog," in Harry Harrison, ed., *Astounding: John W. Campbell Memorial Anthology* (New York: Random House, 1973), p. 239.

Notes for *Asimov, Calvin, and Moses*

[1] Virgil Scott, *Studies in the Short Story* (New York: Holt, Rinehart, Winston, 1971), p. 3.

[2] A small part of Asimov's "considerable output" appears in *Opus 100* (New York: Doubleday, 1970), along with the demurrer as to "deep meanings" in his work. He gracefully acknowledges, however, that others may be better qualified than the author to "interpret" his works.

[3] "The Endochronic Properties of Resublimated Thiotimoline" *Astounding*, 50 (March 1948), 125. Perhaps the same inept scientist who perpetrated "Thiotimoline" subsequently performed the experiment that catapulted Joseph Schwartz, of *Pebble in the Sky,* into the future.

[4] Asimov, *The End of Eternity* (New York: Doubleday, 1955).

[5] Asimov, *I, Robot* (Greenwich, Conn.: Fawcett Crest Book, 1970).

[6] *Opus 100*, pp. 65-69. See also Asimov's "Social Science Fiction"; Susan Sontag, "The Imagination of Disaster"; and Kingsley Amis, "Starting Points," in Dick Allen, ed., *Science Fiction: The Future* (New York: Harcourt, Brace, Johanovich, 1971).

[7] Though the Three Laws are too well known to warrant citation, it is possible that some who confine themselves to "new" science fiction may not know them. So: "1. A robot may not injure a human being, or, through inaction, allow a human to come to harm. 2. A robot must obey the orders of a human, except where such obedience conflicts with the First Law. 3. A robot must protect his own existence as long as self-protection does not conflict with the First or Second Law." See *I, Robot*, Frontispiece. For more of the robots, of Donovan and Powell, and of Susan Calvin, see *The Rest of the Robots* (New York: Doubleday, 1964).

Most writers who "borrow" the Three Laws, either by statement or by allusion, do so in order to utilize the Asimovian type robot. One interesting example of a short story designed to satirize the Three Laws is "A Code for Sam," by Lester del Rey, *Worlds of IF* (November 1966). Lester del Rey labels his robots as "Asimovian."

[8] Powell and Donovan, subordinate to the robots in that group of stories that primarily concern the latter, branch off into the world of cybernetics on their own, providing a cross between man and robot. Donovan,

"killed" in an accident, becomes the brain of a spaceship, and the partnership continues with Powell as pilot of "Donovan's Brain."

[9] An excellent study of the economic factors involved in robotics occurs in Frederik Pohl's "The Midas Touch," in *The Case Against Tomorrow* and in *Gladiator at Law*, with C. M. Kornbluth.

[10] As representatives of the Law (Old Bailey), Elijah Baley and Daneel are inspired by the Old Testament prophets, the indestructible and gentle Daniel of the Lion's Den, and that Elijah, who ascended to Heaven without benefit of death. Both prophets were involved in international intrigue, and both served as "spies" for their nation. The name "Baley" (cf. Bail Channis of Second Foundation) fits Webster's definition of "bail" as "delivery or transfer of property for special purposes without transfer of ownership."

[11] Asimov, *The Caves of Steel* (Garden City, New York: Doubleday, 1954) and *The Naked Sun* (Garden City, New York: Doubleday, 1957). All quotations are from the Lancer paperback editions of 1970.

[12] Cf. Michael Valentine Smith in Robert Heinlein's *Stranger in a Strange Land* in the handling of alien experiences, especially Smith's first encounter with grass.

[13] The influence of Aldous Huxley's *Brave New World* is evident in Asimov's handling of the Baby Farm.

[14] Asimov also stresses "smell imagery"; Solarians believe that Baley gives off an unpleasant odor. The social allusion is plain here.

[15] In *Opus 100* Asimov tells about the discovery of DNA in 1953 by Francis Crick and James Watson: "That was the biochemical analogue of reproduction. But it was in 1953 that I had been writing *The Chemicals of Life* and I had missed it" (p. 182).

[16] The Foundation trilogy blends together, in addition to the Asimovian philosophy, the technologies of economics, psychology, mass psychology, statistics, politics, cyclical history, and, of course, chemistry and atomic physics. Though I describe the plot of the Foundation group in terms of a transistor, the transistor was not developed until shortly after the series was published.

[17] Asimov, "The Last Question," appears in *Opus 100*, but is better found in *Nine Tomorrows*.

Notes for *The Frontier Worlds of Robert A. Heinlein*

[1] Cf. Frederick Jackson Turner, *The Frontier in American History* (New York: Holt, Rinehart, Winston, 1962); George Russell Taylor, ed. *The Turner Thesis Concerning the Role of the Frontier in American History* (Boston: Heath, 1949); Walker D. Wyman and Clifton B. Kroeber, eds., *The Frontier in Perspective* (Madison: University of Wisconsin Press, 1965); C. Merton Babcock, ed., *The American Frontier: A Social and Literary Record* (New York: Holt, Rinehart, Winston, 1965); Philip Durham and Everett Jones, eds., *The Frontier in American Literature* (New York: Odyssey,

1969); Lucy Lockwood Hazard, *The Frontier in American Literature* (New York: Ungar, 1961); Harold P. Simonsen, *The Closed Frontier: Studies in American Literary Tragedy* (New York: Holt, Rinehart, Winston, 1970); Robert L. Heilbroner, *The Future as History* (New York: Grove Press, 1960); and Getthard Günther, "Die Enteeckung Amerikas und die Sache der Weltraumliteratur (Science Fiction), aus der Amerikanische übersetzt von Otto Schrag," pamphlet (Düsseldorf, 1952).

[2] General facts about Heinlein's biography are available in the following sources: *Current Biography* (March 1955); *Contemporary Authors*, v. 2 (1963); *Twentieth Century Authors*; Sam Moskowitz, *Seekers of Tomorrow: Masters of Modern Science Fiction* (Cleveland: World, 1966); Alexei Panshin, *Heinlein in Dimension* (Chicago: Advent, 1968). In addition, I spent six hours on the phone with Heinlein on June 21 and 22, 1974, after sending him a draft of this paper; any comments on what Heinlein says or claims which are not otherwise documented refer back to these conversations.

[3] Besides Moskowitz and Panshin, see also Robert A. Heinlein, "Preface," *The Man Who Sold the Moon* (Chicago: Shasta, 1950); Robert A. Heinlein, "On the Writing of Speculative Fiction," *Of Worlds Beyond: The Science of Science Fiction Writing*, ed. Lloyd Arthur Eschbach (Chicago: Advent, 1964); Robert A. Heinlein, "Science Fiction: Its Nature, Faults, and Virtues," *The Science Fiction Novel: Imagination and Social Criticism* (Chicago: Advent, 1959); Robert A. Heinlein, "Introduction," *Tomorrow, the Stars* (Garden City: Doubleday, 1952); Robert A. Heinlein, "Channel Markers," guest editorial (transcript of April 5, 1973, James Forrestal Memorial Lecture, U. S. Naval Academy, Annapolis), *Analog Science Fiction/Science Fact*, 92 (January 1974), 5-10, 166-178.

[4] For a full and accurate bibliography (as far as I have been able to confirm), see Panshin. A good article on Campbell's work is Albert I. Berger, "The Magic that Works: John W. Campbell and the American Response to Technology," *Journal of Popular Culture*, 5 (Spring 1972), 867-943.

[5] Although Campbell is given a lot of credit for developing young writers, Heinlein maintains that he developed himself, and I see no reason to doubt him. Campbell was the younger man, less experienced, more likely to fly off on tangents and get swept up in fads, and by no means as good a writer. But I suspect their relationship involved a good deal of flow in both directions.

[6] That speech was recently reprinted in *Vertex*, 1 (June 1972), 46-49, 96-98.

[7] Heinlein's attitude toward his "juvenile" novels is described in Robert A. Heinlein, "Ray Guns and Rocket Ships," *Library Journal*, 78 (July 1953), 1188-1191. His growing dissatisfaction as expressed in 1961 is cited in Panshin, p. 185. The overall ambivalence of science fiction toward science and technology is described at some length in Berger, *passim*.

[8] In addition, according to Panshin and Heinlein himself, he wrote and sold a number of light-hearted stories for girl's magazines during the 1950's, which is reflected, in some measure, in *Podkayne of Mars*, "The Menace from

Earth," and " 'All You Zombies,' "

[9] I have not seen or heard the speech, but I have seen the newspaper advertisement in the *Colorado Springs Telegraph Gazette* of April 13, 1958, to which Panshin refers. Heinlein says it was one of several ads run in a number of newspapers, to which the response was insufficient to warrant continuing the membership drive.

[10] Although Heinlein maintains that he is now in perfect health, with the same weight and blood pressure as when he graduated from the Naval Academy, he did not look well at the Nebula Awards convention of the Science Fiction Writers of America, held at the Century Plaza Hotel in Los Angeles, April 26-27, 1974, and he does admit that he was near death in the winter of 1970. His claim that some of his most admired work was written in ill health does not diminish their vitality, nor would his living another thirty years remove from his latest novels their reflection of a concern with death.

[11] The four novels are *Double Star* (1956 award), *Starship Troopers* (1960), *Stranger in a Strange Land* (1962), and *The Moon is a Harsh Mistress* (1967). These awards, for which nomination and election is held among interested fans (including writers), were instituted as recently as 1953, and the competition in a given year may not be too strong, but Heinlein's popularity among fans is still very high according to most polls. Cf. Donald Franson, "A History of the Hugo, Nebula, and International Fantasy Awards," pamphlet (Dearborn, Michigan: Howard De Vore, 1971). It may also be of interest in this regard that two of Heinlein's short stories were voted among the twenty all-time bests, and two of his novelettes placed in the top ten, in recent polls of the Science Fiction Writers of America leading to the publication of *The Science Fiction Hall of Fame*, v. 1, edited by Robert Silverberg (Garden City: Doubleday, 1970), v. 2A and 2B, edited by Ben Bova (Garden City: Doubleday, 1973).

[12] As of 1974, all of Heinlein's books are in print in paperback, most in hard covers, as well. First editions of the juvenile novels, 1947-1958, were published by Scribners; of novels since 1959 by Putnam. Shasta first published the Future History stories, which Putnam put into the omnibus; Doubleday published *Waldo* and *Magic Inc.*, *The Puppet Masters*, *Tomorrow, the Stars* (anthology), *Double Star*, and *The Door into Summer*; Gnome Press published *Sixth Column* (since retitled *The Day After Tomorrow*), *Methuselah's Children*, and two story collections, *The Menace from Earth* and *The Unpleasant Profession of Jonathan Hoag* (since retitled *6 X H*); Fantasy Press published *Beyond this Horizon* and the collection, *Assignment in Eternity*. Additional information on earlier versions and revisions of Heinlein stories is available in Panshin.

[13] Robert A. Heinlein, *Revolt in 2100* (Shasta, 1953; NAL, 1955). Although Heinlein claimed at the time to have abandoned these stories, their outlines bear distinct resemblances to materials used in *Stranger in a Strange Land*, *The Moon is a Harsh Mistress*, and the novelette, "Free Men," published in *The Worlds of Robert A. Heinlein* (New York: Ace, 1966).

[14] This subplot and the "happy ending" were dictated by John Campbell, over the futile objections of Heinlein, who saw the plot and science as too facile and preferred the alternative of shutting down the power; but, in preparing the omnibus for publication, Heinlein's only changes were a few small ones updating terminology.

[15] This is not to say that there are not such wheeler-dealers in the real world; rather, that they don't get what they want so easily in board-room conversations which carry such a heavy load of (reader-oriented) information.

[16] Although "Requiem" was Heinlein's third published story, he points out that it was the first one he ever wrote; this may explain some of its faults, but hardly its popularity.

[17] Although Heinlein says this story was intended for the *Saturday Evening Post*, its theme of real vs. misguided patriotism, its motif of the ordinary man becoming a hero, and its military context seem tailor-made for the American Legion audience.

[18] She also, of course, corresponds to the heroines of the girls' stories Heinlein was turning out in the 1950's, entirely outside the conventions of science fiction.

[19] Cf. Heinlein's comments on the remote control handling devices called "Waldoes" and his so-called prediction of them, in *The Science Fiction Novel*, p. 31.

[20] Lloyd Eschbach, *Of Worlds Beyond*, pp. 14-16. In conversation, Heinlein maintained that he used basically two formulas in most of his writing. In his early stories, he would create two or three good characters, get them into an impossible jam, then start writing the story, making them get out of their fix by means of brain power, not a *deus ex machina*. In his juvenile novels, he would begin with an adolescent, defined more by attitude than physiology, get him into a fix, separated from all adults and/or mentors (the means of separation being the most difficult aspect of the book to keep coming up with); the story then would end when the main character was no longer a boy, but a man, thinking as an adult. I'm not at all sure that his characters always get out of a jam by means of using their intelligence, or that they emerge as adults, but the basic outline seems to fit.

[21] Heinlein's objections that the world was still afraid of Nazis after World War Two and that the Germans had, after all, had the most advanced rocket engineering around may be well taken, but he admits he misgauged his audience (although the book is still being reprinted). I would suggest that he misgauged his material, which no one could have made much out of.

[22] Cf. William B. Johnson and Thomas D. Clareson, "The Interplay of Science and Fiction: The Canals of Mars," and William B. Johnson, "A Checklist to Articles on the Martian 'Canal' Controversy," *Extrapolation*, 5 (May 1964), 37-39; 40-48.

[23] Cf. Brian W. Aldiss, ed. *All About Venus: A Revelation of the Planet Venus in Fact and Fiction* (New York: Dell, 1968).

[24] *Astounding* (January 1974), p. 176.

[25] Heinlein maintains that he had so much fun writing "The Menace

from Earth" that he wanted to try a more extended narrative in the first person female. Of course, *Podkayne* was not sold or published until five years later than the other piece.

[26] For a more extended treatment of Heinlein's solipsism, see Panshin, pp. 160-177.

[27] In fact, Heinlein says, his cat's antics, like those described, gave him the inspiration for this novel which he wrote non-stop in thirteen days.

[28] Charles Manson, convicted in 1970 for the 1969 Tate-La Bianca murders in Los Angeles, seems to have borrowed from *Stranger in a Strange Land* to buttress his attitudes toward love and death, as well as some of the behavior of his twisted "family" of "love." See Ed Sanders, *The Family: The Story of Charles Manson's Dune Buggy Attack Battalion,* revised edition (New York: Avon, 1972), for what sketchy details there are (esp. pp. 32-33, 36, 386). This information, made public in the newspapers and *Time* Magazine, caused Heinlein some notoriety at this time, when *Stranger* had become an "underground classic," due in part to youthful readers' taking dead seriously the novel's love religion.

[29] Moskowitz, *Seekers of Tomorrow*, p. 210. Heinlein, however, contends that while the novel was outlined in the late 1940's, it was written in three large chunks in the late 1950's, which no one has been able to differentiate. The break between the early action and the late philosophy, according to him, was intended from the beginning; if the apparent changes in style and content are only coincidental, it is nonetheless convenient that this novel makes a significant turning point in Heinlein's career, as the philosophizing in his novels takes over and the wider reading public begins to pay more attention to him.

[30] Contrast the following critiques, which seem to indicate that it is difficult to stay neutral about this novel: Robert Plank, "Omnipotent Cannibals: Thoughts on Reading Heinlein's *Stranger in a Strange Land*," *Riverside Quarterly*, 5 (July 1971), 30-37; Ronald Lee Cansler, "*Stranger in a Strange Land*: Science Fiction as Literature of Creative Imagination, Social Criticism, and Entertainment," *Journal of Popular Culture*, 5 (Spring 1972), 944-954.

[31] Heinlein's sensationalism in *Farnham's Freehold* apparently drew fire from a number of quarters, as is indicated by an exchange of correspondence in *Riverside Quarterly* in 1966: Franz Rottensteiner complained of the gratuitous incest motif (2: 144) and of the incredible naiveté of Barbara, *a biology major*, who retches at seeing the mother cat eat her afterbirth, thinking that she might have to do the same thing (2: 220). The scenes occur on pages 93-94 and 100-101 of the novel's paperback edition. Leland Sapiro, editor of *Riverside Quarterly*, responded to Rottensteiner's first letter with a reference to another fanzine critic's argument, in 1964, that Heinlein had set out "deliberately to exhibit our nastiest fears and revulsions." Cf. Plank's article on *Stranger in a Strange Land*.

[32] This dialect, or argot, which is supposed to identify Manny as no intellectual in a culture derived from three generations or more of criminal

and political exiles from many countries, uses words and phrases from several tongues in a grammar ostensibly modified by Russian influence (though my Russian colleague, Prof. Joseph Cvrtlk, strongly questions the legitimacy of Heinlein's usage). The real effect, too often, is of simple dictionary substitution in English sentences. See also Panshin, p. 115.

[33] Algis Budrys, "Galaxy Bookshelf," *Galaxy*, 29 (July 1968), 64-67.

[34] Heinlein assures me that *I Will Fear No Evil* has sold more copies than any of his other books, though *Time Enough For Love* may surpass it and *Stranger in a Strange Land*. But this box office success may only underline that Heinlein is now competing more with Harold Robbins and Jacqueline Susann than with Isaac Asimov and Arthur C. Clarke.

[35] It may be argued, of course, that this dual consciousness may be only a figment of the imagination of the old man's brain, unable to cope with its changed body, but I think we need at least the ambiguity of whether Eunice is really present, or most of the contents of the book lose their meaning, if not their titillating effect.

[36] Heinlein maintains that the reviews of his book, outside the science fiction community, have been predominantly favorable. Not having access to all the reviews, as an author and his publisher have, I did check out those I could find in *Booklist, English Journal, Library Journal*, Los Angeles *Times*, and New York *Times*, all of which paid sentimental homage to Lazarus Long, the Heinlein canon, and the "future history." Most, however, felt that the novel was too long and too garrulous, although they might be willing to put up with that for old times' sake. The only unpatronizing praise came from Harrison J. Means in the *English Journal*, 72 (October 1973), 1060, who found it "a nearly 600-page delight for the avid SF reader who never wants a story to end. . . . With the publication of *I Will Fear No Evil* [in paperback] Heinlein's concern with longevity and with more liberal mores has marked a change in his novels. Both are excellent reading."

[37] This common criticism of Heinlein he disclaims, largely on the grounds that he has always tested the conventional limits of the pulp magazines, pushing for "adult" sexual relationships. But, having taken this freedom since *Stranger*, he has not taken advantage of it yet to portray what I would call an adult sexual relationship. There are adult relationships, as in "The Unpleasant Profession of Johnathan Hoag," and there are regressive relationships, as in *The Door into Summer*, but where there is explicit sex, there seems always to be the cooing, giggling, or sniggering of adolescence.

[38] The idea of a musical analogy is, I think, a good one, allowing Heinlein to pick out of an unwieldy two millennia various moments which might serve as "Variations on a Theme" (a chapter title he uses four times), or conceptual themes which blend or contrast. But the analogy really seems to stop with the contents page, appearing to be superimposed over what is still an unwieldy narrative; to be sure, the last seven subchapters are "titled" with punning bugle calls (as Lazarus goes off to fight in World War One), but that rather changes the shape of the analogy. Unlike the internal monologue, which Heinlein seems more comfortable with than in *I Will Fear No Evil*,

these "modernist" devices do not appear to me to be fully under his control.

[39] This thesis is defended at some length in Alfred Bester, "Science Fiction and the Renaissance Man," *The Science Fiction Novel*, pp. 102-125.

[40] An excellent study of the way that aliens, specifically, meet our fantasy needs is Robert Plank's *The Emotional Significance of Imaginary Beings: A Study of the Interaction Between Psychotherapy, Literature, and Reality in the Modern World* (Springfield, Illinois: Charles C. Thomas, 1968). For an analysis of what readers were willing to accept as science, see any of the articles in the series "The Science in Science Fiction" by Greg Benford and others, in *Amazing*, beginning in November 1969.

[41] Besides Berger, see also Heinlein's sober predictions in "Where To?" *Galaxy*, 6 (February 1952), 13-29, revised and updated as "Pandora's Box," *The Worlds of Robert A. Heinlein*, pp. 7-31.

[42] Cf. Judith Merril, "What Do You Mean Science/Fiction?" *SF: The Other Side of Realism; Essays on Modern Fantasy and Science Fiction*, ed. Thomas D. Clareson (Bowling Green, Ohio: Bowling Green University Popular Press, 1971). Although Heinlein has shown a preference for the term "speculative fiction," his use of it is quite restrictive. See especially his essay in *The Science Fiction Novel, passim*.

[43] In 1973 (*Analog*), as in 1947 (*Of Worlds Beyond*), he maintains that perserverance is the most important ingredient of a writer's success. In 1958, he dismisses "Henry Miller, Jean-Paul Sartre, James Joyce, Francoise Sagan and Alberto Moravia" as representatives of "the ash-can school of realism" in *The Science Fiction Novel* (p. 54). His aim, in style, he maintains, is to write lucid prose, for which he takes as his models Sir Winston Churchill, Justice Holmes, T. H. Huxley, and Rudyard Kipling. Yet in *Farnham's Freehold* he comes close to writing a mainstream novel such as he had six years before classified as sick, in *I Will Fear No Evil* we find him playing with stream of consciousness techniques, and in *Time Enough for Love* the emphasis on juxtaposition and counterpoint is positively obtrusive.

[44] For an even dozen, compare Heinlein's best with *A Canticle for Leibowitz, The Crystal World, Davy, The Dream Master, Dying Inside, The Einstein Intersection, The Left Hand of Darkness, The Man in the High Castle, Mission of Gravity, More than Human, No Blade of Grass,* and *Stand on Zanzibar*. For icing, of course, you can add the best sf works by Anthony Burgess, William Golding, C. S. Lewis, George R. Stewart, and Kurt Vonnegut, along with the great dystopias of Huxley, Orwell, and Zamiatin and the best of Wells's "scientific romances."

[45] In preparing this paper, I have also read but not made significant use of other articles on Heinlein. Two are largely source-tracings, J. R. Christopher's "Methuselah, Out of Heinlein by Shaw," *The Shaw Review*, 6 (May 1973), 79-88, and Diane Pankin Speer's "Heinlein's *The Door into Summer* and *Roderick Random*," *Extrapolation*, 12 (December 1970), 30-34. Three others strongly emphasize character-studies of Heinlein through his writing, a general survey (through 1957) by Damon Knight, "One Sane Man: Robert A. Heinlein," *In Search of Wonder: Essays on Modern Science*

Fiction, revised edition (Chicago: Advent, 1967), 76-80; a study of the first-person narrator by James Blish, "First Person Singular: Heinlein, Son of Heinlein," *More Issues at Hand: Critical Studies in Contemporary Science Fiction* (Chicago: Advent, 1970), 51-58; and an amateur psychoanalytic study by Alexei and Cory Panshin, "Reading Heinlein Subjectively," *The Alien Critic,* 23 (May 1974), 4-17. Doubtless there are numerous other fanzine articles I have not come across which might be illuminating, but, unlike the Panshins, I have attempted a consciously "objective" reading (in that I have tried to relate his work to the real world, as I—subjectively—understand both the work and the world), one which I hope will still stand up when later Heinlein works are published. He claims there's a lot yet to come.

Notes for *The Sturgeon Connection*

[1] Theodore Sturgeon, "The Silken-Swift," *Magazine of Fantasy and Science Fiction,* 5 (November 1953), 104-120.

[2] Sturgeon, "Microcosmic God," in Robert Silverberg, ed. *The Science Fiction Hall of Fame* (Garden City, New York: Doubleday & Company, Inc., 1970), p. 92.

[3] Sturgeon, "Foreword," *Sturgeon Is Alive and Well . . .* (New York: G. P. Putnam's Sons, 1971), p. ix.

[4] Sturgeon, "Thunder and Roses," in Harry Harrison and Brian W. Aldiss, eds., *The Astounding-Analog Reader* (Garden City, New York: Doubleday & Company, Inc., 1973), 2: 38.

[5] Sturgeon, "To Here and the Easel," *Sturgeon Is Alive and Well . . .,* p. 52.

[6] For the novel he wrote a first part, "The Fabulous Idiot," and a final section, "Morality." The novel has now been reprinted by Ballantine, 1974.

[7] Sturgeon, "Baby Is Three," in Ben Bova, ed., *The Science Fiction Hall of Fame* (Garden City, New York: Doubleday & Company, Inc., 1973), 2A: 380.

[8] Robert Bloch, "Imagination and Modern Social Criticism," in Basil Davenport, ed., *The Science Fiction Novel* (Chicago: Advent, 1959), pp. 118-119.

[9] William Nolan, "Introduction to One Foot and the Grave," *Three to the Highest Power* (New York: Avon, 1968), p. 59.

[10] Sturgeon, "Galaxy Bookshelf," *Galaxy,* 33 (March-April 1973), 153.

[11] Sturgeon, "How to Kill Aunty," *Starshine* (New York: Pyramid Books, 1966), p. 174.

[12] The publication of the story in *Universe* may be a measure of its controversial nature, and Sam J. Lundwall, *Science Fiction: What It's All About* (New York: Ace Books, 1971), comments upon the reception given the story, p. 157.

[13] Sturgeon, "The World Well Lost," *Starshine* (New York: Pyramid Books, 1966), p. 82.

[14] Beverly Friend, "Virgin Territory: Women and Sex in Science Fiction," *Extrapolation*, 14 (December 1972), 54.

[15] Sturgeon, *Venus Plus X* (New York: Pyramid Books, 1960), pp. 151-152.

[16] Sturgeon, "If All Men Were Brothers, Would You Let One Marry Your Sister," in Harlan Ellison, ed., *Dangerous Visions* (New York: NAL, 1967), p. 342.

[17] Lundwall, *Science Fiction: What It's All About*, p. 157.

[18] Sturgeon, "Mr. Costello, Hero," *A Touch of Strange* (Garden City, New York: Doubleday & Company, Inc., 1958), p. 15.

[19] Sturgeon, *The Cosmic Rape* (New York: Dell, 1958), pp. 142-143.

[20] Alfred Bester, "Science Fiction and the Renaissance Man," in Basil Davenport, ed., *The Science Fiction Novel* (Chicago: Advent, 1959), p. 90.

[21] William Atheling, Jr. [James Blish], *The Issue at Hand* (Chicago: Advent, 1964), p. 14.

[22] Sturgeon, "Chromium Quaint—and Oddment," *National Review*, 11 (August 1964), 693.

[23] Sturgeon, "Maturity," *The Worlds of Theodore Sturgeon* (New York: Ace Books, 1972), p. 229.

[24] Sturgeon, "A Saucer of Loneliness," in Robert P. Mills, ed., *Worlds of Science Fiction* (New York: Paperback Library, 1963), p. 163.

Notes for TWO VIEWS: I. Ray Bradbury—Past, Present, and Future

[1] All manuscripts of the different versions of this story are now located in the Special Collections Library, California State University, Fullerton, California. Material in this article and otherwise uncited quotations from Bradbury were collected during his stay as artist-in-residence at the same University, 1972.

[2] Bradbury maintains that for nearly 20 years he was unaware that he derived the name "Montag" from the paper company, uncounted reams of whose product he had run through his typewriter.

[3] William F. Nolan, "BRADBURY: Prose Poet in an Age of Space," *F&SF*, 24 (May 1963), 8.

Notes for TWO VIEWS: II. The Past, The Future and Ray Bradbury

[1] Ray Bradbury, *The Martian Chronicles* (New York: Bantam, 1951), p. 37.

[2] Bradbury, *Dandelion Wine* (New York: Bantam, 1959), p. 17.

[3] Bradbury, *I Sing the Body Electric* (New York: Bantam, 1971), p. 126.

Notes for *Henry Kuttner, C. L. Moore, Lewis Padgett* et al.

[1] The quotations from C. L. Moore, unless otherwise identified, occur in a series of private letters written to me over the past several years.

[2] C. L. Moore, "Introduction," *Fury* (New York: Grosset & Dunlap, 1950).

[3] Donald B. Day, *Index to the Science Fiction Magazines 1926-1950* (Portland, Oregon: Perri Press, 1952), pp. 37, 47.

[4] Sam Moskowitz, *Seekers of Tomorrow* (Cleveland and New York: The World Publishing Company, 1966), p. 330.

[5] It had not. Featured as the lead story, it was described as "a new, powerful novel by one of science fiction's finest writers . . . C. L. Moore." *Astounding,* 31 (August 1943), 9.

[6] Lewis Padgett, "Mimsy Were the Borogoves," in Robert Silverberg, ed., *The Science Fiction Hall of Fame* (Garden City, New York: Doubleday & Company, Inc., 1970), 1: 180-208; Lawrence O'Donnell, "Vintage Season," in Ben Bova, ed., *The Science Fiction Hall of Fame* (Garden City, New York: Doubleday & Company, Inc., 1973), 2A: 214-252.

[7] "A, B, and C. The Significant Context of SF: A Dialogue of Comfort Against Tribulation." Transcribed and edited by Darko Suvin, *Science Fiction Studies,* 1 (Spring 1973), 47.

[8] Lewis Padgett, "Piggy Bank," *Astounding,* 30 (December 1942), 118.

[9] William Atheling, Jr. [James Blish], *The Issue at Hand* (Chicago: Advent Publishers, 1964), p. 78.

[10] Lewis Padgett, "Piggy Bank," *Astounding,* 30 (December 1942), 117.

[11] Lawrence O'Donnell, "Clash by Night," *Astounding,* 31 (March 1943), 11.

[12] *Ibid.,* 31: 12.

[13] Lewis Padgett, "When the Bough Breaks," *Astounding,* 34 (November 1944), 82.

[14] Lawrence O'Donnell, "The Children's Hour," *Astounding,* 33 (March 1944), 142.

[15] C. L. Moore, "No Woman Born," *Astounding,* 34 (December 1944), 177.

[16] Lewis Padgett, "What you Need," *Astounding,* 36 (October 1945), 146.

[17] Lewis Padgett, "The Fairy Chessmen," *Astounding,* 36 (January 1946), 7.

[18] Lawrence O'Donnell, "Vintage Season," in Ben Bova, ed., *The Science Fiction Hall of Fame,* 2A: 239.

[19] *Ibid.,* 2A: 250.

[20] Lawrence O'Donnell, "Fury," *Astounding,* 39 (July 1947), 158, 159.

[21] *Ibid.,* 39: 159, 160.

[22] "Land of the Earthquakes," *Startling Stories* (May 1947); "Lord of the Storm," *Startling Stories* (September 1947); "Trouble on Titan," *Thrilling Wonder Stories* (February 1947); "The Power and the Glory," *Thrilling*

Wonder Stories (December 1947); "The Mask of Circe," *Startling Stories* (September 1948); "Time Axis," *Startling Stories* (January 1949); "The Portal in the Picture," *Startling Stories* (September 1949); "As Your Were," *Thrilling Wonder Stories* (August 1950); "The Well of the Worlds," *Startling Stories* (March 1952).

Notes for *The Cosmic Loneliness of Arthur C. Clarke*

[1] Jeremy Berstein, "Profiles: Out of the Ego Chamber," *New Yorker*, 9 August 1969, p. 40.

[2] Clarke's *Earthlight* was first published in *Thrilling Wonder Stories* (August 1951), but not issued in book form until the Ballantine edition (1955).

[3] Clarke, "Introduction," *Report on Planet Three and Other Speculations* (New York: Harper & Row, 1972), p. xi.

[4] Clarke, "The Challenge of Space," in *The Challenge of Space: Previews of Tomorrow's World* (New York: Harper & Brothers, 1959), p. 16.

[5] Clarke, *The Sands of Mars* (London: Sedgwick and Jackson, 1951; New York: Gnome Press, 1952); *Islands in the Sky* (New York: Winston, 1952).

[6] Clarke, "The Star of the Magi," in *Report on Planet Three*, p. 32. "The Star of the Magi" was first published in *Holiday* (December 1954), and then included in *The Challenge of Space*, pp. 77-86.

[7] Clarke, *Prelude to Space* (New York: Harcourt, Brace & World, Inc., n.d.), pp. 208-209.

[8] Clarke, "Across the Sea of Stars," in *The Challenge of Space*, p. 130.

[9] Clarke, "When the Aliens Come," in *Report on Planet Three*, p. 107.

[10] Clarke, "The Challenge of the Spaceship," in *The Challenge of Space*, p. 8.

[11] *Ibid.*, p. 11.

[12] Clarke, "Across the Sea of Stars," in *The Challenge of Space*, p. 127.

[13] Clarke, "Of Space and the Spirit," in *The Challenge of Space*, p. 211.

[14] Clarke, "H. G. Wells and Science Fiction," in *Voices from the Sky: Previews of the Coming Space Age* (New York: Harper & Row, 1965), pp. 218-219.

[15] Clarke, *The Exploration of Space* (New York: Harper & Brothers, 1951), p. 195.

[16] Clarke, *Childhood's End* (New York: Ballantine, 1953), p. 127. Like so many science fiction novels *Childhood's End* was first published in paperback; it was not published in hardback until the omnibus volume, *Across the Sea of Stars* (New York: Harcourt, Brace & World, Inc., 1959), pp. 247-434.

[17] *Ibid.*, pp. 214-215.

[18] David N. Samuelson, "Clarke's *Childhood's End*: A Median Stage in Adolescence?" *Science Fiction Studies*, 1 (Spring 1973), 7.

[19] David Allen, "*Childhood's End*: Arthur C. Clarke (1953)," *SF an Introduction* (Lincoln, Nebraska: Cliffs Notes, 1973), p. 55.

[20] *Ibid.*, p. 47 ff.

[21] Unpublished letter from Arthur C. Clarke to Thomas D. Clareson, dated 1 January 1974.

[22] Samuelson, 1: 11.   [23] Allen, p. 47.

[24] Clarke, "Guardian Angel," in *Famous Fantastic Mysteries*, 11 (April 1950), 129.

[25] Clarke, *Prelude to Space* (New York: Harcourt, Brace & World, Inc., n.d.), p. 93. The paperback edition issued by Lancer Books (1969) was entitled *The Space Dreamers*.

[26] Clarke, "Preface," *Earthlight* (New York: Harcourt Brace Jovanovich, Inc., 1955), p. ix.

[27] Clarke, *Prelude to Space*, p. 175.

[28] David Young, *The Heart's Forest: A Study of Shakespeare's Pastoral Plays* (New Haven & London: Yale University Press, 1972), p. 199. My thanks to Professor Raymond G. McCall of the College of Wooster for pointing out this passage to me.

[29] Clarke, "Introduction," *The Lion of Comarre and Against the Fall of Night* (New York: Harcourt, Brace & World, Inc., 1968), pp. viii-ix.

[30] *Ibid.*, p. 189. The passage is absent from *The City and the Stars*.

[31] Clarke, "The Road to the Sea," in *Tales of Ten Worlds* (New York: Dell, 1964), p. 209.

[32] Clarke, *The City and the Stars*, pp. 156-157. Yet Clarke later says of the Master, "He was a good man, and much of what he taught was true and wise. In the end, he believed his own miracles, but he knew that there was one witness who could refute them. The robot knew all his secrets: . . ." (p. 204). On one of the worlds they visit, Alvin and his companions find an obelisk honoring the Master (p. 243).

[33] Clarke, "Science and Spirituality," *Voices from the Sky*, pp. 181-182.

[34] Clarke, "Out of the Sun," *The Other Side of the Sky* (New York: NAL Signet Book, 1959), p. 124.

[35] Clarke, *Childhood's End*, pp. 171-172.

[36] Clarke, "Transcience," *The Other Side of the Sky*, pp. 128, 131.

[37] Clarke, "The Star," *The Other Side of the Sky*, pp. 118-119.

[38] Clarke, "Before Eden," *Tales of Ten Worlds*, p. 148.

[39] Clarke, "Moon-Watcher," in *The Lost Worlds of 2001* (New York: NAL Signet, 1972), pp. 61-62.

[40] Clarke, "When Aliens Come," in *Report on Planet Three*, pp. 99-100.

[41] Clarke, "The Sentinel," in *Expedition to Earth* (New York: Ballantine Books, 1953), p. 164.

[42] Clarke, "The Dawn of Man," in *The Lost Worlds of 2001*, p. 50. Clarke explains that he wrote "a short story about a meeting in the remote past between visitors from space and a primitive ape-man." It was given the title "Expedition to Earth" when Ballantine published it in 1953. Clarke

preferred the title, "Encounter in the Dawn"; it was also entitled "Encounter at Dawn." Significantly, the alien astronaut has retained the name Clindar through all of the stories dealing with this encounter. Significantly, too, in that it suggests the importance of the theme, Clarke had already written "The Sentinel" in 1948. *The Lost Worlds of 2001*, p. 18.

[43] Clarke, "Expedition to Earth," in *Expedition to Earth* (New York: Ballantine, 1953), pp. 136-137.

[44] Clarke, "The Dawn of Man," in *The Lost Worlds of 2001*, p. 51.

[45] The quotations have been taken from the four stories in *The Lost Worlds of 2001*, pp. 52-75 *passim*.

[46] Clarke, *2001: A Space Odyssey* (New York: NAL, 1968), p. 185.

[47] Clarke, *Rendezvous with Rama* (New York: Harcourt Brace Jovanovich, Inc., 1973), p. 214.

[48] Clarke, "A Meeting with Medusa," in *The Wind from the Sun* (New York: Harcourt Brace Jovanovich, Inc., 1972), p. 193.

[49] Clarke, "Science and Spirituality," in *Voices from the Sky*, p. 184.

Notes for *The Swiftian Satire of Kurt Vonnegut, Jr.*

[1] Max F. Schulz, "The Unconfirmed Thesis: Kurt Vonnegut, Black Humor, and Contemporary Art," *Criticism*, 12 (1971), 8. Subsequent references are cited in the text.

[2] Maynard Mack, "The Muse of Satire," *Yale Review*, 41 (1951), 80-91.

[3] Willis E. McNelly, "Science Fiction the Modern Mythology: Vonnegut's *Slaughterhouse-Five*," *SF: The Other Side of Realism*, ed., Thomas D. Clareson (Bowling Green, Ohio: Bowling Green Popular Press, 1971), pp. 193-198; David H. Goldsmith, *Kurt Vonnegut: Fantasist of Fire and Ice*, Popular Writers Series No. 2 (Bowling Green, Ohio: Bowling Green Popular Press, 1972); Glenn Meeter, "Vonnegut's Formal and Moral Otherworldliness: *Cat's Cradle* and *Slaughterhouse-Five*," and John Somer, "Geodesic Vonnegut; Or, If Buckminster Fuller Wrote Novems," both in *The Vonnegut Statement*, ed., Jerome Klinkowitz and Somer (New York: Delacorte Press, 1973), pp. 204-254.

[4] Tony Tanner, "The Uncertain Messenger: A Study of the Novels of Kurt Vonnegut, Jr.," *Critical Quarterly*, 11 (1969), 297-315, repr. Tanner, *City of Words: American Fiction 1950-1970* (New York: Harper & Row, 1971); and Alfred Kazin, "The War Novel: From Mailer to Vonnegut," *Saturday Review*, 6 February 1971, pp. 13-15. Tanner is aware of much of what Vonnegut is doing, states his own misgivings honestly, and suspects that Vonnegut may share them; he does. Kazin thinks the space fiction element "too droll . . . a boy's fantasy of more rational creatures than ourselves"; Vonnegut, I think, agrees with him.

[5] Schulz is discussed above; see also Robert Scholes, "Fabulation and Satire," *The Fabulators* (New York: Oxford University Press, 1967), pp. 35-55. Scholes, as his title suggests, tries to see Vonnegut as a development of a

continuing satiric tradition, but he sees modern satire as abandoning the traditional method of attack; Vonnegut, he says, accepts the pointlessness of life, lets us in on the cosmic joke, and helps us take it with the gift of laughter; Scholes may be describing Vonnegut, but he confuses the comic with the satiric mode.

[6] Peter J. Reed, in *Writers for the Seventies: Kurt Vonnegut, Jr.* (New York: Warner Books, 1972), sees more clearly than anyone yet in print the multiplicity of Vonnegut's targets, but he does not see the extent to which the narrator of *Cat's Cradle* and Billy Pilgrim are themselves objects of Vonnegut's satire.

[7] J. Michael Crichton, "Sci-Fi and Vonnegut," *New Republic*, 26 April 1969, p. 35.

[8] Citations to all Vonnegut novels will be from the Seymour Lawrence/ Delacorte Press "standard" (their own claim) editions; the pagination of this edition of all the novels is the same in the Delta paperbacks.

[9] Martin Heidegger, *An Introduction to Metaphysics*, tr. Ralph Manheim (New York: Yale University Press, 1959), p. 21.

CONTRIBUTORS

Thomas D. Clareson *was chairman of the Science Fiction Research Association (SFRA). He was elected to a five-year term on the Executive Committee of the MLA Section of Popular Culture. Since 1959 he has edited* Extrapolation: A Journal of Science Fiction and Fantasy *for the MLA Seminar on Science Fiction.*

He received his doctorate from the University of Pennsylvania and teaches in the fields of American literature and 19th and 20th century fiction. Among his publications in the area of science fiction are SF: The Other Side of Realism *(Bowling Green Popular Press, 1971),* SF Criticism: An Annotated Checklist *(Kent State University Press, 1972), and* A Spectrum of Worlds *(Doubleday, 1972), an historically-oriented anthology intended for classroom use.*

On leave-of-absence in 1976-1977, Professor Clareson hopes to complete Some Kind of Paradise, *a history of American science fiction, primarily, up to the advent of the specialist magazines in 1926.*

Beverly Friend *has long been a book reviewer of science fiction for the* Chicago Daily News. *She is a member of the SFRA Executive Committee and co-editor of the SFRA* Newsletter.

James Gunn *of the University of Kansas is one of the best known contemporary writers of science fiction, as well as a critic and historian of the field. He originated a .film series of interviews with outstanding writers and editors. A past president of Science Fiction Writers of America, he is also a member of the Executive Committee of SFRA.*

Willis E. McNelly *of the California State University at Fullerton has long been active in academic criticism of science fiction. He is editor of the new* CEA Chapbook, Science Fiction: the Academic Awakening, *and is chairman of the committee giving the annual John W. Campbell Award for the best science fiction novel of the year.*

Maxine Moore *is a member of the English Department, University of Missouri at Kansas City. Professor Maxine Moore has long had an interest in science fiction and American literature. Her most recent book is* That Lonely Game: Melville, Mardi, and the Almanac *(1975).*

David N. Samuelson *is a professor in the English Department at the University of California—Long Beach. He has served on the Executive Committee of SFRA and has chaired several MLA Seminars on Science Fiction. He is interested in the field of futurology as well as literary criticism. His* Visions of Tomorrow: Six Journeys From Outer to Inner Space *was included in the Arno Press Science Fiction Collection (1975).*

Curtis C. Smith *of SUNY—Albany has written extensively on Stapledon and is now at work on a full-length biography of that writer.*

Alfred D. Stewart *is Assistant Professor, Departments of English and Philosophy, Midwestern University, Wichita Falls, Texas. His special hobbyhorses in literature are Edgar Allan Poe and the "Berserker" stories of Fred Saberhagen.*

A. James Stupple *is Associate Professor of English at California State University, Fullerton where he has taught American Literature and Science Fiction, including a pro-seminar in Bradbury. His publications include "Towards a Definition of Anti-Utopian Literature," in* Science Fiction: The Academic Awakening.

Jack Williamson *of Eastern New Mexico University is the recipient of the 1973 Pilgrim Award in recognition of his contribution to science fiction both as a writer and a scholar.*

Thomas L. Wymer *of Bowling Green State University has been particularly active in organizing the interest of the Popular Cutlure Association in the field of science fiction.*